William Dear is well known for his investigation and solution of many difficult cases. He heads his own private investigation firm in Dallas, Texas. *The Dungeon Master* is his first book.

The Dungeon Master

The Disappearance of James Dallas Egbert III

WILLIAM DEAR

SPHERE BOOKS LIMITED
London and Sydney

First published in Great Britain by
Sphere Books Limited 1985
30-32 Gray's Inn Road, London WC1X 8JL

First published in the United States of America 1984
by Houghton Mifflin Company

TRADE
MARK

Set in Times

Printed and bound in Great Britain by
Collins, Glasgow

To my parents, James and Lucille Dear, and to the most important person in the world to me, my son, Michael.

Acknowledgments

The Dungeon Master means a great deal to me. I would like to acknowledge the many gifted children all over the world. I hope someday the funds are made available to help these children properly.

I originally wanted to keep the acknowledgments to a minimum, but once finishing the book realized that was unfair. There have been so many people who have made my life what it is that I want to recognize them.

Robie Macauley, my editor who has believed in this project from the very beginning. Sandy Goroff, and the many other people at Houghton Mifflin who have helped so much.

My friends, and associates Dick Riddle, Bill & Judy Hoffman, Lea, Ethan, Micah, Lewis, Jim Gosdin, Joe Villanueva, Boots Hinton, Frank Lambert, Jim Hock, Bob France, Billy Bowles, Carol Morello, Sgt. Larry Lyons, Sgt. Bill Wardwell, Preston DeShazo, Dr. Melvin Gross, Cliff Perotti, Rick Rapaport, Connie Bergus, Tom Styer, Mike & Nancy Furlich, Gregg Happ, Dan McBride, Jerry Forrester, Pat Beraducci, Mike & Donna Phipps, Karen & Jacquie Moseley, Nancy, Steve & Andy Dixon, Tom McBride, Lt. Larry Momchilov, Dick & BJ Merket, Lt. Bob Scalise, Richard Stallings, Don Tucker, Dr. Charles Hirsch, Betty Kisor, Judge Francis Christie, Bill Courson, and Willard Green.

Also Waylon McMullen, John Spillman, Thomas G. Hight, Richard & Diane Eubanks, Tony Bauer, Dr. Joe Phipps, J. P. Snaps, Doris Haegerman, Col. Lee Simmons, Harry, Joan, Ron, Jody, Brenda & BoBo

Eubanks, Priscilla Hollis, Mike Wolff, John Lambert, Mr. & Mrs. Eli Momchilov, Teri Hurley, Lynn Ferguson, Blue & Helen Clark, Alese Alders, Andy Sebastian, Al Ellis, Bob Woodruff, Andrea Kuracki and family, Marge McGill, Lee Bennett, Harry, Linda & Tiffany Tinnerella, Bud & Judy Isenhart, Mark Martin, Sally Foster, Kim, Bobby & Stacy Rourk, Sol & Martha Freedberg, Ann Marie Biondo, Stu Bonnett, Dave Salyers, Jeff Brown, A. J. Love, Ellen Gunter, and Patsy Caldwell.

Ron Chamness, Ruth Thornton, Arvin & Glenda Clark, Ray & Emily Cornelius, Richard Craven, Peggy Curry, Dr. Marilyn Ceblin, Al De Jordy, Bob & Dixie Dunn, Kay Dalton Mable, Jackie & Judy Eads, Sylvia Forbes, Avon Franks, Sol & Patty Gambino, Garland & Carolyn Gibbs, Dr. Earl Rose, Leon Johnson, Jay & Martha Hand, Sue Kollinger, Bill Key, Paul Kunde, Ray & Mary Lambert, Judy Marcinkewicz, Billejo Mills, Lynn Furlow, Fritz Lewis, Doug & Marilyn Jenney, Kevin Vandiveer, J. T. Blackmor, John Adamek, Det. John Bailey, Mark Delk, Rev. Dixon Rial, M. C. White, Joe & Gene Witenhafer, Larry Price, Tommy Fallin, Jimmy Furr, Cheri Kennedy, Brandon Sailor, Kristi Lynn Wester, and especially to someone very dear to me, Gini Clement.

Publisher's Note

In William Dear's account of his investigation of the disappearance of James Dallas Egbert III, the author and individuals interviewed during the investigation speak of 'Dungeons & Dragons' or 'D&D,' a reference to a fantasy role-playing game thought to be a possible key to unlocking the mystery of the disappearance of Dallas Egbert, an avid player of the game. The Dungeons and Dragons game is manufactured and distributed under these trademarks by TSR, Inc., of Lake Geneva,

Wisconsin. References to 'Dungeons & Dragons' or 'D&D' in the book represent the author's recollections of the way people talked, and his own thoughts, about a possible relationship between the playing of the game by Dallas and others in the East Lansing area and Dallas's disappearance. Readers should be aware, however, that such reported references to the game may not accurately describe the fantasy role-playing game published by TSR, Inc., and reports in the book that individuals played games in actual tunnels under Michigan State University or other potentially dangerous locations should not be interpreted to be suggestions that such practices are part of the Dungeons & Dragons game or are recommended by TSR, Inc., or its Licensees.

Preface

The James Dallas Egbert case didn't begin in any bizarre way.

In my fifteen years as a private investigator, I have handled thousands of cases, some perfectly commonplace, some exceptionally strange. As I look back, I think of an attractive nurse in Dallas named Norma Heistand. One day, with a sheet of her master's thesis still in her typewriter, she vanished without a trace. The police search turned up not a single clue, and in the end I discovered her in her own house, where she'd hidden herself in a boxboard carton. I remember the great imposter – I mean the *great* one, not the infamous Fred Demaris, but Jack Bradford, a.k.a. Jack Brown. Before I unmasked him, this remarkable-looking man, who was a karate pro with red hair and a superb command of language, had filled a dozen roles. Once he'd posed as a doctor and performed some sophisticated surgery; another time he had been CEO of a couple of large corporations; then he'd served as warden of a major prison. He had even acted as commandant of a U.S. military base. There was the fourteen-year-old daughter of a southern governor who ran away from home, which led to my being knifed during a peace demonstration in Berkeley. Later I found the girl and returned her. And I've had other intriguing cases, in England, South Korea, Italy, Hong Kong, Thailand, the Netherlands, East Germany, and China, some of which were used as the bases of 'Simon & Simon' and 'Matt Houston' TV episodes. Yes, I've had my share of the strange ones.

In Raymond Chandler novels and in Humphrey Bogart movies it often begins with a telephone call. Strange to say, in real life it often begins that way too.

Chapter 1

On August 22, 1979, I had a call from a Dr. Melvin Gross. All I knew about Melvin Gross was that he was the prominent Irving, Texas, surgeon for whom my sister worked. On the few social occasions when I'd seen him, he had shown an intelligent interest in my investigations.

'My nephew has disappeared,' he said in a voice that quavered. 'He was taking a summer course at Michigan State University, in East Lansing, when it happened.'

'Where's his permanent home?' I asked. I knew that students sometimes get despondent over grades and vanish from school. But usually, after a detour, they turn up at home. Criminals on the run exhibit pretty much the same pattern.

'The family lives in Dayton, Ohio.'

'And he didn't just run off?'

'He's not that kind of kid. He loves school; in fact, he's considered to be a genius. He has a wonderful analytical mind, and the professors have been amazed at his mathematical skill and how much he knows about computers. I just can't see him as a runaway.'

'How old is he?' I wasn't much impressed so far. Uncles tend to exaggerate a bit about favorite nephews. I still thought, Bad grades.

'Dallas is sixteen.'

'Dallas?'

'James Dallas Egbert the Third. We call him Dallas. He graduated from high school at thirteen, entered college at fourteen, and he's a sophomore now. I'm telling you, Dear, he's not the type to just go on the road.'

Now I was interested. Maybe because at thirteen I was in the eighth grade and my chief worries were acne and my shyness with girls. The name Dallas fascinated me too. On the other hand, I had to think for a minute before I could decide about getting involved. I'd just returned from handling an extortion case in Tokyo, and I was looking forward to taking my eleven-year-old son to Disney World. I looked at his picture on my desk and I thought about lost boys. I didn't want or need another investigation right now, but something led me to ask more about this one.

'What do you want me to do?' I asked.

'Would you be interested in handling the case? I've talked with Jim and Anna Egbert – Anna is my wife's sister – and they are very unhappy about the police in East Lansing, who think it's just another missing-person case. Anyway, the Egberts very much want to retain your services.'

'Maybe,' I said. 'But let me talk with the Egberts first.'

That is a rule with me. Before I take any case, I want to be sure that my clients will tell me all details, good and bad, about the person involved. My standard warning to clients is that if they withhold anything, I walk off. That all stems from the 3:00 A.M. call I once had from a man who told me with great emotion that he had just shot a man who was trying to rob him. I took this fellow as a client and put myself on the line for him – only to discover that what he had actually done was to shoot *and stab* the victim in a fight over a woman. The police in his town still give me a hard time when I try to work with them. Nevertheless, as a private investigator I often get the kind of trust and information that people don't give the police. That's why I can solve cases that the police can't.

I got Jim Egbert in Dayton, and he put his wife on the

telephone extension. She took over immediately. 'Mr. Dear, thank God you called. I'm so desperate about my son. I don't know if he's committed suicide and is lying in some ditch or what. Maybe he's been kidnapped. I hope so. That would be better than what I've been thinking: that he's been murdered. Oh my God, I'm out of my mind.'

I could sense her hysteria and her frantic anxiety about her son. I said some soothing words and finally, 'Tell me about Dallas.'

'Will you help, Mr. Dear? Please God, tell me you'll help us.'

'I need to know something about the boy, Mrs. Egbert.'

'Anna,' said Jim Egbert, 'I know he'll help. Just calm down and tell him what he wants to know.'

'That's what I'm doing,' she replied, sobbing.

It was that kind of conversation. I've had quite a few of them, and I've learned how to be patient. 'Let me do the worrying for you,' I said. 'I'll find your son.' I was a little surprised to hear myself saying that, but as I took in the words, I realized that I meant them. I would take the case. Half of my cases in the past fifteen years have concerned missing persons, and not once have I failed to find an individual.

'Can you really?' she pleaded.

'How long ago did Dallas disappear?'

'Eight days ago, on the fifteenth. But nobody notified us until the twentieth. That upsets me even more than the way the police are acting. How could a school be so irresponsible about a minor child? They promised me he'd be looked after.'

Eight days. It was a long time for any kind of small fling.

'Now, please tell me about Dallas,' I said, 'and begin anywhere you like.' This would be the first step in the vital process I always go through in searching for someone. For me, it is always essential to think myself into the mind of that person, in the way a good actor thinks himself into a character. When I'm most successful, I begin to reason like the person I'm looking for; to anticipate his moves, to be conditioned by his past experiences. I even begin to walk like him, in some instances; at least, an Ohio prosecutor once told me that I'd taken on a real physical resemblance to one of the key figures in a murder case. The topflight investigator becomes the person he hunts.

Anna Egbert's voice was cracking and she talked between sobs, but what came out was a point-by-point description just as logical as a police report. 'Mr. Dear, he was reciting his alphabet when he was only two. He was reading at three and, can you believe it, finished kindergarten at four. He grasped things so quickly, the teachers were amazed. He was a quiet and passive boy. Grade school didn't challenge him, and he graduated high school in two years. He repaired the computer in the school office when it broke down. Had a scholarship offer from M.I.T. – just think of that, he was only thirteen. But he chose Michigan State because they have special courses for gifted children.'

'Please describe Dallas physically.'

She started to sob in great gasps, and for a few moments she couldn't say anything. Jim Egbert was trying to calm her down. He wasn't hysterical, but he waited for her to give the information. I was fairly certain now who was the spokesperson for the family.

'My son is just a little boy,' Anna said at last. 'He's five feet five inches tall, weighs only a hundred and thirty pounds. He looks a lot younger than sixteen. Brown hair. Soft brown eyes.'

'Complexion? Any acne?'

'A little.'

'How does he usually dress?'

'Oh, jeans and a T-shirt. I'm telling you, Mr. Dear, that Dallas is just a little boy in lots of ways, but with a great mind.'

I had begun to sense a lead here. 'Does Dallas enjoy playing games? Please tell me more about his mind.'

'Well, it's interesting that you ask that. Dallas loves science fiction, and he attends every convention he can. He has played with calculators and computers since he was ten. At twelve he programmed a computer to play games. Dallas *is* a genius, Mr. Dear.'

The Egberts and I wound up the conversation by agreeing on some practical moves. There was still an enormous amount I wanted to learn, but that would have to come in East Lansing. We agreed that Jim and Anna would go there immediately and that I would send an advance team of detectives and arrive myself in a few days.

I sat back in my chair and began the process of trying to imagine myself in another's shoes. I was Dallas Egbert, sixteen, a shy and lonely kid sitting alone in my dormitory room in a giant university. I was a game-player, and I was obsessed with images from science fiction and fantasy. I always remember these first attempts at identification, and much later I compare them with the final outcome of a case. Little did I know on that August day how little I knew and sensed about James Dallas Egbert III.

I called in three of my best detectives and we sat in the office for a tactics session. Dick Riddle, who was thirty-seven, had been my chief investigator for the past five years. He is a former police lieutenant – he served in a Louisville, Kentucky, suburb – and he has the tenacity of a pit bulldog. He has never heard of a time clock. He is loyal, absolutely honest, and incredibly persistent. Once Dick and I recovered a child from a religious cult that had kidnapped her in Erie, Pennsylvania. We put our helicopter down in an empty schoolyard and got the girl, but then we had to deal with armed cult members. I handed the child to Dick and told him to run for the copter, and I saw the struggle of loyalties in his face: he wanted to stand by my side, but as a good policeman and a member of my agency, he knew that the client's safety came first. So he ran with the child, and I stood there to take a beating. I might have been killed if Dick hadn't forced the frightened helicopter pilot to wait for me.

James Hock was twenty-eight and had the street smarts (and the back-alley smarts) of a patrol sergeant along with the finesse of a detective. Jim held both these jobs in Arkansas before he joined my firm. He is solid, husky, and hasn't an ounce of fat on his five-foot ten-inch, 220-pound body. One of Jim's great talents is the ability to blend into crowds and become virtually invisible. He is an excellent man for surveillance, and he has the all-important quality of endless patience.

The third man was Frank Lambert, a thirty-year-old, former Green Beret who served as a sniper in Vietnam. He is five feet eight, weighs in at 160 pounds, and at times has the temper of a wildcat. Most people will never know this, however, because Frank's usual manner is reticent and soft-spoken. I hired him as a pilot to fly my private plane. I like Frank's courage and resourcefulness, but I prize beyond gold his ability to land a plane virtually anywhere, even in the most hazardous conditions. Once Frank had himself lowered into a deep cave to find a body. Another time, while searching for a map we'd been hired to find, he spent fourteen days on a sailboat, most of the time without food or water. He is almost eerily strong. On another occasion, when I had to approach three very large and very rough men in order to tell one of them that he was accused of murder, Frank was the only backup I wanted or needed.

As the four of us sat in my office, I explained what I knew about the Egbert case and sketched out some scenarios. If Dallas Egbert had killed himself, I said, we could expect to find the body fairly near the campus, since Dallas did not drive a car. The exception would be if someone had helped Dallas out by giving him a lift somewhere. My expectation, I said, was that the boy had committed suicide.

A second possibility was that Dallas had been kidnapped. If so, we were better equipped to deal with it than the small campus police force was. I'm convinced that no police force has better men than the three I was talking with, but we had state-of-the-art technical equipment as well. I said that I wanted to be on the scene before any possible kidnapping leads were followed up. Kidnapping is both delicate and difficult to handle.

Third, murder couldn't be ruled out. If the boy had been killed, I fully intended to solve the crime, although nothing had been said about that when I talked with the Egberts. It was the kind of challenge I couldn't avoid, even though I knew it would require three good investigators to do the necessary digging into Dallas's past.

The fourth possibility was the simplest: Dallas was a runaway, and his disappearance was a hoax. This would be the young prodigy's way of crying out for attention. A runaway, however, invariably tells someone that he's going, and even though the campus police had no one named Poirot or Holmes on the force, I knew they could have found the person Dallas had confided in.

Suicide, kidnapping, murder, runaway/hoax – which? How could I have known that the answer would not be singular?

We planned for Frank Lambert to fly my C-55, twin-engine Baron up to East Lansing. It is splendid for surveillance work, and it gives us a mobility that the police seldom have. Dick Riddle and Jim Hock would drive company cars, two more examples of our technological capability. Each car is equipped with magnetic tracking devices and two-way radios with a dead FM frequency, which enables us to hear conversations that come through planted listening devices as much as five miles away. We can, of course, tape these conversations. We also have two briefcases with concealed tracking devices, which come in especially handy when a kidnapper is making off with a case full of ransom money. Two more briefcases contain concealed tape recorders that are activated when the cases are opened. Thus, when I stroll outside with a witness or informant or speak with someone in a home or office, I can tape what is said. The recorders can even be activated by a hand movement when the briefcase is not opened.

We can use the plane and the cars in tandem. Say that we attached a magnetic chip beneath a car to be followed and that this car somehow went beyond the five-mile range of the trailing cars. The plane would still receive the magnetic-chip signals, from a much greater distance.

Other equipment included fingerprint kits and numerous cameras, including a subminiature that is smaller than a pack of cigarettes, another that doubles as a cigarette lighter, a motorized binocular camera that can photograph at remarkable distances, and a 35mm camera with zoom, telephoto, wide-angle, and fisheye lenses. A metal detector. Two portable, rubberized magnets for use on land or water (very good for pulling a gun out of a river). A book that isn't a book but a case full of recording equipment. Ultraviolet lights to locate scratch marks or other clues invisible to the human eye. Miniature walkie-talkies so that we could keep in touch with one another.

As we stood on the cement at Red Bird Airport to see Frank off, we each made a guess as to the solution of the Egbert case. I stuck with suicide. The others wrote their answers on scraps of paper and folded them, and I stowed them away in my billfold. 'When it's over, we'll see who's the best detective,' I said.

'Do I get to own the company if I'm right?' Lambert asked.

'No, but you might still work for it if you're wrong,' I said.

Chapter 2

Seven days later I flew from Dallas to Detroit and then on to East Lansing. I had kept in touch with the investigators, who had phoned me four or five times a day with reports that were beginning to sound like elements of fantasy fiction.

The three were at the airport to meet me, along with about eight reporters and two television crews. The story of the disappearance had first been published in the campus newspaper, had spread to the local news, and had finally made it to many Michigan papers. This was only an intimation of things to come.

I'd given my investigators strict orders not to talk to the press, and I followed the same rule at first. I wasn't being arbitrary. I know the value of good reporting, and newspaper and TV coverage can often reach potential witnesses whom no investigator, however enterprising, could hope to contact. On the negative side, though, I often must work with the local police, and generally the local police don't like reporters. If I gave out some interesting investigative results I'd had, it would look like I was showboating at the expense of the local law. And sometimes I've furnished information to the local police, only to have them publicize it as their own discovery.

The reporters followed me to Dick Riddle's car. Was the boy kidnapped, or did he run away? No comment at this time. Is the boy alive? Ditto, no comment. Was I going to solve the case? Yes, of course I was. And so it went. Finally, as I was climbing into the car: Do all Texans wear cowboy boots like that? Answer: Sure we do. And we all keep horses in the back yard.

We drove straight to the Red Roof Inn in East Lansing, and at about 3:00 P.M. this August 29, we met with Jim and Anna Egbert for the first time. My room in the Red Roof Inn was to be my headquarters during my stay and was to witness the comings and goings of a very weird set of characters. The Egberts were not at all weird, but they were a study in contrasts. Anna was five feet eight and stout; Jim was an inch shorter and some pounds slenderer. She usually wore a plain, no-nonsense dress, and he always wore either a new suit or a natty sports coat and slacks. Jim, an optometrist, was quiet-spoken and polite; Anna talked forcefully and at considerable length.

'What's your opinion at this point?' Jim began.

'I'm not sure,' I said. 'I need to talk with my men – and I want to hear some things from you.'

'Let me handle this,' Anna interrupted. 'Do you think Dallas is alive?'

'I don't know.'

'I'm aware you don't know. What do you *think*?'

'I won't speculate.' Actually, I had become relatively certain that the boy had killed himself, but I wasn't going to say it to his parents at this point.

There were tears in Anna's and Jim's eyes now. Anna said, 'I know he's dead. I killed him. I pushed him about his grades because I wanted him to be perfect, to have all A's. I never let up on him. There was a bar mitzvah he wanted to attend in Texas last weekend, but I told him he had to study. I guess I just don't know how to cope with a genius.' She was weeping openly now. 'I pushed him until he died.'

I got up from my chair and put an arm around her. 'Listen to me, things work out. There's a good chance we'll find him alive.'

In the course of the years, several people have died in

my arms. I knew that each of them had a life expectancy measured in seconds, but I told them that they were going to be all right. I'll never forget the look of happiness that statement brought to their faces. They trusted me, and they died with hope. Isn't that better than the awful certainty? Anna Egbert needed hope.

'Dallas called me on August twelfth,' she said. 'He was so happy because he got a 3.5 in a computer-science course. I told him it should have been a 4.0.'

Anna was willing to shoulder the entire blame. Of course, parents usually deserve some blame when things go wrong, but I was sure that Dallas's case was not that simple. Numerous people, circumstances, and events had contributed.

My interview with the Egberts came to an end with some more emotional talk on Anna's part and further attempts to soothe on mine.

'I'd give up my life if we could just find Dallas safe. I'd give up my life in a moment,' she said.

'Please try to quit worrying. Get some rest. Stay calm and try to think of any people at all my men may not have talked with yet. Recall everyone Dallas knew, no matter how slightly. Go over his habits – list them. I know you've done this before, but do it again.'

I finally did succeed in persuading the Egberts to go to their room, and as soon as they were gone I called Dick Riddle.

Riddle looks so much like an ideal cop on the stage or screen that everybody takes him for a cop immediately. He is slightly above average height, clean-cut, muscular, and a dedicated investigator. And he has a couple of qualities that perhaps even ideal cops don't often have: a good sense of humor, and something that makes people – even perfect strangers – confide in him. In the old hard-cop/soft-cop scenario, Riddle is a great costar for the physically menacing Jim Hock, who usually seems to be on the brink of losing control. The impatient, snarling Hock or the pleasant, down-home Riddle – for the witness or suspect, the choice is clear.

'It looks like a five-carton case,' said Riddle as he came in the door.

I groaned. He knew that I have a near-fanatical hatred of cigarette smoke. A five-carton case is one that takes a lot of time and a lot of difficult breathing for a nonsmoker.

'You know,' Riddle said, 'we'd usually have something like this wrapped up in a week. The problem is, I don't think we've ever been faced with "something like this" before. Not only do we not have it wrapped up, we don't even know what's involved. We start with choices of kidnap, murder, suicide, or runaway. A week later, any one of them looks just as possible as it did when we began.'

'What about the Egberts?'

'The Egberts have been doing some wondering. They've heard rumors about homosexual activity.'

'Was Dallas gay?'

'At least bisexual. His homosexual affairs are confirmed.'

'You didn't tell the Egberts, did you?'

'Of course not.'

Riddle had talked with Karen Coleman, a nineteen-year-old coed whom Dallas called 'Mother'. She said that Dallas had been a member of the Gay Council, an activist group on campus, and that he had given speeches on 'the fruits of homosexuality' in a social-science course. John Miller, a gay activist, had confirmed Karen's account and had referred Riddle to a Gay Council member named Peggy Hogan, who supposedly had known Dallas well.

Peggy had begun by saying that she didn't believe Dallas had killed himself. Further, she might be able to contact 'some people' who knew where he was or what had happened to him. Riddle immediately asked for names. Peggy was evasive. No, she said, she didn't want any unnecessary hassle; she would prefer to contact the people herself.

Riddle thought he knew how to handle that. 'Look,' he had said, 'the newspapers are going to find out about Dallas's associations. The boy is sixteen, a *minor*. Once this hits the press, everything the Gay Council has accomplished in the past few years is down the tube. The press will tear it apart. Now, I can hold the press off, but if you don't cooperate, I don't know for how long.'

Peggy had been frightened, but not enough. She still wouldn't name names, but she did promise to turn over any information she might get to Riddle rather than to the police.

After that interview, Riddle decided to put a little pressure on Peggy. He made a deal with Carol Morello, a reporter with the *Lansing State Journal*. In one of her forthcoming stories she would make a vague reference to the possible involvement of the gay community in the case, and in return Riddle would notify Morello first when Dallas was finally found. Riddle was going to show the printed story to Peggy, making a strong implication that the press was now hot on the trail of the gays. It was not quite fair, perhaps, but a boy's life was at stake.

In the course of his interview with Peggy Hogan, Riddle learned that Dallas had spent many nights talking with her. He talked constantly about the Dungeons & Dragons game,* which she thought derived from J. R. R. Tolkien's *Lord of the Rings*. Dallas was often depressed when he came to stay overnight at her house, but he perked up when he began to talk about the game. 'I don't know how

*A game produced by TSR, Inc. See the Publisher's Note and trademark notice at the front of this book.

to play it,' Peggy had said, 'but I do know you can't play if you're a dumb-ass.'

Riddle added that he had been trying to follow up the leads offered by Dallas's alleged homosexual associations. He had become generally acquainted with the gay bars and other gathering places in the area. This led to something of an explosion on Riddle's part.

'Know what I think? Michigan State may have its ass in a sling. The school promised the Egberts proper supervision for their boy – and look what happened. They call that supervision? When this is over, if I were the Egberts, I'd get a shrewd, greedy lawyer and go after MSU. I sure wouldn't trust *my* son to their kind of supervision.'

We decided that the next thing to do was to visit Dallas's room in Case Hall dormitory. Riddle gave me a brief description of some of the enigmatic things that had been found there. As for the room itself, I would see it very much as it had been when the first investigating officers had arrived.

One of the foremost oddities found in the room was an unsigned, hand-printed note. Riddle had a copy. It read:

> TO WHOM IT MAY CONCERN:
> SHOULD MY BODY BE FOUND,
> I WISH IT TO BE CREMATED.

The note had been found in a conspicuous place on top of some of Dallas's poems, which were also neatly hand-printed. Riddle had some copies of them too.

Die, Brave Bug, Die
Psychotic Sky

The bug rested
in illusory safety

on the warm, inviting arm.

Impact. Disruption. Suddenly thrust
into a lifeless white plane
with peculiar blue parallels,
the bug crawled . . .

until
a spear came from the sky
to leave behind a pool of blue
with an alarming aroma.

The bug evaded the long thin snag
and continued on his path.
The sky laughed.

The sky then sent a second spear
to blemish the barren flatness.
The bug shunned that pool
with unseemly deliberation.

In a cruel frenzy of formation,
many more spears appeared.
The panicked bug blindly
maneuvered the maze
and bad-smelling blue,
and found there was no escape.

At distant was the sweet scent
of the warm, welcoming arm.
The brave bug risked
the dangers of the evil blue
to return to false friendliness.

That's not fair! said the sky.

Two other poems were found, and although I possess no qualifications to analyze poetry, they seemed to fit my theory of suicide. The one that follows I believe was written by a very lonely boy.

You like our happy babies,
yet you would turn them
into monsters like your own,
by denying them the love of all.

You like our smiling children,
yet you would strike them
when their only crime
was forgetfulness.

You like our quiet teenagers,
yet you would drive them
mad with boredom and
take them away from us.

You like our loving people,
yet you would offer them
the irreversible apple.
Who me? Sure, I'll bite.

And, last, this one, titled 'Final Destination,' to me is just filled with despair:

Sittin' in my Chevy
on a country road,
my engine and my radio
have left me all alone.
What a place to break down,
a thousand miles from home,
where mine are the only tracks
that I see in the snow.

Both hands of my dashboard clock
have frozen near the nine.
Has it been five minutes,
or has an hour gone by
while watching Mother Nature
paint the windows white
and drinking glove-box whiskey
to warm me up inside?

Probably a town up
ahead, maybe a farm.
Probably could make it,
wouldn't be too hard.
If I can find a reason,
then I'll leave the car.
At the moment, though, I just don't know
where the reasons are.

Whenever I decide there's
a place I'd like to be,
soon as I can find there's
a goal to be achieved,
come the time I'm shown that
there's something left for me,
then I'll go, but until then,
I think I'd rather sleep.

I told Riddle to contact Sergeant Bill Wardwell of the Michigan State campus police to arrange for a handwriting analysis. Why wouldn't the note about cremation and the poems have been written by Dallas Egbert? There was no reason to suspect otherwise, but I wanted to be thorough. Nothing, it would turn out, could be assumed or taken at face value in this investigation.

Red Roof Inn was three miles from the Michigan State

University campus, where more than 45,000 students pursued a higher education. It was easy to see how Dallas could be lost in this shuffle – the student population was that of a small city. Case Hall was close to the football stadium, near the middle of the campus, and while I was getting to it on this late-August afternoon I could see how lovely the campus was. The old buildings had character; there were stately trees everywhere, and green grass and gardens bursting with flowers. I wished I had gone to school here. The picturesque grounds were mostly empty now, but they soon would be swarming with students coming for the fall term.

Case Hall was an old brick-and-stone building surrounded by tall trees, but it struck me as strangely cold and forbidding. The inside was in need of paint. *Dallas lived here*, I thought; right up to the moment of his disappearance his days (what were they like?) had been spent in this environment. The last person to see him – his friend Karen Coleman – had eaten lunch with him in Case Hall's first-floor cafeteria. Riddle had talked with Karen, but she was high on my list of someone who needed interviewing again.

Andy Magruder, the dorm supervisor, showed us to Dallas's third floor room. It was very small, and had a double window, bunk beds (though Dallas had no roommate), a small desk with two shelves above it (forty-three books on the shelves), a small refrigerator, a twelve-inch Sony color TV, a portable stereo, two hard-backed chairs, a chest of drawers, and a doorless closet where clothes hung.

Someone had gone to great lengths to make this room immaculate, and I said *uh-oh* to myself. It was almost as if no one had lived here. The room was as neat as one of those model apartments on display in a new condo – the kind you wish you lived in but you know would turn into chaos ten minutes after your family walked in. It reminded Riddle of a military barracks just before inspection. There were no loose papers, no mementos, no class notes, no mail, not even checking-account records.

I recalled asking Anna Egbert whether her son was neat. She answered, 'Mentally, yes. His mind is very ordered. Physically, no. I'm afraid he's a worse-than-average sloppy teenager. Always threw his clothes on the floor. Never made his bed. Paraphernalia from chemistry experiments scattered around. And paper – sometimes you couldn't see his desk, there were so many papers. Up over his head and spilling across the floor.'

My investigators had interviewed a number of students who had been here in the past, and everyone remembered a chaos. Dallas had been experimenting with the extraction of pure nicotine from cigarette tobacco – a smelly, messy, and even dangerous project, and one very hard to conduct in a dormitory room.

The absolutely clean and orderly room stared at me. Anna had said about it, 'Anything that was Dallas's personally isn't there.' It took no Nero Wolfe to realize that this was a clue – but now I had to interpret it.

The room made me doubt my suicide theory. My experience with suicides has been that older people have an urge to put their affairs (or their living quarters) in order, but that young ones do not. They leave long letters, not a brief message like the one that had been found here. I tried to rationalize that maybe the room was telling us, *Hey, I'm sorry my life was a mess, but at least I won't leave a mess behind*. But the more I thought about it, the less that showplace seemed to fit a suicide.

Murder, or kidnapping? I couldn't imagine this room as the scene. For one thing, Case Hall was a coed dormitory and there was no curfew; people came and went at all hours. It would be very risky to try to take Dallas, dead or alive, down two flights of stairs and outside without being noticed. Besides, my team had used lasers and ultra-violet lights to search for bloodstains, scratches, or other evidence that the human eye could not catch, and they had come up empty-handed. A murderer or kidnapper might have come back to eliminate any incriminating evidence, but would he do a housekeeper's job?

For me, the room contained only three clues: the neatness, the cremation note, and a cork bulletin board found propped on a chair in front of the stereo. Thirty-eight blue and white pushpins and thumbtacks were inserted into the corkboard to form something that looked like a map.

That board seemed to say, *Here's a clue as to where to look. Figure it out if you can*. Well, if I had to, I could learn to play this game.

Dallas was a game-player – but with whom had he been playing? And had the game suddenly turned deadly? I mulled over the kidnapping alternative again, and again it seemed like a long shot. The Egberts were not rich; they were on the lower fringes of the upper-middle-class, and just hiring me had been one of the greatest financial commitments they would ever make. Many children, even at a state university, had wealthier parents.

Riddle and I were finished with the dorm room. As we walked down the corridor, we stopped and questioned each student we met. Most of them denied even knowing that Dallas existed. Impossible, of course, but a predictable lie. There are more people in this world who would turn a deaf ear to Kitty Genovese's screams for her life than there are descendants of that Samaritan who came across a half-dead man on the road from Jerusalem to Jericho. The only interesting answer we got was from a student who admitted that he had been in Dallas's room.

'I wouldn't call it a pigpen,' he said, 'but it wasn't going to make *House Beautiful*.'

We returned to the Red Roof Inn just at dusk. Although I hadn't eaten all day, I wasn't going to begin. Eating, or eating any large amount, at least, can slow down your mental processes. I had to be ready for an interview with Jim Hock, who had gathered some interesting psychiatric information about Dallas Egbert.

Chapter 3

'Let me read you from my notes exactly what Dr. Clark said.' Jim Hock had a green 8 by 10½ spiral notebook in his lap as he sat across from me in my room. The first impression Jim gives is that of a pro football linebacker. Before long, however, you realize that he is a studious man with a lot of talent for our work. He studied psychology in college, and he had become a nonpareil interrogator and a patient listener. Unlike the single-minded Riddle, he can be very flexible in the procedures of an investigation.

'That's the MSU psychologist? Were you there when he talked with the Egberts?'

'Yes. And I talked with him alone afterward. He said that although he hadn't talked with Dallas, he was sure that the boy's problem was caused by "parental pressure, criticism, academic pressure, and the failure of all persons to realize that, although Dallas Egbert was a genius, he was socially retardant, and in some respects could be considered mentally retarded." '

'Does Dr. Clark think Dallas is still alive?'

'He said the same thing both in front of the Egberts and afterward: he thinks it's impossible to know anything for certain.'

Later I learned that Dr. Louise Sause, a Michigan State professor who specializes in child psychology and development, had studied Dallas Egbert's case. She called it an example of 'the very costly price asked of some children . . . Their own image becomes one so perfect that they dare not fail to live up to it . . . At the same time, fear of success can become just as great as, or greater than, the fear of failure. It's the constant demand to be a star.'

Dr. Sause went on to emphasize the importance of the stress caused by competition. 'College adjustment is a pressure cooker at best, and eighteen- and nineteen-year-olds find it difficult. For a child, competing on this level and without close friendships within his age group, the tension can build unchecked. It becomes almost intolerable to face the social and academic pressures . . . To expect a sixteen-year-old to have maturity and judgment about living and lifestyles is almost asking more than a child can do. A superior achiever – or any other child, for that matter – deserves the right to happiness and to know other kids.'

Dr. Sause was asked about gifted children at the university. How many sixteen-year-olds were there? Not many, she said, and they were usually isolated even more by the treatment they got. 'A young genius is seen as a mascot or a rarity. Very often, he or she becomes a kind of exhibit. We should be aware that there is a *person* there, not just a phenomenal set of test scores. What kind of setting are we putting such children into?'

As I began to see my way into this case, I realized that I would have to keep in mind that the genius-Dallas, with an IQ of something between 170 and 190, existed in combination with the child-Dallas, a confused little boy perhaps no older than six or seven in his ability to deal with the world.

'You said you spoke with someone named Mark McCrosky,' I said to Jim Hock. 'I want to hear about your talk with him.'

'Well, he's one of the few people who'll even admit he knows Dallas, and he was the one who notified the authorities that Dallas was missing. They got to be friends a year ago, when they both lived in Holmes Hall. He knows that Dallas is bisexual, but McCrosky is straight. And I checked that out. It's true.'

'What else?'

'He talked about Dallas and drugs. There's no question that Dallas took them – marijuana, cocaine, and some stuff he cooked up himself. McCrosky said he knew where Dallas kept his drug equipment, but when we searched the room, none of it was there. No stainless-steel tray, water pipes, Bunsen burner, test tubes, hemostats – nothing.'

'Where did he get the drugs?'

'He made most of his own from chemicals he took from a university lab. Some material he bought over the counter. He could actually make PCP.'

'Angel dust,' I said. 'It can fry your brains.' I'd seen its effect in quite a few of my cases. I still have a picture in my mind of the missing daughter of a prominent Texas family, whom I tracked down to a dilapidated shack in the country, where I found her curled up on the bed in the fetal position. Later that day she died in a hospital. PCP can turn people into murderers, or it can delude them into thinking they can fly from the tops of tall buildings. I knew of a few who had tried those things. Angel dust is very expensive on the street, and Dallas's ability to make it might have made him a target for kidnappers. A young genius in the hands of a drug ring? Stranger things have happened.

I wondered where the university authorities had been while a sixteen-year-old was making – and perhaps giving out – a deadly drug.

'Did McCrosky add anything in your second interview?'

'I pursued the drug matter. He said that Dallas had a book on so-called recreational drugs, and the book recommended various dosages for various highs, and even the dosages to take if you wanted to commit suicide.'

'And you didn't find that book when you searched the room?'

'No. But if it existed, it belonged to Dallas. There's nothing like that in the MSU library.'

Hock, like the rest of the team, had found very few students in Case Hall who would admit even to having seen Dallas Egbert. In my own days as a student, we would have been naively proud to furnish information in such a celebrated case. But these students were the younger brothers and sisters of the Vietnam-era protestors. They still said about adults, 'They always lie to you.' I could see that the sledding was going to be rough.

'You also mentioned Bruce Roberts on the phone to me in Texas. Tell me about him.'

'He lived down the corridor from Dallas last spring, in Holmes Hall. One night Roberts was studying for exams down in the lounge and Dallas happened along. He was on a high, Roberts says, and he began talking about suicide. Bruce didn't take it very seriously. Then Dallas said he might just find a place – anywhere – and go there to commit suicide. He said he'd leave a map that would give directions to his body, but he didn't think anyone could figure it out.'

'Hmm. Any corroboration for that little discussion?'

'Yes, a girl named Karen Byerly, another student. I interviewed her too. She had some additional details, the most interesting one being that Dallas spoke to her and Bruce about the hallucinogenic and poisonous effects of certain mushrooms.'

People who are serious about suicide, folk wisdom tells us, never talk about it. When someone talks about committing suicide, the usual reaction of a listener is to dismiss it as a bit of attention-seeking or a symptom of temporary depression. Because Dallas had seemed to be high, neither Roberts nor Byerly had paid a whole lot of attention. It was only when the newspaper carried the story about the corkboard that they remembered. Even then, Hock had had to track them down.

Professional psychologists disagree with folk wisdom, however. Talk about suicide calls for action – examination and treatment. Here in the statements of Karen Byerly and Bruce Roberts we had three associated elements: a map, a definite but unknown site, and suicide.

'Karen remembered something else very interesting,' Hock added. 'I have this exact quote in my notes. Listen: "Dallas also wondered what it would be like to play a sophisticated game of hide-and-seek with real-life police trying to find him. He said he would leave clues, just to give the searchers a chance, but that he could outwit them." '

Was I now the leader of the pursuers Dallas had imagined? How could I carry out my usual act of identifying with the subject of the case? I was neither sixteen nor a genius, as I had noted before. What we had on our side, though, was that human comforter and failing *habit*. Even geniuses have it. A runaway will change his name, but he'll usually select a new one that has traces of the old, just so he won't lose all sense of identity. Sleeping habits do not change. Rarely do eating habits alter. The type of friends a fugitive makes remains the same. What the fugitive enjoys doing, or what he has ambitions to do, is the same as what he enjoyed or wanted to do before.

I remember a prominent attorney who vanished without a trace. He was discovered years later, living in the country in a rustic house and painting pictures, which was exactly what he had always wanted to do. None of the searchers had ever asked the question, What was this man's dearest fantasy about himself? But this question was becoming very important in the search for Dallas, because a large part of Dallas's life seemed to be made up of fantasy.

For a moment we went back to more mundane matters and talked over what we might deduce about Dallas's movements after he left his room, presuming that he left voluntarily and alone. There were a few things I thought I could predicate. First, Dallas would have a hard time getting a room in a hotel or rooming house. What landlady or hotel clerk wouldn't be suspicious of this childlike creature with no luggage? (The no-luggage assumption was simply a good guess, based on the fact that all of Dallas's clothes except the ones he wore had been found in his room.) I further guessed that he had no money. He'd held no job, and the $500 he'd been given by his parents at the beginning of the summer was almost certainly gone by the third week in August. He had severe limitations on where he might go. Bars would not let him in. Employment offices would be difficult and risky. Shelters? Youth hostels? Nothing had turned up yet. It did seem possible that people in the gay community might be hiding him. But these were routes still to be pursued. It was now 10:30 P.M. and I had to have a talk with Frank Lambert.

Lambert entered the room with his hands in his pockets and an easygoing smile on his face – very laid back. Of course, certain criminals might tell you that Frank Lambert is as laid back and easygoing as a cobra. He loves two things, flying and excitement, more than anything else in the world.

'I guess you've checked the airports,' I said.

'Every one within twenty miles. Some little private ones you wouldn't know exist. Showed Dallas's picture around. Nothing.'

'Bus stations?'

'Same thing.'

'Game rooms?' Dallas loved video games – and this was before they became a rage.

'One guy thought he recognized him as a kid who came in alone, played a long time, and got high scores. If you're good, you get free games.'

'What have you found in the dormitory and around campus?' Lambert could pass as a student, while Hock and Riddle never could.

'The students just won't talk, and the professors won't either. I think it's true that he didn't have many friends. But I also think they're scared. Who wants to talk about sex and drugs when the kid was that young?'

Lambert had put his finger on it. It might be that a felony was involved somewhere, a felony very similar to that of taking advantage of an underage girl – except a lot worse. Prosecutors get very zealous when they go after men who have had sex with male minors. And a prisoner convicted of sexual offenses against children finds prison a living hell, and his fellow prisoners like Puritan judges. Even a mass murderer looks down on a child molester.

'Any luck on the trash detail?' I asked Lambert, bringing my mind back to the matter at hand. Great information comes out of garbage cans sometimes, and I never overlook this possibility. Gold rings, stylish clothes, and all, I did the digging to find a lead in the killing of a multimillionaire from Akron, Dean Milo. And I've seen it work many other times. Peggy Hogan had told Riddle that she might know some people who had some information about Dallas. Of course Peggy would recognize Riddle when she saw him again, but she would never guess the real occupation of the new, young garbage collector.

'Just trash so far. She likes junk food.'

'Okay. Now, the Tolkien Fellowship of MSU – what do you have on that?'

'They read the works of the master and talk about them. They're like the "Star Trek" Trekkies. Dallas turned up at a few meetings, according to Karen Coleman and Mark Hyde, who's the president of the Science Fiction Society. The other members won't say anything. The group is supposed to be having some kind of anniversary celebration soon – it has to do with a *Lord of the Rings* character named Gandolf. I've heard they meet in Party Hollow, a clearing in the middle of some woods.'

'We'll be there.' It seemed just barely possible that Dallas might decide to attend.

'We won't be welcome.'

'I'm not asking for an invitation. You can hide in a tree. Or I will.'

'You do it.'

'Was Dallas a member of the Science Fiction Society?'

'Mark Hyde says so. Dallas was a great reader of poetry, mysticism, and the occult. Lots of sf too. His favorite science-fiction writers were Kurt Vonnegut and Isaac Asimov.'

'Have you learned anything else? You flew the plane over the campus, didn't you?'

'Yes, to see if any configuration conformed to the diagram on the corkboard. I've got twenty or thirty very good pictures.'

I leafed through them. I came to two or three showing a building that from above resembled almost exactly the shape of the tacks clustered together on the corkboard.

'I thought you'd find that interesting,' said Lambert.

The building we were looking at was the old Michigan State University power plant, now almost completely phased out by a new facility. You had to be in the air to see the resemblance to the tack cluster, but then it was unmistakable. I thought of space flight and science fiction, the mind of a sixteen-year-old. I thought hard. It wouldn't come; I couldn't go any further. I didn't know Dallas well enough yet.

But that figure worried me. Did it mean more than just the shape of a building where our search should begin? It looked something like a gun – an Army Colt .45 automatic, for instance. Did it also signify Dallas's method of dying? Was the gun Dallas himself, loaded and ready to explode? And I couldn't forget that there were *thirty-eight* tacks on the corkboard, the rest of them scattered. I thought that those tacks and pushpins might show a path Dallas intended to follow after doing something in the power plant.

It would not be easy. The note left in the room implied, at least to me, that the writer did not expect us to succeed. But we had the starting point; I was convinced of that, and I was determined to follow the maze the rest of the way.

Chapter 4

I'd never had a dream like this one. Dallas's disembodied head appeared, and it said piteously, 'Help me, help me, find me if you can.' His face was gaunt, and etched into it were fear, pain, agony. The voice pleaded; its tone spoke of a terrible ordeal. If this once had been a game, it was one no longer. The game had gone hideously awry. Dallas was alive, and he desperately wanted, *needed*, to be found.

I always dream about my cases. I take them one at a time, never trying to juggle two investigations at once, and the case I'm working on absorbs me. It's not surprising that we dream about what we live during our waking hours, and sleep, of course, can unleash the mind to the nightmare of our worst unconscious fears. On the other hand, I could not cavalierly dismiss this dream, which was more vivid than any that had ever haunted me, because it could well contain meanings that still lay unrecognized in my unconscious.

During a quick shower and shave I realized that this day began the third week that Dallas Egbert had been missing. It was August 30, and Dallas had vanished on August 15. The time elapsed without *any* clue did not bode well. Each day the situation persisted unchanged, experience and common sense told me, we were less likely to find Dallas alive. If this were a hoax, the novelty would long ago have worn off. And as time went on, I thought, the boy's genius and considerable resourcefulness became secondary, almost unimportant. Simple emotional and physical needs would take precedence. He was only sixteen, according to Dr. Clark he was 'socially retardant,' and anyway, how much pressure could he take?

I dressed rapidly, rang Dick Riddle in his room to tell him to meet me in the parking lot, and headed out the door. I wanted to see Karen Coleman, Dallas's friend and confidante, the coed he referred to as 'Mother.'

Riddle and I interviewed her in her neat and orderly Case Hall room. She had shoulder-length brown hair framing a face that was open and friendly, and she showed a genuine concern and affection for the confused, lonely boy who had chosen her as a friend.

'You're the last person we know of who saw Dallas,' I said. 'I know you've already described it to Mr. Riddle, but I'd appreciate if you'd tell me.'

'It was lunch in the cafeteria downstairs.'

'Was Dallas depressed?'

'He didn't seem so. He was quiet, but that wasn't unusual.'

'What did you talk about?'

'Nothing special. I told him I was having trouble with my calculus. I guess now that he's gone I'll have to drop that course. Dallas helped me all the time – it was easy for him. He'd take the time to explain what was going on, show me how to work out problems that were difficult.'

'Did you know he was a genius?'

'Yes. He never talked about it. I mean, never. But it was so easy to tell.'

'Did other students know?'

'Not if they depended on Dallas to tell them. But they must have known. He was so bright and intelligent. And so young.'

'Can you tell me what Dallas was wearing the last time you saw him?'

'Blue jeans and a dark T-shirt. Dallas always wore tennis shoes.'

'What color T-shirt?'

'I couldn't tell you. I have glaucoma.'

Even without Karen's help, I thought I knew what color Dallas's T-shirt had been. Anna Egbert had gone through his room with a fine-tooth comb; the missing T-shirt was brown. 'Try to remember,' I said, 'what kind of mood Dallas was in.'

'Well . . .' she replied, and paused. I could tell she was debating with herself whether to trust us. Her concern for Dallas's fate won out over fears that she was breaking a confidence. 'He was high on something, I think,' she said. 'Probably marijuana.'

'How did it show?'

'Slow, slurred speech, mainly. I knew him pretty well, Mr. Dear. I could tell when he'd been smoking.'

'Do you know where Dallas got the marijuiana?' Riddle asked.

'Why is that important?'

'We've got a boy who has been missing for more than two weeks,' Riddle said. 'He could very well be dead.' He was trying to scare her.

'I'd really rather not say. Is it very important?'

'It could be,' I said. ' Karen, let's understand one thing. We are not police officers. We're not obligated to tell the police everything we know. We're working for Dallas's parents, not the police or the university, and our only interest is finding Dallas. I'm sure you want that too.'

'I don't want to get anyone into trouble.'

'Karen,' Riddle said, 'you may be the only real friend Dallas had on this campus. I know you want to do all you can to help him.'

'Okay,' she said. 'I know that on the first weekend of this month he went to Ypsilanti to visit a friend of his named Betty Martin. When he came back, he said he'd gotten the drugs he wanted.'

'Anything other than marijuana?'

'He didn't say.'

'How did Dallas get to Ypsilanti?'

'He had to hitchhike, or take the bus.'

'Did he do much hitchhiking?'

'Some. But that's not unusual around here. A lot of the students do it.'

'When Dallas left you there in the cafeteria, what did he say? Think hard, Karen. Did he say anything unusual?'

'No. He just said something like "Take care of yourself," and walked out.'

Yes – and vanished from the face of the earth. Where had he gone? To his room? It was lunch hour; the students weren't in class; someone should have seen him. But sixteen days ago Dallas Egbert had walked out of his dorm's cafeteria and disappeared as completely as if a giant hand had reached down from the sky and plucked him off the planet. Nothing had been heard from him since – not a word, not a note, *nothing*.

I said to Karen, 'Tell me what you and Dallas talked about when you were together.'

'A lot of times, about my schoolwork. He helped me. It was like having a professor for a friend.'

'What else? What things interested Dallas?'

'Science fiction. He was a real science-fiction buff. He believed in reincarnation, talked about it a lot. He thought life was a recycling process, and each time you came back it was in a higher state. You wouldn't be a dog or a snake in your next life.'

'What did he believe he would come back as?'

'He never said. Just that it would be something better.'

'Science fiction . . . Did his interest involve more than books?'

'It involved everything. There was an important science-fiction convention he talked constantly about attending. In fact, it starts tomorrow, I believe. In Louisville, Kentucky. Dallas really wanted to be there. He said he wasn't going to let anything keep him away.'

Right. And I knew some other people who wouldn't be kept away either. It was back to the matter of habits. If a person was an avid player of horses before he vanished, a good place to look for him would be a racetrack. Heavy drinkers turn up in bars. When a person disappears, the cause might be a wish for more time and freedom to indulge a habit.

'What else did Dallas talk about? What did he enjoy doing?'

'He loved D & D. Couldn't get enough of it.'

'What's D & D?'

'Dungeons & Dragons. I don't know how to play it. You have to be very smart. Dallas tried to explain it to me, but I just couldn't understand what he was saying.'

'Do you have any idea at all about the game?'

'It has something to do with science fiction, I think. The players assume the roles of certain characters. The characters are always in danger, and unless they think very clearly, they can be killed.'

'This is a board game? A game you can buy?'

'It's a *mind* game. There's no board involved. Dallas said you can make the game into anything you want – as easy or as complicated as you want. And, yes, you can buy it. D & D is very popular, not only at MSU but at colleges everywhere.'

'You sit around a table and play it?'

'Usually. That's what a lot of kids do in the Student Union.'

'There's another way to play?'

'You can play it for real. I mean, you can go out and simulate the situations. That's when you're really involved.'

'Did Dallas go out and play D & D?'

'Oh, yes. He was very much into the game.'

'Where did he play?'

'In the tunnels beneath the school.'

'Tunnels?'

'I don't know . . . pipes. Heating pipes underneath the school. I understand there are miles of them.'

'He'd go into the tunnels?'

'Yes, he said it made the game much more real for him. But it worried me. I remember one Sunday night, late, he came back to the dorm utterly exhausted, mentally and physically. He looked terrible; his clothes were a mess. He'd been playing D & D in the tunnels.'

'Did you ever go down there?'

'No. I would be afraid to. But Dallas said it was just perfect for the game.'

Karen Coleman seemed genuinely worried about Dallas, and I believed that she wanted him found. But I felt that she was still holding information back – probably to protect her friend, but possibly because there was something she didn't want us to know about her. If there was something, I knew I would eventually learn what it was. I saw no reason to push her now. So far she had been more cooperative than anyone else on campus.

'You know, don't you,' I said to Riddle when we returned to the car, 'that you're going to Louisville? I'd like you to go late tomorrow.'

'My old hometown.'

'Take Hock along with you. This science-fiction convention sounds like a big one. It may take two of you to cover it all.'

'I've got a lot of contacts in Louisville,' Riddle replied. 'I'll find Dallas if he's there.'

I had put off talking to the Egberts that morning, but I couldn't delay any longer. I asked Riddle to make one stop along the way – at a local hobby store, to buy the game Dungeons & Dragons – then we drove to the Red Roof Inn and met the Egberts in their room.

'How are you doing?' Anna asked. 'Have you learned anything yet?'

'Nothing concrete. We didn't know Dallas's life was so complex – you didn't tell us.'

'What are you talking about?'

'Dallas's homosexual affairs.'

Anna looked shocked. I couldn't tell whether it was because of the fact or because we'd learned it. I didn't want to have to tell her such things. It would be better if I could just find the boy, and then make decisions about what to reveal. But we weren't getting anywhere with this course, and Dallas's welfare was my prime concern.

'What about his using drugs?' I said. 'Why didn't you tell me that?'

'I didn't know.' It was as if I were beating her. 'I honestly didn't know.'

'It's important for us to find out everything we can about Dallas, so we know where to look. We're going in circles right now.'

'I'd think it could go quicker,' Anna said.

'Anna,' I said, 'we're doing all we can. I know it's terribly hard for you to be patient, but you must try. I've promised you, and I'll promise you again, we'll find your son.'

'I need to be kept abreast of what you're doing. I can't stand not knowing.'

'If I kept you up to date on everything we've done and everything we will do, Anna, I would be spending too much time discussing the matter with you and not enough time on the road, where I need to be. We've got plenty of information to keep us busy. If there's anything you can help us on, believe me, I'll be here to talk to you in a flash.

You remember, a couple of days ago you asked my staff to take you to a wildlife refuge twenty miles away, where you thought Dallas might have gone to kill himself. My men spent all afternoon out there, with negative results. I want to use our time wisely and more efficiently because each day makes the job more difficult. You've given me the responsibility of finding Dallas. I want to do this in a way that's both professional and successful.'

'I guess I shouldn't say please hurry. I know you're doing all you can. But please hurry.'

Riddle and I drove to the Michigan State University public safety building, new and modern, where the campus police were housed. There we talked with Sergeants Larry Lyons and Bill Wardwell of the criminal division, who had been assigned to Dallas's disappearance. Both were young and alert, had attended Michigan State, and were continuing their educations while working full time as police officers. It was immediately apparent to me that they were a cut above most detectives, who are generally a jaded lot made cynical by overwork and poor pay. But Lyons and Wardwell cared. They'd been working extra hours on this case, which was not a normal occurrence, despite what TV police dramas depict.

Lyons and Wardwell knew that I was well thought of by law enforcement agencies around the nation and that I did not intend just to use them and give nothing in return. In fact, they welcomed our appearance in the case. They knew that we had more experience in finding missing persons than they did, and they were weary of fending off questions from the press.

'It's not just the locals,' Bill Wardwell explained. 'The story's gone out on the wires. We're getting calls from out of town. Big-name organizations are picking up on this.'

'Why not let us take the calls from the press?' I said.

'That way you can work on whatever other cases you have. We only have this one case.'

Wardwell glanced at Lyons. Both were clean-cut, wore business suits, and radiated efficiency. Lyons shrugged. Why not?

'We'll put out the word,' Wardwell said, 'that you're the people to talk to on this case. We'll tell our switchboard to refer calls from the press to you.'

'That's fine,' I agreed. 'And we'll keep you informed of what we learn.' It was a promise I fully intended to keep. I was once a police officer myself, and I know what it means to be short-staffed.

But I had another reason for volunteering to talk to the press. If I could keep drugs and homosexuality out of the papers, fine. I wanted to spare the Egberts the embarrassment, and Dallas himself, if he was alive. Also I hoped we could use the press to find Dallas. If he was portrayed as I was beginning to know him to be, we would have the public looking for him too, rather than just a handful of detectives. His desire, or the desire of those who led him, to remain out of sight would be enormously more difficult to satisfy if the public was searching for him. Of course, if he was alive, he was a little boy fighting for survival in a dark world, and if this was successfully explained to people, they would *want* to help.

A third reason was something the Egberts had done at my request – they had put up a $5000 reward 'for information leading to the recovery or whereabouts of James Dallas Egbert III.' The wording of the reward notice promised that no questions would be asked and all information would be kept strictly confidential. I made certain that I had the ultimate say about who received the money. I also obtained instant access to the $5000, since a really good informant might want cash right on the spot.

Offering a reward can be of tremendous value. It had

helped me solve several cases in the past, and I believed it might be an enormous help in this instance. College students don't want to violate their code and cooperate with the 'enemy' – the police – and often they are not sophisticated enough to understand the difference between private investigators and cops. But they are like the rest of the population in their appreciation of money. Five thousand dollars is more than most of them have ever seen. And if Dallas's fellow students could get that money, in cash, without their peers knowing . . .

I hoped the reward offer would bring results. We would run it in local newspapers and student publications, paste it up in washeterias, student hangouts, and game rooms, on storefronts in the gay community, in the Student Union where Dungeons & Dragons was played, even on those lovely campus trees. Soon, with the arrival of the national and international media, much of the world would know about the reward.

When I said calls could be channeled through me, though, I had no idea what I'd let myself in for. Soon ten Bill Dears working around the clock couldn't have kept up with the incoming calls – not just from the media, but from informants, concerned citizens, psychics, crackpots, anonymous tipsters, corporation heads who played Dungeons & Dragons on the company computer, and just plain decent people offering their support and saying that Dallas was in their prayers.

Outside the campus police station, I used our car's telephone to call Frank Lambert. 'I've heard there are tunnels beneath the entire MSU campus,' I said. 'I want you to scout around the university, talk to students without letting them know what it's all about, and learn all you can about the tunnels. It's possible these tunnels are being used to play games. I want to know what kind of games, who is playing them, and what kind of people they are. Are they just students? Or students and faculty? Are there outsiders involved?'

'Tunnels,' Lambert said. 'I've got bad memories of tunnels.' He had crawled through a few in Vietnam.

'Get a map of them if you can. Find out where you get into them.'

I cut the connection. I knew that if there was anything to learn about those tunnels, Lambert would find it for me. I had a hunch about the tunnels. They had been on my mind ever since Karen Coleman had mentioned that Dallas had gone down into them to play Dungeons & Dragons. It made me think of that corkboard with the colored tacks. The gun-shaped configuration seemed identical to the shape of the old power plant, but to recognize that, one had to be in the air. Perhaps to understand the rest, one needed to go underground.

'Next stop: Ypsilanti,' I said to Dick Riddle.

'Betty Martin,' he agreed, and started the car in motion.

It was about thirty miles from East Lansing to Ypsilanti, and I used the time to study the Dungeons & Dragons booklets we had stopped to buy. They seemed to contain almost everything you needed to know about the game. Karen had told me that the character Dallas most liked to play was called the magic-user. This was the role he chose in his fantasies, the form he took to confront the countless monsters awaiting him along the path.

In Dungeons & Dragons, each character has assigned abilities and a point score for each ability (unless players choose to make up their own rules). These ability scores tell the player how strong his character is in each area; for instance, a character might be rated very high where a strength is concerned but very low in intelligence. Knowing your character's capabilities helps you survive in the dangerous world of Dungeons & Dragons, where the object is to slay enemies – the most formidable being dragons – and stay alive while you find treasure.

The magic-user possesses extremely high intelligence – his forte. His weakness is his fighting ability; under all circumstances he should avoid physical combat. The magic-user can cast spells, such as bringing down lightning bolts on his enemies. He starts the game as the weakest of players, but if he is properly shrewd, resourceful, and inventive, he can end up the most powerful of all. Still, the magic-user is advised never to enter a dungeon alone, for his lack of physical strength, and the fact that he is the only character who cannot wear armor, make him extraordinarily vulnerable.

I studied the magic-user's basic ability points. (The ability score of each character is measured by numbers from three to eighteen. A three means you're a hopeless incompetent; an eighteen is the highest anyone can achieve.)

Intelligence	17
Dexterity	16
Constitution	14
Wisdom	11
Charisma	9
Strength	8

Yes, the character Dallas chose to play was himself. Strength and charisma he did not possess, but intelligence and dexterity, yes. Like many small people, Dallas was agile. Apparently he had gone down into the tunnels – not dungeons of the mind, but real ones – to play this game. I wondered if he had done what the magic-user should never do: go down alone.

An individual can play the game by himself, but usually there are more than two participants, and in this case a dungeon master is needed. The dungeon master referees the game and creates different obstacles, such as trap doors, hidden doors, and monsters. The dungeon master is a sort of god, with total authority to resolve disputes. The best of them are absolutely impartial.

A group of players gathering in a given spot is called a dungeon, and usually more than one game is going on at the same time at these dungeons. Incredibly, there were more than one hundred dungeons in the East Lansing area along when Dallas disappeared. On the weekend of August 19, 1979, just a few days before we were called into the case, *thousands* of college students attended a game convention at the University of Wisconsin at Parkside to play Dungeons & Dragons. The national Sunday supplement magazine *Parade* called the game 'the hottest craze on college campuses since streaking.' But D & D's appeal cut across all occupations and social classes, and all ages. The only common denominator among players was a higher-than-average IQ. Later, when Dallas's case became an international *cause célèbre*, Dungeons & Dragons became even more popular.

I stopped thinking about the game as we reached Ypsilanti, a quaint, quiet, pretty town near Ann Arbor and the University of Michigan. Betty Martin lived in a single-story white frame duplex. She was by herself when we arrived, and invited us in when I made the introductions. A slender and attractive woman with long black hair and a fair complexion, she was perhaps twenty-one years old, an office clerk at General Motors, in the division where automobile transmissions are made.

'We've been told,' I began, 'that Dallas Egbert visited you on the first weekend of this month, before he disappeared.'

'I didn't even know he was missing,' she said.

'Don't you read the papers?'

'I haven't had time. I don't pay much attention to the papers.'

'Was he here on the third of August?'

'Yes. I wasn't expecting him – he showed up on the doorstep. He caught me off guard. My boyfriend was with me.'

'How did you come to know Dallas?'

'I met him at a science-fiction convention last year, in November, I think. Afterward he wrote me a couple of times.'

'Sounds like he was taken with you.'

'I don't know why. I liked Dallas, but I never led him on.'

'What did he want? Why was he at your door?'

'He needed a place to stay for the night. I couldn't let him stay here – you know, because my boyfriend was here.'

'Did he come this far just to visit? Especially unannounced . . . You sure there's not something you're not telling me?'

'No. He just showed up, that's all.'

'Seems strange to me. You sure he's not buying drugs from you?'

'I don't know what you're talking about.' She was not angry. She revealed no reaction at all.

'Do you know Karen Coleman?'

'Not personally. Dallas talked about her.'

'Do you know Peggy Hogan?'

'No.'

'That's odd. You're from Ypsilanti. Karen Coleman is from Ypsilanti. Peggy Hogan is from Ypsilanti. All of you know Dallas, yet none of you know each other. Ypsilanti isn't a very big place.'

'It doesn't seem so odd to me.'

'When you told Dallas he couldn't stay here, what did he do?'

'He asked if he could use the phone. I told him sure. He made two or three phone calls.'

'Who did he call?' This is the right way to ask this question. You shouldn't ask, 'Do you know who he called?' That makes it too easy to say no. The right way implies that it's the most natural thing in the world that the person you're talking to would know.

'He called Karen Coleman. In the other conversations, I remember, he mentioned the names Lee and Judith. That's all. He talked about taking a bus back to East Lansing.'

'Do you know who Lee and Judith are?'

'No idea at all.'

'How long did Dallas stay after making the phone calls?'

'Maybe thirty minutes. It was obvious that my boyfriend wanted to get rid of him.'

'What was Dallas's mood? Was anything bothering him?'

'He was depressed. He was always depressed.'

'Was he high on anything?'

'Yes, he was – I don't know what. And he smoked a joint before he left.'

'You said you didn't sell him drugs. Do you know who did?'

'No, I don't know who did. Will you stop trying to make me look like a pusher?' Now she was showing some emotion.

'We're just trying to find out what happened to a sixteen-year-old boy. He picked up drugs in Ypsilanti. We *know* that.'

'Well, I can't help you. And I don't like your

insinuations. I haven't seen Dallas since that day. You can take it or leave it.'

We left it. As we were walking out the door, Betty asked, 'Do you think he's dead?'

'It's a possibility,' I said.

On the way back to East Lansing my mind raced. Why didn't anyone want to talk about Dallas and his or her involvement with him? The students. The professors. Members of the gay community. And now Betty Martin. She knew more than she had told us, I was sure of that.

'I want you to check her phone records,' I said to Riddle.

'I'm going to Louisville,' he reminded me. 'Why not have Lambert do it?'

'Right.' Including myself, we had four men on this investigation full time, and still there weren't enough. Lambert already had plenty of work to do. *Four full-time men*. Does anyone wonder why the police often can't devote to a case the attention that it deserves?

'I'll have him check Karen Coleman's phone too,' I said. Many of the students in Case Hall, Karen included, had their own telephones – another change from when I was a youth.

Karen Coleman. My mind always came back to her. She hadn't told us that Dallas had called her from Ypsilanti. Dallas's 'mother' was going to receive another visit from me – very soon.

When Riddle and I were back in East Lansing, I contacted Frank Lambert on our two-way radio. 'What about the tunnels?' I asked.

'Incredible information,' he said. Lambert is not the sort to use a phrase like that loosely. 'But there's something else. Something even more important.'

'What's that?'

'I just talked with Wardwell. About the cremation note. Dallas didn't write it.'

Chapter 5

State police handwriting analysts had discovered discrepancies between the cremation note and the printing in Dallas's poems, especially in the way the *i*'s and the *e*'s were drawn. So many conflicting thoughts went through my mind that no single one was appropriate. If Dallas hadn't written the note, the chances that he had committed suicide seemed much less likely. This was the good news; the bad news was that others were involved. Because fifteen days had elapsed since the disappearance, the possibility that a joke was being played or that the motives were innocent was greatly lessened.

Handwriting analysis is a fairly precise and accurate science, but there is room for error. I recalled the time I'd been retained by the parents of a high school student who received a 'You are going to die' note in the mail. The parents took this note very seriously, as well they should have. The handwriting experts I called in came to the conclusion that the student had written the note himself. I couldn't accept this. I had gotten to know the boy involved, and I didn't believe he was lying. Further investigation proved me right. I discovered the person who had sent the note, a boy who had serious emotional problems and felt spurned in his attempts to befriend my client's son. If he had not been caught, writing that note might very well have been a first step on the way to a much more serious action. Like the Dallas Egbert investigation, this case featured parents who really did not adequately understand their son. They were prepared, on the basis of the handwriting analysis, to put their son in psychiatric care.

Generally, handwriting analysis is admissible in courts as evidence, whereas a lie-detector test is not. I put a lot of stock in handwriting analysis, *if* the experts have enough samples of the individual's penmanship with which to draw comparisons. The state police analysts had copies of the three poems Dallas had written, plus some letters and schoolwork. This should have been enough; it certainly would have been for the firm I usually employ in Texas, which is made up of former Secret Service agents.

In any case, the news about the cremation note hardly cleared the muddy waters, but it did explain away the one major doubt I'd felt about my suicide hypothesis. Why hadn't we found the body? Bodies smell. Animals and birds find bodies and call attention to them. In wooded areas, bodies are found by hikers and hunters; in fields, by farmers. The odds said we should have found Dallas's body. There are woods all around Michigan State University, but students on walks tramp through them continually.

Was the person who wrote the note the same one who cleaned up Dallas's dorm room? And why did he or she write it?

The note had to be part of a coverup. It made no sense otherwise. We were being misdirected. For what purpose?

The whole case was maddening. If Dallas's aim had been to confuse his pursuers, if Dallas the magic-user had been casting a spell, he had succeeded. But he'd needed help. Who would have written that note for him? Wouldn't a friend have come forward by now? Kidnappers might have wanted time to set up a plan . . . but *fifteen days*?

In my opinion, murder became more of a likelihood with the news from the handwriting analysis. A murderer might have found an ideal hiding place for the body and reasoned that interest in the matter would eventually die out. A murderer would hope we'd conclude that the boy had simply been clever enough to devise a resting place where he would never be found. No one would go beyond that and start looking for a killer.

But that was just the point. *Dallas was clever*. We knew he had given considerable thought to disappearing, in fact had talked about it with Karen Byerly and Bruce Roberts that night in Holmes Hall. We couldn't underestimate Dallas. I remembered a fact about him: when computers broke down at Wright-Patterson Air Force Base, Dallas, then aged twelve, was called out to repair them. Still, I now had to concede to myself that murder or a hoax was more likely than suicide. The only thing to do was learn more.

'What about the tunnels?' I asked Lambert when he arrived in my room.

'They're there, all right,' he said. 'Miles and miles of them. They cobweb everywhere underneath this campus.'

'How accessible are they?'

'If I believed what I heard, you can't get into the tunnels. All the adults I asked said the same thing. But I snooped around the school administration building today.'

'Well?'

'They're lying. Or they've got their heads in the sand.'

'How do you know?'

'Hell, Bill, I was in those tunnels.'

I'd figured he would go in if they were there. As I've said, Lambert loves risks. He'd taken them in Vietnam, and he was attracted as a moth to flame by anything that looked like excitement.

'What was it like?' I asked.

'Miserable. Hot like hell, wet, cramped. Steamier than a Saigon whorehouse. I can see why you wanted me to go down there.'

'I didn't want you to go down there,' I said. I couldn't help smiling.

'Well, I did. But I didn't stay long. It's a hellhole.'

'Dallas played Dungeons & Dragons down there.'

'I was afraid you'd say that.'

'Why?'

'It means we're going in. And we'll be staying a lot longer than I'd care to.'

'Imagine Dallas playing a game in the tunnels.'

'I can't see its being any fun. And if he went where I did, he wouldn't be playing very long – heat exhaustion would set in. He'd be dead.'

Would he? Lambert's description of the tunnels reminded me of the game booklets I'd read that afternoon. 'Hiding' was an important tactic to success in the game, as was 'dodging,' at which small creatures were especially adept. Other headlines in the Dungeons & Dragons booklets included 'Evasion and Pursuit,' 'Characters Flee,' 'Delaying Pursuit,' and 'Length of Pursuit.' Here is what is written under 'Length of Pursuit': 'If nothing is dropped to cause them to stop, monsters will pursue for any length of time . . .'

As I thought about it, I could imagine Dallas playing a real-life version of the game with us. The tunnels seemed eerily to fit the descriptions I'd read of the dungeons where adventures took place and monsters lurked and pursued. A cremation note intended to throw us off the track could refer to 'If nothing is dropped to cause them to stop . . .' Everything about this case could be a mammoth ruse orchestrated by an erratic but brilliant magician.

Another idea could not be completely rejected: Dallas might actually have begun to live the game, not just to play it. Dungeons & Dragons could have absorbed him so much that his mind had slipped through the fragile barrier between reality and fantasy, and he no longer existed in the world we inhabit. If this had happened, he might be much more difficult to find. The physically weak but intellectually gifted magic-user, all alone, trembling, frightened, could be a resourceful fox with giant hounds in pursuit. Who knew how long he might hide, perhaps leaving his lair to scavenge for food each night? If, in the manner of Jekyll and Hyde, he had become a dual personality, Dallas might hold out a very long time. Surely he would not show himself to his pursuers.

'You just walked into those tunnels?' I said to Lambert.

'You don't walk into them, at least from where I entered. Would you believe going through a manhole cover?'

'Why were you told they were inaccessible?'

'You'd say they were inaccessible too, if you knew the problems this university has. There have been robberies on campus, and rapes. They haven't been solved. I can't prove it, but I'd wager that those tunnels played a role in some of these crimes. God knows where they lead.'

What a way to get inside the buildings! And to effect an escape! It seemed to me that administration officials might very well want to look the other way where the tunnels were concerned. Several people had made it clear to Lambert that a search would not be welcome; I expected to encounter opposition, but I also intended to raise a fuss. My mind kept going back to something Anna Egbert had told me with resentment: 'One of the reasons we sent Dallas to MSU was because of the network of security they told us about. They told us they could handle a young boy because they have had other very young students on campus before.'

'Dallas could be down there,' I said to Lambert.

'He's dead, then.'

'I'm not so sure. He's a very unusual boy.' If anyone could find a way to survive in that maze of tunnels, Dallas was that person. 'I'm going down there,' I said. 'If Dallas is in the tunnels, we'll find him. If he's not, we'll prove he's not. It doesn't matter whether the university cooperates. Let them deny permission – I'll give the press such an earful, the administration will have to bend to the pressure. If I have to, I'll bring in more men from Texas.'

I was finished with Lambert for the moment, and he was about to leave when Hock and Riddle appeared at the door. I wanted their opinions. I brought them up to date on what Lambert had learned, then asked, 'What do you think, is Dallas dead or alive?'

'Dead,' Lambert reiterated. 'I think he committed suicide.'

'Why? He didn't write that note.'

'The state police can make mistakes. Everything else points to suicide.'

'All right. Hock, what about you?'

'Alive. Remember, I was there when the Egberts talked with Dr. Clark, the psychologist. I think a lot of animosity built up between Dallas and his parents. I think he just split and is running us around in circles. I keep thinking, though, after what I've learned, that maybe he's better off dead.'

'What does that mean?'

'All the pressures he had – I couldn't have taken them. But I still vote alive. I think this is the way he's chosen to get even.'

'Riddle?'

'Dead. The drug involvement scares the hell out of me. I think he could be OD'd somewhere. Especially if he ran away, like Hock believes. The report on the cremation note bothers me, because it indicates that somebody kidnapped him, maybe on a drug deal, and then left a note to misdirect us. Of course, Dallas had every reason to commit suicide. Either way points to dead.'

'I say alive,' I said, though I respected everything the men had told me. 'I know that I started off believing that he was a suicide, but now I just have a gut hunch that when we find him, he'll be alive.'

I winced when I said 'gut hunch.' I was supposed to be the leader of this elite pack, and the best I could do was 'gut hunch.' In contrast, Hock, Lambert, and Riddle had offered sound reasons for their beliefs. Regardless, I'd had so-called gut hunches before, and they usually turned out to be right.

The three men left, Riddle and Hock to check out gay bars, Lambert to spend more time trying to pick up something new at the university. I lay back on my bed and said, 'Talk to me, Dallas. Tell me where you are.' We had some of the pieces to the puzzle. I tried to fill in the rest with my imagination, by pretending that I was Dallas walking out of that Case Hall cafeteria. Where had I gone? Straight to the tunnels? Had I been preparing myself for months to go into that incredible maze? I would have gathered food to survive on, and taken a blanket and a few personal items to which I'd become attached. I'd have to be prepared to hold out against my enemies for a long time. For as long as I had breath. Forever. And my magic would make me powerful down there.

I – Bill Dear – was sweating, and my breath came in gasps. Yes, Dallas had gone into the tunnels. He went straight from the cafeteria to the tunnels. It was almost as if I *knew*. I felt I had made that walk with him, gone across the green grass beneath the stately maples, my mind absorbed by the perilous, soon-to-begin, real-life adventure.

Everything that was Dallas was missing from his room, Mrs. Egbert had said. That fit the profile of someone intending to leave, and leave for a long time. As I've said, people simply do not seem to be able to break completely with their past, no matter how miserable they might find it. Dallas might have taken his few precious personal possessions with him.

As yet I had no idea what had happened next, but I believed that something had gone tragically wrong. Had Dallas met someone in the tunnels? Had a betrayal taken place? Had that person, or persons, returned to Dallas's room to tidy it up and print the cremation note? And what had they done with Dallas himself?

I'd done enough musing; it was time for more prosaic actions. I called the front desk for the day's messages.

'Mr. Dear,' the clerk said, 'there are three people sitting down here waiting for you. They seem to be willing to wait for the duration. And I have some phone messages for you. It might be best if you picked them up.'

'Why is that?'

'I can't spare the two bellmen it would take to carry them.'

She was a wise guy. 'Why don't you bring them?' I said.

'Seriously, Mr. Dear, the switchboard has been lit up all day. Other people are having trouble getting calls through.'

'Ummm,' I said. I needed a moment to think. The three people downstairs had to be reporters. I couldn't talk to the press right now, which meant that I couldn't pick up the messages. But if there had been as many calls as the clerk indicated, a few of them might be important.

'Bring them up,' I said, 'and I'll give you a dozen of the most beautiful roses you've ever seen.'

'That would be nice. I've never had roses.'

There were more than fifty messages. Except for a few

from my office and two from the Egberts, I had no idea whom they were from. The Michigan State detectives, Lyons and Wardwell, had kept their promise: all information on the disappearance was being channeled through me.

In some areas of daily existence I'm not very organized. An example is phone calls: unless I know something is very important, I run a sort of lottery with messages. I spread them across a desk and grab one, which is what I did with this batch.

'Mrs. Reeves, this is Bill Dear. You called me.'

'I think I know where Dallas is.'

'Please tell me. I can use any help I can get.'

'I'm a psychic,' she said.

I groaned. There are a lot of people in the world who are anxious to help out on a case like this, but it's always hard to tell the sincere ones from the loonies. Although I didn't know it at the time, Mrs. Reeves was only the first of hundreds of psychics who called me about the disappearance of James Dallas Egbert III, which must have set a world record for unleashing odd characters. I always talk to the psychics, though. They generally seem sincere to me, though none has ever helped me on a case. Also, talking with a psychic – well, maybe just talking with anyone – can bring to mind an idea that could prove helpful.

'What information do you have, Mrs. Reeves?'

'The boy is lying near water, a pond. He's near trees. He's hurt, but he's alive. It's somewhere near the university. That's all I can see right now, but I'll keep trying. Would you mind if I call you when I know more?'

'I wouldn't mind at all, Mrs. Reeves.'

I hung up and put the message in what would become a pile. I would have many of these. Reporters. Psychics and anyone else who wanted to be helpful. People who knew

Dallas. Police officers. Those who played Dungeons & Dragons.

The next message I took at random had 'IMPORTANT' written across the top in capital letters. There was no name, just a telephone number, which I dialed.

'This is Bill Dear,' I said.

The voice was young and female. 'I'm glad you called,' she said. 'I've got something I need to tell you.'

'Who is this?'

'Mr. Dear, I can't get involved. I'm in school here. The university will tell you that you can't get into the tunnels, but don't believe that. I know you can – I've been there.'

'Why would you go there?'

'I play Dungeons & Dragons. Many kids do. If you're familiar with the game, you'll know the tunnels are as close to the real thing as you can get. The students aren't the only ones who play the game there. So do professors.'

'Do you know Dallas?'

'I don't think so. But I know he played the game in the tunnels. The reason I'm talking with you is to tell you that the game is very dangerous. You can be hurt. I think Dallas may have hurt himself and got trapped. I think you should go into the tunnels.'

'How could he get hurt?' I could think of a hundred ways.

'It's terrible down there, Mr. Dear. That's why it's so good for the game. It's hot and wet, and there's slime on the walls. You never know when the steam will be released. You can fall and crack your head. One night five or six of us were playing, and suddenly we came across this guy who wasn't one of us. I shined my flashlight in the guy's face and he ran. Later I learned that a girl had been attacked in one of the dorms. We never said anything because we would have been expelled, and the professor who was with us would have been fired.'

'I'd like to meet you,' I said.

'I can't. I'm afraid. I'm going to be a senior – I couldn't stand to get in trouble.'

'Well, I'd like you to stay in touch with me. I'd like you to find out who played the game with Dallas. Would you do that for me?'

'Yes. I just don't want anyone to know my name.'

'You have my word. But work on this – help me. I'm afraid Dallas is in great danger. I need to find him.'

'I'll call you, Mr. Dear. Good-bye.'

I picked another nameless message from the pile. I was just beginning to see that this case would also set some sort of record for anonymous phone calls. Nobody wanted to talk openly about Dallas; everyone was afraid.

'This is Bill Dear,' I said. 'You called me.'

'I know Dallas. I know a place where you should look for him. It's where he trestled.'

'Trestled?'

'Right. Trestling is when you lie on railroad ties and let a train run over you.'

'Dallas did *that*?'

'I saw it a couple times. He did it to get attention.'

'You were going to tell me where.'

'It's at the south end of the campus. You go through the woods, follow the path – the only path there is – to the C & O railroad tracks. Walk east. You'll come to a trestle bridge with a stream underneath. It's about a twenty-five-foot drop from the tracks to the water.'

'You saw Dallas play this game?'

'Yeah. You can do it one of two ways. You can dangle from the track, and if you get scared you can let go and fall into the water. Or you can lie across the ties and let the train run over you. That's a lot more dangerous. It's what Dallas did.'

'Will you take me to this place?'

'You're the detective – you can find it. But go out there. Dallas could have been hit by a train, or he could be in the water.'

I decided to go tomorrow. I'd feel like a fool, but I'd go trestling. I'd do that, and one other thing too. I was going to talk to 'Mother' again.

Chapter 6

Riddle and I sat across the table from Karen Coleman, whose room was still as neat as the proverbial pin. This time I was going to get some answers.

Riddle and I are so used to the soft-cop/hard-cop routine that we felt no need to rehearse; we simply slipped into it naturally. Riddle was talking about the pleasant autumn weather, or some such subject he didn't care about, when I got up from my chair and started to pace. I've learned that you can dominate someone if you stand while they sit. They feel uncomfortable, a little afraid. They have to look up at you.

'Listen, Karen,' I said, 'this has gone too damn far. I want to know, and I want to know right now, every piece of information you have about Dallas's disappearance.'

'I don't know where he is. I don't know what happened to him.'

'Don't give me that.' I flared up, staring at her hard. 'He didn't call you Mother for nothing. He phoned you from Betty Martin's home.'

'You know, he did,' she said, the tone of her voice indicating how remarkable it was that she could have forgotten.

'It seems there are a lot of things that you've forgotten. But let's stay with this. Why did Dallas call you?'

'He asked if I knew somewhere he could stay in Ypsilanti. It was too late to catch a bus back to school.'

'Why would he call you?'

'I'm from Ypsilanti. I have a lot of friends there.'

'Did you find him a place to stay?'

'He stayed with a friend of mine named Tim Privett. Dallas came back the next day. He hitchhiked, I think.'

This sudden flood of remembrances would have seemed amazing, except that I had seen it so often in other investigations. People simply don't want to volunteer information to investigators; you have to dig it out.

'What was he doing in Ypsilanti?'

'I'm sure I told you this before. He went to get drugs – marijuana, I would guess.'

'My God,' I said. 'A sixteen-year-old boy. Didn't anybody care about Dallas? Didn't you?'

'Yes, I cared. But what could I do? I'll tell you this, he was looking for attention. He wanted to belong, to have friends. That's why he did a lot of things. And I blame his mother, because no matter what he accomplished, she always expected more. I was Dallas's friend. I think I was his best friend, maybe his only friend. He talked with me a lot, told me how much he wanted to please people. But nothing was ever enough. He said he always felt used.'

'Did he talk about his father?'

'He loved his father, and he missed him a lot. His father never took him places. I think his father is dominated by his mother. I'll tell you another thing – Dallas felt that his parents didn't want him around. He didn't go just to Michigan State, you know; he attended Northwestern before. He thought his parents didn't know what to do with him, so they gave the job to someone else.'

'I knew about Northwestern. What did Dallas say life was like there?'

'Pretty much the same as at MSU. He didn't make friends, didn't get any special attention or help either. He was so brilliant, I guess people didn't realize he had needs. You know some of the things he accomplished, don't you?'

Yes, I did. At age thirteen, when he graduated from

high school, he placed second in the Ohio math competition, competing against much older youngsters, and received a commendation from the Ohio Council of Mathematics Teachers. He also received a commendation in the National Merit Scholarship competition, placed in several other math competitions, and was a member of the National Honor Society and the Dayton Honors Seminar. At Michigan State he had been accepted into the Honors College.

Of course Dallas's mind was the key to this case. Captain Ferman Badgley of the MSU campus police later agreed with me. 'All his hobbies had to do with challenges to his mind,' Captain Badgley said. 'Competition for him was in his brain. Without a challenge, he got bored. Consequently, he turned to the bizarre.' And Sergeant Wardwell said that Dallas's faculty adviser 'had seen him only a few times to work out class schedules. It's hard to think that a guy pulling mostly 4.0's in computer and math class was under pressure. But a 3.5 can be traumatic for someone accustomed to doing better.'

Karen Coleman had been close to Dallas, and she had seen how Dallas's accomplishments had affected him. But I felt that she still wasn't telling us all she knew. I did not enjoy playing the role of tough interrogator with a young woman, but it was necessary if that was the only way to get information, and this time I was determined to get from her what she knew.

'I think it's damn strange,' I said, 'that whenever I pursue anything, the path leads back to you. I look for his best friend, I find you. I want to learn about drugs, I come to you. I go to Ypsilanti, the trail comes back here. I'm interested in Dungeons & Dragons; you tell me he's played the game in the tunnels. As far as I know, you're the last person he talked with. Karen, let's stop this. No more covering up. No games. I don't want to keep coming back for answers that you can give me right now. I'll try to protect you, if there's something you're worried about, but I won't help you a bit if you don't tell me everything.'

For just a moment, that room might have been frozen in time and space, so quiet and still did it become. A visitor might have thought we had been there for a very long time. The first movement was a little flutter of Karen's hands. She was nervous and very frightened, but I knew she didn't wish Dallas ill, that her motivation for holding back was not a desire to see her young friend hurt.

She wouldn't look me in the eye. Instead she turned to Riddle, Mr. Sympathetic, who had said very little since those opening pleasantries. She needed help, and this kindly father-figure gave it to her.

'Karen, you know he's right. He won't give up. He'll find Dallas one way or another. It might be a game with you, but it isn't with him.'

'Mr. Riddle, it's no game with me.' Tears glistened in her eyes. 'I really care for Dallas. I don't want anything to happen to him. I want him to be alive, to be well.'

'Karen,' Riddle pointed out, 'the more time that goes by, the less chance there is that we'll find him well. If you want to help him, it's time you helped us.'

'You have no idea what the Egberts are going through,' I added.

'I don't care about the Egberts! If it wasn't for them, he'd be okay. It's funny, why didn't they care when he needed them?'

'Karen,' I said. 'You care. I know you do.'

'Well, I do care. I haven't stopped worrying since he disappeared. I swear to God I care.'

'Now is the time to prove Dallas is your friend,' Riddle urged. 'To prove you care and want to help.'

'Let's start with Dallas's room,' I said. 'Did you have anything to do with cleaning it?'

The tears were really beginning to form. 'All right,' she said. 'I straightened it up.'

'In what way?'

'His room was a mess, like it always was. I made his bed and hung up his clothes.'

'When did you do this?'

'The day he disappeared. I had no idea that he wasn't coming back to his room. He was terribly depressed – I thought it would brighten things for him if he came back to a clean room.'

'He didn't indicate that he was in trouble?'

'No, he was just terribly depressed. He was depressed so often. His eyes made me so sad. Unlike his family and other so-called friends, I wanted to help him.'

'Did you ever clean up his room before?'

'Yes. He helped me with my studies. This was a way of repaying him.'

'Did you see the note in his room? The one saying he wanted to be cremated?'

'Yes, but I really didn't know what to make of it. It occurred to me it might be part of his poetry. I guess I should have realized by the way he'd been acting that something was wrong.'

She was very emotional, and I felt that I would not get the entire story of her involvement. Once a person has been persuaded to open up, a good interrogator usually doesn't let up. The idea is to get everything in one session; it's called milking, and once the opportunity is lost, it may never return.

'Where was the note when you saw it?' I had been told that the note had been found on Dallas's desk, next to some neatly stacked calculus papers belonging to Karen.

'It was on the desk.'

'Did you touch it? Did you move it?'

'I probably did when I was putting his desk in order.'

'Did you notice anything strange about it?'

'Except for the message, wanting to be cremated and all, no. And I didn't find that particularly strange. At least, I didn't take it seriously. Oh God, no one ever took him seriously.'

'Did you read the note carefully?'

'I read it, but no more carefully than anything else I'd read. I just didn't stop to think.'

'Well,' I said, removing a copy of the note from my pocket, 'read it now. Read it carefully.'

Karen brushed hair off her forehead and tears from her eyes. Her hands shook as she read the scrap of paper.

'What do you notice?' I asked.

'It's a copy of the note I saw.'

'Do you notice anything different about it now?'

She looked at it, looked at me, dropped her eyes. 'You don't think he wrote it, do you?' she said.

'Why don't you tell us?' Riddle said.

'I really can't be sure.'

'You know Dallas's handwriting,' I said. 'Look at these.' I handed her copies of Dallas's poems. 'Does the writing on the note seem the same as that on the poems?'

'How can I tell? I'm not an expert.'

'Did you write that note, Karen?'

'No. So help me God, I didn't.'

'Do you know who did?'

'No, I don't know. I wish I hadn't cleaned his room that day.'

'Karen, let's say Dallas didn't write that note. Who could have written it, if it wasn't you? You cleaned up his room that very day.'

'Dallas never locked his door,' she said, her voice shaking. 'Anyone could have walked in.'

'Does that seem likely?' I asked sarcastically.

'Not really. But I swear, Mr. Dear, I had nothing to do with his disappearance.'

'Well, let me tell you, Karen, the state police don't think Dallas wrote that note. You say you didn't write it. Then someone had to come into his room in the few hours between when you last saw him and when you cleaned up, and write what most people would take to be a suicide note. That doesn't make any sense to me. Does it to you?'

'I don't know what makes any sense at this point.'

Neither did I. Karen seemed to be telling the truth (and I pride myself on being able to tell). But I intended to get a copy of her handwriting and have it compared with the cremation note.

'Why the hell didn't you tell what you knew from the beginning? It's been sixteen days.'

'I thought he'd show up. I thought he was in the tunnels playing Dungeons & Dragons. When he wanted to get away, that's what he did.'

'*Sixteen days*, Karen. You realize that from the beginning you've withheld information that might help us to locate Dallas? If it turns out to be murder or kidnapping, you're in a lot of trouble. Even as it stands right now, withholding information is a crime. Is there anything else that you haven't told us? We still can help you, but we won't if you hold anything else back.'

'There's nothing else, Mr. Dear. If Dallas isn't in the tunnels, and if he isn't at the science-fiction convention in Louisville, I have no idea where he might be.'

'Let me get one thing into your head, Karen. I'm on your side right now, but I can only protect you to a point.' Although I did not intend to tell the campus police that she had cleaned up Dallas's room, I would have to report my information if we learned that Dallas had been murdered; otherwise, *I* would be breaking the law.

I continued. 'You know which professors and students have been playing Dungeons & Dragons in the tunnels. You know which faculty members and students are gay and have associated with Dallas. You also know who is dealing and buying drugs on campus. You know the inner workings of this entire university. I want this information. You can find out things that I can't, because you are a student. People who won't talk to us will talk to you. Believe it or not, you're part of the establishment here. We're not; we're outsiders trying to do the best job we can. Let me again guarantee you that we don't intend to cause any problems for anyone unless they're involved in Dallas's disappearance. But I do expect you to help. I'm helping you. What you did is serious. I want your promise that you'll help me.'

'What I tell you will be confidential?'

'You can count on that. But what you tell me had better be the truth.'

'I'll do what I can. I'll do it more for Dallas's sake than my own. I do think, Mr. Dear, that you very much want to find him.'

'Good,' I said. 'Now let's get back to the day Dallas disappeared, the day you cleaned his room. You must have done more than make his bed and hang up his clothes. That room was in perfect order.'

'I swept the floor, emptied the trash. I made it as nice as I could.'

'And you say there was nothing unusual about him when he left you in the cafeteria?'

'He was just depressed. There was nothing unusual about that. I know how it must look to you, but if I'd had a suspicion something was wrong, I'd never have cleaned the room. But when he did disappear, I saw how bad it looked. I was afraid to speak up. I was his best friend and just trying to help.'

'You were his best friend. You mean he wouldn't have confided in you if he'd planned to commit suicide or run away?'

'I think he would. I knew of his involvement with the gay community, the Tolkien society, drugs. That's why I'm so worried – I think he would have told me. He always did in the past.'

'The past? He did this before?'

'When he became very depressed, he would take off for a few days and go to a hotel downtown. Just to be by himself.'

'Which hotel?'

'He didn't say. But he would tell me not to worry. He'd just go to relax, to listen to music and read a book.'

'How many times did he go to a hotel?'

'Three or four.'

'He could just come and go as he pleased?'

'The school's pretty liberal.'

'How could a young boy get into a hotel?'

'I think he had help.'

'From whom?'

'I don't know, Mr. Dear, I really don't.'

'Did he take off for other places?'

'He went to a science-fiction convention in Romulus. This was last year.'

'How did he get there?'

'He took a bus.'

'Did he go alone?'

'As far as I know.'

'How long was he gone?'

'Two days, I think. He was never gone more than a few days.'

This was amazing. But evidently a university spokesman quoted by the *Detroit Free Press* seven days earlier didn't think so: 'We don't have bed check,' he said. 'Kids are free to pretty much come and go as they want.'

'Karen,' I said, 'I still don't understand why you didn't report Dallas missing. It was five days before anyone said a word, and then it was Mark McCrosky.'

'At first I thought he'd just gone to get his head straight. Then I thought maybe he was playing a game.'

Her answer was the same as before – another indication that she was telling the truth. It's often good to ask the same question twice, because frequently you won't get the same answer twice.

'Dungeons & Dragons – can't you tell me anyone he played the game with?'

'I never asked and he never told me. I understand there were some pretty far-out people. I didn't want to meet them.'

'What do you mean by "far-out"?'

'People with their heads somewhere else. I never met them, but I could imagine. Weird hairdos. In a world of their own.'

'Think carefully, Karen. Were there signs of a struggle in that room when you went in to clean it up? Chairs turned over? Typewriter on the floor? Trash cans upside down? Anything that might have been blood?'

'Nothing like that. The room was disorganized, but that was its natural state.'

'Do you remember seeing the corkboard?'

'Yes.'

'Where was it?'

'When I first saw it, it was on the floor, propped against the desk. I picked it up and put it on the chair next to the stereo.'

'What was on the corkboard?'

'It was the same as when the police found it. I saw a picture of it in the paper.'

'What did Dallas normally use the corkboard for?'

'It was a message board. People would come into his room and leave messages for him, and he'd leave messages for people who might be looking for him. You know, tell them where he was.'

'Don't you think it's strange that the suicide note wasn't on the corkboard? That it was on the desk?'

'I really didn't think of that. But maybe that's why I figured it was just some of his poetry.'

'But the corkboard wasn't found by the police where it was originally left?'

'No. I moved it.'

'When you walked into the room, was the corkboard clearly and immediately in view?'

'Yes. I saw it right away. I couldn't miss it.'

'In relation to the corkboard, where was the note?'

'On top of the desk, right behind the corkboard.'

'Was it in plain view?'

'Yes. You would see it if you just looked.'

'There was a typewriter on that desk. Was there any paper in the typewriter?'

'No.'

'Any books opened? Like maybe to a certain passage?'

'No.'

'Did you move any of the tacks on the board? This is very important, Karen.'

'I didn't touch the tacks at all.'

'Was there anything else besides leaving and receiving notes that he used the corkboard for?'

'He'd lie on his bed and play with the tacks. He said he was trying to build a new computer design, or something like that. He also said he designed mazes, difficult mazes where it was hard to get from point A to point B.'

'Look at this picture.' I handed Karen a photograph of the corkboard. 'This doesn't look like a maze to me. Does it to you?'

'It could be a puzzle he dreamed up.'

'It could be,' I said thoughtfully. 'It very well could be. But does it look like anything to you? Anything you're familiar with?'

'It might be a gun shooting bullets in crazy directions.'

Bingo! That's what it looked like to me.

'Could the configuration of those tacks be a message?'

'You mean, telling us where he is? Yes, that would be like him.'

'Look at the picture closely. Does it suggest anyplace where Dallas might be?'

'If it's a maze, like he used to construct, those tacks might be spots in the tunnels. I just don't know.'

'Let me change the subject for a minute, Karen. Did Dallas ever mention trestling to you?'

'You're finding out a lot, aren't you?'

'You knew about it, then?'

'Yes, Dallas bragged about trestling. I think it made him feel manly. He wasn't big enough for something like football, of course. Trestling was another way to gain attention and to prove his courage.'

'Did you ever go with him?'

'No. That's hardly my idea of having fun.'

'It sounds very dangerous to me.'

'I'm sure it is.'

'And Dallas said he wanted to prove his courage?'

'Yes. I told him he didn't have to prove anything to his real friends. I told him I wished he'd stop.'

'He enjoyed the danger, thought it required courage.' I speculated out loud. 'Sounds a lot like the appeal Dungeons & Dragons has, if you play it for real.'

'The train could have been the dragon bearing down upon him.'

'Yes,' I agreed. I was about to say more when a beep came over my pager.

'Call the Red Roof Inn,' said the voice. 'It's an emergency.'

I dialed the motel's number. 'We've got an enormous amount of messages piling up here,' the woman on the phone said, 'and maybe a dozen reporters crowding the lobby. But that's not why I'm calling. There's something I think you should know: a heavyset young woman has been up to your room several times. The maintenance people have seen her. She doesn't knock at the door, she just tries to peer in. Of course, your curtains are drawn, so I doubt if she's seen anything. What concerns me, though, is what happened a few minutes ago. She'd been sitting in her car for maybe ninety minutes, just sitting there and looking up at your room, and we began to wonder about her. Anyone would, her just parked out there for that long. So I sent a maintenance man out to check. As he approached her car, she started her engine, gunned the motor, and almost ran him down getting out of here. I mean, she was traveling. I thought you should know.'

'You did the right thing, calling me.'

'Well, I didn't know. You said to hold your messages. But this woman was something else. When she sped off, it was like hounds were at her heels.'

'Did you notice what kind of car she drove?'

'A red Vega.'

'You are terrific – you should work for me. You didn't get the license tag, did you?'

'No, I'm sorry. I tried, but I didn't think of it until she was doing an imitation of a rocket.'

'You did very well. I'm sorry about all the calls you're receiving, and about the logjam in your lobby.'

'Hey, don't talk that way – this is exciting. Why, CBS called today. And Europe. I can't remember ever getting calls from Europe.'

'Maybe your boss isn't so happy, though, with the routine being disrupted and all.'

'Who cares what he thinks? Besides, he's not that upset. A lot of the reporters are checking into the motel. Business is good.'

'Well, you keep up the good work. When this is over, I'll get something nice for the entire staff from Neiman-Marcus. You have my promise.'

I said good-bye to Karen Coleman, telling her that I would see her soon and emphasizing how important it was for her to learn anything more she could about Dallas's friends and activities. Everything considered, it did not seem likely to me that Dallas was entirely a lone wolf in this case. Someone knew what had happened to him.

'We've got a mystery woman,' I said to Riddle as we headed through the lobby of Karen's dorm.

'I don't like mysteries,' he said.

'Neither do I,' I replied.

We emerged into a stunningly bright, orange-brown autumn noon. The leaves were just beginning to turn, against a clear, serene blue sky; a warm breeze brushed my face. It would turn cool soon. How I'd love to be here on a November Saturday for the Purdue football game, with a pipe stuck in my mouth and a pretty, fresh-faced girl on the arm of my silly fur coat, flask of brandy safe inside.

I guess I'm too old for that now, but it seemed that someone else wasn't. I blinked my eyes, then looked again. Standing nearby in tennis shoes, jeans, and a varsity jacket, in the midst of four girls and four young men who seemed older than he was, apparently so at ease that you just knew he belonged here, was Frank Lambert. Eating my heart out, I managed a frown and a signal that he should meet us around the corner of Case Hall.

'You ought to pay me for this kind of assignment,' I said to him when we were out of sight.

'We're not going to solve this case real quick, are we?' Lambert asked. 'I can get used to this life.'

'Well, get used to something else: we're going to go lie underneath a train.'

'That sounds like fun too.'

'Not to me,' said Riddle.

Chapter 7

The woods were thick now, and narrow shafts of sunlight penetrated where I walked. The sunlight made all the leaves appear yellow, but I was more concerned with the stickers, thorns, and burrs biting my legs than with the sylvan beauty of my surroundings. Gnats and other unpleasant insects made me a target of buzz-bombing dives. In places the weeds and grass were over my head; it would be easy to sprain an ankle or break a leg on the uncertain, treacherous terrain. The worst, though, was the wild unruly bushes, big, nasty creatures that traced ugly red scratches across my arms.

Dallas had gone into these woods – at night, when the perils were greatly multiplied. Dallas could have come out here when he was depressed, fallen and hurt himself, suffered a slow and terrible fate. He could have been brought out here and murdered. It was not impossible that Lambert, Riddle, or I, because of our experience with such macabre matters, might detect the telltale odor of a dead body, even at a considerable distance. That's why the three of us had entered the woods from widely separated points, agreeing to rendezvous at the trestle bridge.

At first the woods had not been so dense. I'd encountered perhaps a dozen students – several couples on nature walks, another holding hands and necking on a log – and to each I showed a picture of Dallas and asked whether he or she remembered seeing him. Where the trees grew more closely together, I heard someone coming along what passed for a path, and I waited behind a bush until he was almost upon me. I nearly scared him to death when I materialized in front of him. He was an Audubon Society member, a bird watcher, and I owed him an apology.

I eventually found the railroad tracks and walked along them perhaps a quarter of a mile to the trestle bridge. The bridge was some twenty-five feet above the water. I couldn't believe my eyes. Dangling like a monkey from one of the ties was Frank Lambert.

'Keep it up,' I said. 'Hang there till the train comes.'

'This is fun,' he said.

'Right,' I said. 'So is playing chicken with an eighteen-wheeler.' I picked up a rock and threw it at him.

Lambert pulled himself up to the tracks and we took stock of our surroundings. Below was a slow-moving stream about thirty feet across and apparently four to eight feet deep. The stream was clear, and we could see fish and, in most places, the sandy bottom. On all sides of us were woods. The area seemed more isolated than it was, since we were only a mile from the campus. It was not a beautiful spot, nor was it godforsaken and ugly, because the trees were a riot of color. I could imagine Huckleberry Finn fishing from this bridge. Unfortunately, I could also imagine Dallas hanging from it, and that frail boy could not have resembled Frank Lambert less. But Dallas had done more: he had laid down on the tracks and let trains run over him.

I wondered how often the trains ran. Fairly frequently, I'd heard. I'd come out here to trestle, but as I stood with Lambert on the bridge, I could think of a thousand reasons why the idea was idiotic. Still, I wanted to know how Dallas felt, and what better way than to experience what he had?

Where was Riddle? He should be here by now. Well, I was going ahead even if he didn't arrive. I kept looking at those railroad tracks, imagining a freight train running over my body, sparks flying, the noise bursting my eardrums, and I could feel my resolve wavering. Did it take courage to lie on those tracks? For Dallas, it probably did. For me, I kept thinking, it just took stupidity. Still, if I didn't do it, I had better stop taking pride in getting into the mind of the person I pursued. It's easy to talk about doing things. *Doing* them is something different.

I don't believe that I am qualified to challenge the master, Ernest Hemingway, but his definition of courage as grace under pressure is not entirely satisfactory for me. I think that courage is doing something important, something dangerous and difficult, something *you don't want to do*. This eliminates, I believe, endeavors such as skydiving, bronco busting, and going over Niagara Falls in a barrel. Sadly, it also shuts out taking care of a terminally ill spouse for many years, which should be classified as love, not courage.

Anyway, I was setting records in the sport of rationalizing. One rationalization that seemed stronger than any other was that there was a line between courage and stupidity, and that trestling at age forty-two put me in the latter category. Frankly, I didn't know what I was going to do.

I saw Riddle in the distance, coming up the tracks. I thought of remarks I could make about shaping up, about the direct relationship between good physical condition and a long life, about a healthy mind and a healthy body going hand in hand, and so on, but before I could bore him with any of this he spoke.

'You won't be able to guess who I met on the railroad tracks.'

'Tell me.'

'Jim Egbert. I feel so sorry for that man. I was coming

out of the woods when I heard someone calling "Dallas, Dallas, Dallas!" I didn't know what to make of it, so I followed the voice, and I saw him walking on the railroad tracks, between the rails. His back was to me. His hands were in his pockets, and he was shouting out into those woods. I've never seen anyone look so forlorn.'

'He was alone?' I asked.

'I've never seen anyone so alone. He heard me coming up behind and turned around. "Hi, Dick," he said. His shoulders were slumped, and he had tears in his eyes. I said that I thought he and Mrs. Egbert were returning to Dayton. He agreed, but he said that he just wanted to make one last effort to find Dallas. He asked if you were with me, so I told him you and Frank were at the trestle bridge.'

'I think they're doing the right thing. It probably will be better if they go back to Dayton.'

'We talked for twenty minutes. I tried to be as sympathetic and understanding as I could. He said that if Dallas were dead, he would still have Doug to take care of, and he wouldn't let the mistakes he'd made with Dallas be repeated.' Doug was the Egberts' only other child. He was thirteen at this time.

'I just loaned him my ear,' Riddle continued. 'He's filled with guilt. I agreed with him that it would be a good idea to make a lot of adjustments, no matter how this turns out. I told him that it wasn't my business to tell him how to run his family, but as an objective third party, and as a parent, I would face any problems a kid had head-on, instead of ignoring them and hoping they would go away. I'd try to recognize what the kid's needs are.'

'How did you part?'

'He said he was going to keep looking for Dallas. I told him I thought he should go back to the motel.'

'And?'

'I think he went back.'

'Well,' I said, 'why don't you go back too, pick up Hock, and get a start for Louisville? I wanted you to come out here so we could cover more ground, but Lambert and I can handle it from here.'

'Okay,' said Riddle. He turned and headed back down the tracks. He'd gone perhaps fifty feet when he faced us and called, 'Good luck!' I knew what he meant. Finding Dallas had turned out to mean a great deal to all of us.

Now my attention switched back to my dilemma with those damnable railroad tracks. Why hadn't I sent Lambert to Louisville? The solid, middle-class Riddle would have understood if I backed down from a confrontation with a train, but not Lambert – he *liked* this stuff. As I tried to find a way out of what I increasingly saw as madness, I began to fantasize that Lambert really wanted me to get killed. But why would he want that? I had perhaps the most successful and lucrative private investigative business in the nation, but surely he didn't believe he was going to take that over? Yet it seemed that every time I was with Lambert, flying through some insane thunderstorm or rowing through rapids, my life was in danger.

Maybe the train wouldn't show up. That seemed a vain hope. From what I'd heard, we were lucky that one hadn't gone past already. I put my right hand on one of the rails. I knew you could feel a train before you heard it, and hear it before you saw it. But I felt nothing.

It turned out I'd misjudged the situation. 'Bill, please,' said Lambert, 'let me do it.' His eyes had the hopeful, pleading look of a dog.

'Do what?'

'I know you want to lie under that train.'

I did? But I knew what he was saying.

'Right,' I said. 'But you see . . .'

'*Please*. It's not fair. You have all the fun.'

'Rank has its privileges.' What rank? Was I really saying this? When I was twenty, a year under the minimum age even to be in law enforcement, I was chief deputy constable in Miami, Florida, and took totally ridiculous chances – like singlehandedly transporting two murderers and an armed robber six miles, from the jail to the courthouse, *in a car*, not a paddy wagon. But I was twenty years old then. I hoped I'd grown older and wiser.

Actually, I *couldn't* let Lambert trestle; it wouldn't accomplish anything. My purpose was to feel what Dallas felt, not to see whether it could be done.

I lay down on the railroad ties and tried to imagine myself as Dallas. I had to forget who and what I was. Now I was a troubled student, and I was thinking that if I could go through with this, other people would see what a really remarkable person I was. They would accept me . . . *I'm super-intelligent. I can make computers dance to my tune, and I can work mathematical equations that stump and baffle professors. Oh God, my head hurts. Nobody cares about that. I can't take people not caring about me. Without that, is anything worth living for? I can't take the pressure anymore. There is no reason to. Why am I here? Why am I anywhere? Maybe this time it will be all over. Am I real, or just a figment of someone's imagination? Anyway, the world I'll be reincarnated in will be better than this one.*

Was this how Dallas felt?

I was face down on the railroad ties. People talk about cold sweat, but it's not really cold. I know. I've felt it several times. Once I raced around a corner in pursuit of a murderer and ran right into his gun, which was pointed at my chest; 'I've killed two,' he said, 'one more won't make any difference.' It was happening again now. But the sweat is not really cold. Clammy is a better word.

I was face down on the railroad ties not because it brought me closer to the ground but because I preferred for any flying sparks to burn the back of my head rather than my face. Had Dallas felt this way? He was much smaller than I. Did it matter to him? Again, *why* did he do this? His mind, I knew, was preoccupied with a fantasy world. Science fiction. Dungeons & Dragons. The dangers his mind could conjure up in Dungeons & Dragons had not been enough; he had had to play the game for real. Perhaps trestling was just another step further. And if he had survived trestling – and I was not absolutely convinced that he had – what new fantasy adventure could he be living out now?

The rails trembled, ever so slightly. While I had been lying there, the world had seemed to me absolutely quiet. Even the birds seemed not to chirp. I hadn't even been aware of Frank Lambert, standing perhaps four feet away from the rail on my right. But that first tiny tremor made me aware – oh, how it made me aware. It was as if my senses had become supernaturally perceptive. I could see the veins in one of the pebbles beneath my face. I heard a leaf rustle. No one ever has smelled creosote as I did then.

'Train's coming,' I said to Lambert. I tried to get closer to the ground.

'Why don't you call this off?' he said. 'This isn't worth it.'

Well, I wasn't sure. Maybe if I went through with trestling, it would give me insight into what the next thrill might be. I thought I knew. With trestling, you might, just might, come out alive. The next step would be designing a situation in which you *had* to die.

The rails vibrated. At virtually the same time, my nerves tingled as if jolted by electricity. My mouth went dry as cotton. I knew a surge of adrenalin would come next, and that would be worse, because adrenalin spurs you to action. I needed to lie as still as a stone.

The rails were humming now, like high-tension wires drawn tight against the wind. I couldn't hear the train, though, and that was worst of all. If I could hear it, I would have some basis of measurement, something real with which to calculate how long I had. I think firing-squad officers do a condemned man no favor when they blindfold him; it's far better, I think, to know *when* it is coming (if you are sure it *is* coming). A person can prepare himself even for instant death. How do you prepare yourself for a moment that is uncertain?

The hum grew louder. I could see the tracks trembling. One side of me, the rational side, tried desperately to gain control. *Am I really going to do this? What kind of epithet will this earn ? 'Crazy Middle-Aged Man Dies While Lying on Railroad Tracks.' How about that? You're an adult, Dear,* I said to myself. *Get your body off these tracks, or they'll have to spoon it into a bag before they can ship it home to your son.*

But the other side, the insane side, had its own arguments. *You say you're an adventurer, Dear. You've made a pretty comfortable living, at least partially because of that reputation. Is it all glitter? Are you a phony, Dear? Here's an adventure. You gonna back away from it? Back away from what a terrified little boy could do?*

I heard the train's whistle. I knew the train was closer than it sounded, because time had to elapse while that noise traveled to my ears. It was time to end this argument between the sane and the insane Dear. I didn't move. I tried to get closer to the ground. A sixteenth of an inch might be the difference between life and death.

Now I heard the train itself, a rumbling sound, growing louder. Big diesel engines.

'Get the hell off that track!' Lambert yelled.

The tracks were alive underneath my chest, pounding against my heart, which pounded back as though it knew every beat might be its last. A songwriter said you gotta have heart. That's nonsense. My heart would have fled from this scene a long time ago. It was my mind that was keeping me here. And that mind was working terrifically fast, like a motion picture speeded up, except that each frame was blindingly clear. I had only seconds now, if that. Staying required no action at all: just lie there and leave the rest to the Fates. I thought of Dallas. I thought, *You'd better move NOW if you're moving.*

The train's whistle screamed in my eardrums. The blast was urgent: *Get out! Get out!* it said. The engineer had seen me, I could tell. He couldn't stop, there wasn't time, all he could do was shrill that whistle and hope it penetrated a very thick skull. But I might not have moved even then, if the words *cattle catcher* hadn't appeared, apparently from nowhere, in my brain. *Cattle catcher. This train has a cattle catcher. You came out here knowing you might die. Not that you would die.*

I just knew that the engine had a cattle catcher, one of those slanted, gratelike, steel protrusions that are attached to the front of trains in order to keep the tracks clear. The cattle catcher knocks aside anything in the train's way. Its purpose, of course, is to protect the locomotive from being undermined from below, and it is also insurance against a derailment caused by hitting a heavy object.

I've often wondered about that moment on the tracks. I could not have known that the train had a cattle catcher, though indeed it did. Lambert had yelled a warning, but I couldn't hear him over the racket of the train, so the tricks of my mind must have saved my life. My mind believed that the cattle catcher existed; it left no room for me even to wonder. I saw the thing banging me, sweeping me up, tossing me aside.

I've also wondered how much time I *really* had to get off that track. In my mind it is in millionths of seconds. So too in Frank Lambert's memory, but he is not a reliable witness. He is a friend, and the moment was too frightening for him to be objective.

Anyway, I sprang up and saw the train coming from the direction in which my head had been pointed. I guess it was a little less than a football field away. It loomed like a rushing monster charging straight for me, growing before my eyes as it came. I could not have stood on the tracks for more than the merest fraction of a second before I stepped to my right, off the tracks and over the rail, and stood perhaps six feet away, watching the freight train hurtle by. Forty miles an hour, which is my estimate of the train's speed, is probably not 'hurtling,' but that's how it seemed to me.

I waited for Lambert to say something wiseacre-ish, and he didn't disappoint. 'Don't feel bad,' he said. 'It's natural for old men to lose some of their nerve.'

My clothes were dusty. My face was smudged with dirt. 'Your turn's coming next,' I replied. 'We're both going to trestle from the bridge, and we'll see who hangs on the longest.'

Lying on the tracks beneath the train was clearly more dangerous than hanging from the cross-ties over the stream, but I didn't expect the latter to be a Sunday stroll in the park. We were going to hang from those ties, though, and not just so I could experience what Dallas had, important as that was. If we were frightened and fell into the water, or if the shaking of the railroad ties made it impossible to hang on, I wanted to know what happened as we plummeted into that stream. Real life isn't like it appears in old films, in the throw-the-victim-off-the-mountain scene. People going off mountains do not react as dummies do. People flail when they fall; they reach, grasp, try to catch themselves, sometimes all the way to the bottom. There was no telling what would have happened to Dallas if he had unintentionally plunged into that stream. It was not impossible, I knew, that we would find his body down there, caught against a rock or a tree limb.

The second train (also a freight but with no cattle catcher) came an hour later. Lambert and I had gone over every inch of the trestle bridge and decided that the most likely place for Dallas to have hung was near the center, where the water was deepest below. We had been sitting on the rails waiting for the first vibration, and when I felt it we lowered ourselves into a chin-up position, hands gripping the ties. Lambert was to my right and two ties behind me. I thought it was important to get into position early so the train's engineer wouldn't spot us. A little earlier a helicopter had made five or six passes over our heads, and I imagined that the engineer on the previous train had reported that there was a madman on the tracks.

The second train came as the first had: first the rails trembled almost imperceptibly, then they vibrated, then hummed; we heard the train's whistle (how far off?), the diesel engines pounding *bam bam bam*, the constant roar – a noise Dante couldn't have imagined, loud, sustained, awesome. Despite all of this I was surprised when the train was over us. It suddenly just was *there*. And there. And there. I suppose in my secret heart I had hoped the train would be a short one that would provide a few moments of insight and then be gone, but this was the kind you always get stuck by at intersections on hot days or when you're in a hurry.

The noise (and I am still amazed by this) became

bearable, though surely not less loud. What was most difficult was hanging onto my railroad tie. It bucked like a rodeo bull, and there were moments when I thought I'd lost my grip. Pebbles were flung hard against my knuckles, and into my face when I looked up. Steam and heat and sparks flying from the wheels almost scalded me. I imagined that I resembled a side of beef, hanging from a hook and being cooked from above.

The train rolled along overhead – I would say that Lambert and I were beneath it for about four minutes – and I thought I had an idea of what Dallas had felt. Neither of us had fallen into the water, although of course we still might. I thought I had fulfilled two of my purposes, that is, trying to re-create an incident from Dallas's life and seeing whether a person was easily jarred off those tracks, but Lambert's 'old men' remark had provided me with a third goal. It was going to hurt, but it was worth it.

Gripping the pulsating tie, I swiveled my head. 'Old man, huh!' I yelled, though surely Lambert couldn't hear me. 'Fall, you wise-ass kid! I know you want to!'

When the last of the cars had passed the tie to which I clung, I shouted at Lambert, 'How you feel?'

'Aww, shit!' he said.

'I'm climbing up,' I said. 'You stay there for a minute. I want to come up and stomp on your fingers until you fall into the water!'

Scrambling like a squirrel, Lambert pulled himself up to the tracks a moment before I could. It made me sad to look at him. His face and hands were blackened, as mine were, but he had an 'I-kinda-enjoyed-that' look. I consoled myself by suspecting that most people begrudge lost years – but I'd spent those years, and as a wise man said, if you do not spend them, they cannot be saved.

I explained my next idea to Lambert, and we slid off the

bridge to the edge of the woods and began gathering paper, sticks, and leaves. These we mushed together into a mass and stuffed into the Windbreaker I'd worn out to the woods. I knotted the sleeves, neck, and bottom of the Windbreaker so none of the contents could escape. I wished the package were heavier so the experiment would be more realistic, but it just wasn't possible. This would have to suffice. What I wanted to know was what would happen to a human being if one of those freight trains hit him.

I carried my dummy up to the tracks and laid it between the rails. 'Go down three hundred yards,' I said to Lambert. 'Wave at the train engineer when he passes. Act real friendly. I'll do the same thing when he approaches this spot. We don't want to scare him, like we did the first guy. We'll divert his attention and he won't see that dummy.'

That was one reason for waving; I didn't want to disrupt the operation of the railroad any more than I already had. But there was another. Dallas had trestled at night, when the engineer couldn't have seen him and therefore wouldn't have tried to slow down. I wanted that train going at its regular speed. If Dallas had been hit by a train, he just might be where that dummy would be knocked or dragged to. I thought of the corkboard in Dallas's room. Couldn't the gun shape represent a train? And all those other tacks – in their scattershot fashion, couldn't they be telling us that even Dallas was unable to compute where his body would come to rest? That truly would be a mystery: arranging for your body to be in a place not even you can know.

As these thoughts went through my head, I wondered whether I had taken leave of my senses. How bizarre could this disappearance be? Pretty bizarre, every bone in my body told me. I had to follow my instincts.

But as Lambert began his trek down the tracks to wait for the next train, it occurred to me that if I had not taken leave of my senses, I might be accused, with justification, of acting irresponsibly.

'Frank! Come back here!' I called.

'What's wrong?' Lambert asked.

'This may not be my greatest idea,' I said.

'I was thinking the same thing.'

'We've got no assurances that we can divert that engineer.'

'What do you want to do?'

'I want to run this test. But I don't want to be responsible for someone else's taking chances. Maybe I'll contact the railroad, tell them what I need, and ask if they'll cooperate. If they know the reason, they might go ahead. Besides, it would be better that way – we could make this operation more true to life. That dummy, for one thing. It should be Dallas's weight, 125 pounds.'

Lambert agreed with me, so we decided to put off our experiment and concentrate on exploring the area carefully. Dallas might have been knocked into the water by a train, or simply fallen in and drowned. The water was deep enough in spots, though I know of people who have drowned in just a few inches of water. Given the wrong circumstances, even a good swimmer can drown in a bathtub.

Earlier I'd spotted an old, rotting rowboat tied beneath the trestle bridge on the stream's bank. I decided to putter around in that for a while, to see what we could find. The boat had one paddle, and I put Lambert, who is from one of those small Texas towns that is too dry and rugged to support camels (as the U.S. Cavalry learned in the last century), in charge of navigation. The best I can say is that he was enthusiastic. He attacked the water with gusto. What was needed, of course, was finesse, and if the boat hadn't had one of those wide, flat bottoms, he'd have capsized it. He never did get the hang of paddling, but with perseverance we managed to cover every area where a body falling, or flung, from those tracks might come to rest.

To my relief, we did not find Dallas in the slow-moving stream beneath the trestle bridge. We had about an hour of good sunlight left, so when we got back to the railroad tracks, I told Lambert I wanted him to travel a mile in one direction while I went in the other. Each of us would walk down one side of the track, then come back to the starting point walking on the other side, searching for Dallas's body all the while. I was literally praying that this grisly search would prove empty.

Two things can happen when a person argues with a train, each of them hideous. He or she can be smashed off the tracks and propelled through the air, a broken, mangled, shattered mass of flying debris, or he or she can be hooked by the train and be dragged along, here the head squishing like a watermelon, there the back torn open to the spine, then a leg or an arm sailing through the air. I can't say which is the worst way to die: I've never seen anyone live very long after such an encounter. I do know which is the more stomach-turning to look at – the body that has been dragged along.

As a police officer and deputy sheriff in Florida and later as a private investigator in Texas, I handled a number of train-death cases. I remember how many: seven. One was a drunk who wandered up on railroad tracks and passed out. Another involved two teenagers who were playing on a trestle when a train came; one saved himself by jumping, the other froze. There was a father of three with domestic problems, who perhaps figured that getting hit by a train was easier than pulling a trigger, and a deputy sheriff from Broward County,

Florida, who was hit broadside by a locomotive he never saw or heard on his first day on the job, *first call*. The fifth involved a car stalled on railroad tracks and a driver who was confident that he could start it in time (a mistake, though I can understand how this can happen – the train is coming at you much faster than you think.) The sixth was a deaf black man fishing off a railroad bridge. And the last was still another teenager, high on a hallucinogen, who thought he was Superman and could stop a train. Yes, I remembered how many, and what they were like. And that's why I prayed that Lambert and I were doing nothing more than taking a late-afternoon walk.

Neither of us found anything, and when we met back on the trestle bridge it was dusk. Lambert had a nine o'clock meeting with a student who knew a student who might have information about Dallas (one of that kind of lead), and I imagined that I had a mountain of commitments waiting for me at Red Roof Inn, so we returned to my car the same way we had come, taking separate paths through the woods. Our return hike was as Dallas would have known it: dark, much more hazardous in the dense underbrush, and with night creatures chirping in their fascinating language. Much of the time I walked as Frankenstein's monster had, my arms straight out in front to avoid colliding with a tree.

Lambert, being much more at home than I was in this sort of terrain, had arrived at the car ahead of me. We were headed for the motel before either of us spoke.

'You think we accomplished anything?' Lambert asked.

'I don't know,' I said. 'We've been too busy acting to reflect. I need to think about what we know.'

But it didn't appear that there would be any time for thinking. When I stepped into the lobby of the Red Roof Inn, caked with grime from my experiences on the tracks and in the woods, I was swallowed up by a sea of reporters, each with a question to ask, and each question different. Which one should I answer? Or should I answer any of them? Over the reporters' heads I could see the night desk clerk, with a concerned expression on her face.

'Any leads yet?' I heard a woman ask.

'Yes.'

'What are they? What are you looking for? We know you've been gone all day. Where were you?'

Three questions and a statement. I'd try to answer the questions in order. 'I can't tell you what the leads are. Some things are pending. If I tell you what's going on, it may stop going on. You ask what we're looking for. We're looking for Dallas. We're going to find him. I'm not at liberty to tell you where I was today. Put it this way: this is an unusual case, and I'm following unusual leads.'

'You've been deluged with phone calls.' This from a youngish local man. 'What are they about?'

'I don't know.' This was true enough. 'I've answered a few of them. I haven't gotten to every one.' Every one? I'd gotten to three. From the expression on the desk clerk's face, there must be more than a hundred by now.

'AP and UPI are running continual and detailed stories. Are you giving them information you're withholding from us?'

'No.' I was trying to push closer to the desk, to get those messages, without appearing to push. But I was surrounded.

'Do you believe Dallas is alive?'

'I'm not sure. I am sure we'll find him.' I made it two steps closer to the desk.

'What about Dungeons & Dragons?' There was no sense trying to keep track of which reporter asked which questions.

'Yes, Dallas was an avid player of the game.'

'Could he be playing it now?'

'No comment.' This can be a good reply when you don't know the answer.

'How are the Egberts holding up?'

I didn't know. Except for Riddle's report about Jim Egbert on the railroad tracks, I had no idea what they were doing. 'They're very worried about their son. I think they're holding up wonderfully under the circumstances.'

'The Egberts have been very critical of the campus police and the school administration. Do you have any comment?'

'The police have been most cooperative. I totally agree with the Egberts about the school. The lack of supervision for the boy is appalling. Even now, with Dallas missing seventeen days, the faculty and administrators are hardly rushing forward to offer assistance. And Dallas was their responsibility.' I didn't add, though I could have, that certain professors with whom my investigators had talked not only were reluctant to volunteer information but seemed to be holding it back.

'What's your feeling about the suicide note?'

'I'm in no position to argue with the state police handwriting report.'

'Do you know who wrote the note?'

'No, I don't.' I was six feet from the desk.

'Doesn't the information about the note point to murder?'

'No comment.' I handed this reporter a card I always carry. On one side it reads 'No Comment'; on the other side, 'Investigation Pending.'

'Are drugs involved?'

'No comment.' This can also be a good reply when the answer is yes, or when it is no – or just about any time. It's not that I try to deceive the press, as the public has come to expect from certain politicians. Politicians, in almost every instance, should tell the whole truth and nothing but. They work for the people. I work for private citizens. And the truth is that there are many times during an investigation where my interests may not dovetail with those of the press. Informants will surely be reluctant to come forward if they read their comments in the newspaper the next day. But more than that – if this case turned out to be a kidnapping, we didn't want the bad guys kept abreast of our progress. Likewise with a murder. Even if this were discovered to be a hoax perpetrated by Dallas, or by Dallas and others, full disclosure in the media before the boy was found could deflect the course of events in totally unpredictable directions.

'What about the corkboard?' another reporter asked. 'Does it have any significance?'

'Both the police department and my staff have compared the pushpins and thumbtacks on the corkboard, their pattern, to the configuration of some of the buildings on campus. We've reached no final conclusions. This is just one of the possibilities we're following through on. I might add that some of the people we've talked to who've played Dungeons & Dragons feel that the tacks may represent a game of D & D laid out by Dallas.' This was true enough. Riddle, Hock, and Lambert, while unable to locate anyone who would admit to playing Dungeons & Dragons with Dallas, had shown pictures of the corkboard to a number of participants in the game.

'Do you believe that Dallas is in this area?'

I'd reached the desk! Several news cameras were running, and I wanted to make a dignified exit. 'I'd rather not answer that at this time.' This was vague enough, I thought. I didn't want anyone involved in the disappearance to know we were stumped. Conversely, I didn't want to panic anyone by indicating that I was moments away from swooping down on them.

I looked into the desk clerk's eyes. She was excited, and a little bit scared by the frenzied crush of attention. She pushed an envelope into my hand, and a stack of more than a hundred loose messages. 'Thanks a lot,' I whispered, and then I moved quickly toward a side door through which I could reach my room. I very much needed to be alone. For all I knew, the solution to the case was right in my hands, on one of those messages.

I had the door open and was going through it when a question shouted loudly, above all the others, brought me to a halt.

'When are you going into the tunnels?'

Damn! I was hoping I could get away before that question was asked. Getting the university's permission to let us into those tunnels would be tough enough. If this reporter had figured out that the tunnels might be important, others could also, and pressure from the press might stiffen the school's resistance. I had hoped to make my search as painlessly as possible for all parties involved. I wanted to employ the press only as a last resort. However, I admired the way that reporter asked his question: '*When* are you going?' not '*Are* you going?' Of course I would do it. One way or another, I was going into that maze.

'Soon, I hope,' I said.

'Why aren't you going now?'

Double damn! *Why wasn't I?*

'We need permission from the university.'

'They haven't given it?'

'Not yet.' Everything my men and I had learned about the school's administration indicated that when I did ask, the answer would be no. My investigators had mentioned the existence of the tunnels to school authorities. So had the campus police. The reply was always a brusque, 'They don't go anywhere.'

How far from the truth this would turn out to be!

In any event, those tunnels should have been searched many days ago. It could not be a mystery to school authorities that hundreds of students played Dungeons & Dragons in them, or that they were dangerous. If officials were acting responsibly, with Dallas's best interests at heart, they would insist on just such a search. Well, I would try to get permission, but only the most heartless individual would allow the petty threat of a trespassing charge to stand in the way of possibly finding the boy.

That sharp but annoying reporter had another question to ask, but I didn't want to answer. I slipped through the door, and as I hurried toward my room I heard it close behind me. So far, I felt, we hadn't been lacking for leads. What I needed was time alone to understand them.

Chapter 8

George I. Thomas and Joseph Crescimbeni, in their book *Guiding the Gifted Child*, came up with the following statistics, based on a population of 200 million:

IQ	*Category*	*% of Population*
Below 60	Trainable	.6 (1.2 million)
60-69	Educable	2 (4 million)
70-79	Very slow learners or high educables	5.6 (11.2 million)
80-89	Low average or slow learners	14.5 (29 million)
90-99	Average learners	23 (46 million)
100-109	Average learners	23.5 (47 million)
110-119	High average, bright, and fast learners	18.1 (36.2 million)
120-129	Superior	8.2 (16.4 million)
130-139	Gifted to highly gifted	3.1 (6.2 million)
Above 140	Highly gifted to genius	1-1.5 (2-3 million)

Thomas and Crescimbeni concluded that *one in a million* people have an IQ of 180 or above, and it was in this rarefied atmosphere, I'd heard and read, that Dallas breathed. One in a million! If the U.S. population is 226,504,825, as the Census Bureau reported it to be in 1980, there were 225 others 'like' him in the entire nation.

I was sitting in my Red Roof Inn room reading about gifted children, hoping but not really believing that I would learn something about Dallas. I was relaxing after an arduous day, getting my mind off what looked like an impending all-weekend session of catching up with messages and analyzing what I already had (plus what Lambert, Hock, and Riddle would have to report). But what I was learning didn't relax me at all. I was getting steamed.

One in a million. I couldn't stop thinking about that. Was this country so rich in talent that it could afford to treat its geniuses cavalierly, like so many pieces of meat on an assembly line? No, worse than that. A hunk of meat would get attention; Dallas had been ignored, provided with no direction, permitted to transmogrify haphazardly into God only knew what. I had some clues: the gay experiences, the playing of Dungeons & Dragons in tunnels, the lying beneath speeding trains. Could not some caring, competent person have taken Dallas under his or her wing and channeled what should be considered a great natural resource into activities that might well benefit all of us? Dallas was even more valuable than one in a million. Was I not hearing about the arrival of the Computer Age? Be first with computers and you're on the way to being first on the planet. Not all of those 225 others, I was sure, were classified as geniuses because of towering aptitude with computers.

The great Roman philosopher Seneca wrote, 'There is no great genius without some touch of madness.' Modern studies show that at the lower IQ ranges of the gifted, students tend to be no more or less troubled than other youngsters their age, but the highest scorers indeed experience frequent difficulties. For these few, special and expert nurturing is needed if their talents are to reach full flower. What special and expert nurturing had Dallas received?

'The most important part of education,' said Plato, 'is right training in the nursery,' and modern educational studies are proving him correct. Owenita Sanderlin, author and expert on gifted children, describes the influence of parents on a child's life as 'awesome.' Nonetheless, because necessary research on ways in which gifted children should be raised and guided is sadly lacking, and because there is a singular absence of means to find assistance in this area, it is unlikely that many parents in this great land are able to cope ideally with an exceptionally gifted child.

Second to parental influence in importance is that of schools. Albert Einstein, who knew about such matters, said, 'It is in fact nothing short of a miracle that the modern methods of instruction have not yet entirely strangled the holy curiosity of inquiry.' Study after study has shown that gifted children *want* to learn, yet the norm appears to be that these youngsters are notorious for missing classes. The reason, of course, is that the classes do not challenge them. Owenita Sanderlin also wrote that 'bored geniuses and undeveloped leaders and creative artists are potential dropouts, delinquents, criminals . . .' The possibility that Dallas was involved in criminal activity was something I had not really seriously considered, but it was an area I could perhaps no longer overlook.

The experts I read unanimously favored moving gifted children ahead in grades, given the right circumstances. But that is a big given, the experts all agree. A gifted child's mental age is often far in advance of his or her social age. If a child is moved ahead, as Dallas was, the adults involved must exercise great care to meet needs besides the intellectual ones. Individualized tutoring, individualized guidance is a must. Dallas had received very little, if any, of such attention. For instance, one of the many advisable measures if a youngster is moved ahead is to assure that he will not be alone in his new environment, that others his age share the same milieu.

At Michigan State, what peer did Dallas have?

Book after book about gifted children, it seemed to me, might have been written after a series of interviews with Dallas. The highly creative child, for example, usually is not neat. Sanderlin wrote: 'Creative children need *things* to create with; the highly regarded English "infant schools" call them *stuff*. Heaven help the creative children of a compulsive housekeeper. They make things, they collect things, they do experiments, and they don't want you to throw them away. Even worse, they don't want you to move something they are making, like a bridge of blocks in the middle of the living room floor.'

The extraordinarily gifted tend not to be braggarts. If you wait for them to tell you of their genius, the cows might come home first. Dallas certainly fit this mold. He was exceptionally modest, never talking about his gifts and generally embarrassed when someone brought up the subject with him. The gifted also possess an extraordinary degree of honesty. A high-IQ child who cheats on exams is almost unheard of. It is not enough to brush this aside by saying that these youngsters don't *have* to cheat. Often the pressure laid upon their shoulders to excel is far heavier than that put upon average students to 'do well.' If Dallas fit this mold – and I had every reason to suspect that he did – then the cremation note might be an honest statement of his wishes and a straightforward reference to suicide. That is, if he had written it.

Most significant to me as far as Dallas was concerned was that one authority after another wrote about the tremendous pressure applied to gifted youngsters to conform. If they do not, they might find themselves *without any friends at all*. This is why farseeing educators emphasize the need for these geniuses to have social relationships with their peers; studies have shown that high-IQ children are stimulating to one another. It seemed crystal clear to me that Dallas had not had associations with his peers, and the results had been disastrous. Conforming, for him, had led to relationships in which he was exploited and activities that were dangerous and self-destructive.

Interestingly, several unrelated studies gave case histories of gifted children who were absorbed by the fantasy world created by Tolkien. Fantasies are important, of course, and perhaps more so for the creative person, but what occurred in some instances went far beyond mere daydreaming. These youngsters took their fantasies to extraordinary lengths, almost becoming the characters they read about and practically living in the world they imagined. Today, parents of video-game addicts worry about the influence these games seem to exercise on their children. Although this is not a concern to be taken lightly, it hardly compares to the transformation that can occur when a lonely, brilliant child retreats inside himself and becomes someone or something else.

As I looked through these books, I learned that Dallas was highly unusual, but not unique. There were others like him, though not so many that we could afford to make blunders with their lives. Dallas's story had revealed instances of failure after failure, right from the beginning; if anyone had done anything right, I had yet to discover it. I hoped that maybe his life could still be salvaged. If not, perhaps what people learned from his case might spare other Dallases.

It was about 11 P.M. on August 31 when I began answering the messages that had piled up, and 10 A.M. on September 1 – a bright, sunshiny Saturday – when I put down the phone for the last time. It did not bother me in the least that I woke many of the people I called from a sound sleep. What I was doing counted more than their rest.

The majority of messages were from newspapers and radio and television stations. With these I was polite but brief. I couldn't orchestrate a media show and find Dallas at the same time. Several of the radio callers wanted to do live or taped interviews; there just wasn't time for this. Several calls were from overseas. It was clear that Dallas's disappearance had begun to capture the attention of the national media; among those who had called were NBC, CBS, *Time* magazine, AP, and UPI. Soon the people, and not merely in this country, would be just as interested.

Most of the calls amounted to nothing. There was an overrun of messages from psychics. Many of these had called collect. One, a middle-aged woman from Texas, wanted me to drop everything and find a way to watch a rerun of a 'Starsky and Hutch' episode she was convinced would solve the case for me. Besides the psychics, a number of just plain good people called to offer support and sympathy, and neglected to tell the switchboard why they were calling. One man, refusing to identify himself, said I should check a cache of explosives buried near Mount Hope. Calling Dallas 'the boy,' he intimated darkly that the missing youngster would be found near a service road not far from the campus. Since explosives were involved and I no longer do bomb work (robots are often used for this activity), I called the police, who checked out the lead. Nothing was found.

Only three of the phone calls I made that night resulted in information that might prove important. One of these was to Professor Joseph Baum, who taught a racquetball course that Dallas had taken.

'There are some things I probably should have told you before,' Baum said. 'It just didn't occur to me earlier that they might be important. Do you know about the seizures Dallas had?'

'No, I don't. Go on, please.'

'I know of two separate instances, both while he was playing racquetball. The first was last February. Dallas was totally unconscious for sixty seconds. He just keeled over and collapsed. I wanted to call an ambulance when he revived, but he said that it was simply caused by studying too hard and a lack of sleep. Much of this "study," Dallas said, was helping other kids in the dormitory with their class work. I had no reason not to believe him.'

'When was the second seizure?'

'About the middle of March. All of a sudden Dallas just collapsed on the racquetball court. I saw it happen. I ran over to him and he was totally unconscious. Very pale. I told one of the students to call the campus police department and an ambulance. I remained with Dallas until the ambulance arrived. He was unconscious for eight minutes that time. I was very worried.'

'What kind of seizure was this?' My mind immediately focused on those tunnels. What if Dallas had been stricken down there?

'I didn't know at the time. Later I was told that it was a severe epileptic seizure. Anyway, Dallas was taken to Olin Heath Medical Center and held for a couple of days. Extensive tests were run. I called Dallas at the hospital, and he told me he would be all right. Said he would be able to finish the course, which wasn't what concerned me. He blamed the episode on lack of sleep, studying, and helping others study. He said he was drinking too much coffee, and the caffeine was bad for him. Anyhow, he did return to the course, and he did complete it.'

'Is there anything else you can tell me about Dallas?'

'He took only the one course from me, and I really didn't get to know him very well.'

'I thank you for calling,' I said.

This conversation made me very angry at the Egberts. I

had explained to them how absolutely essential it was for them to tell me *everything* they knew about Dallas, yet they had withheld this vital information. And it wasn't because they didn't know; later I saw a letter that Dallas had written them in November 1978, talking about the seizures.

I could understand why they might withhold this information, but understanding in no sense meant condoning. Many parents are embarrassed that an offspring suffers from epilepsy, despite the obvious fact that there is nothing whatever to be embarrassed about. No one is embarrassed because someone has a cold or an attack of hay fever. Yet some parents believe that a stigma is attached to epilepsy; their child is less than perfect. It is true that children can be cruel, and parents might have cause not to broadcast news of the disease to everyone. The sufferer of epilepsy might be looked on as a pariah, or be made fun of or jeered at, if parents and schools haven't instilled in children a sensitivity to others.

But assuming such cause, there was no logical reason to keep the information from me.

Professor Baum's news did, however, clear up one question that had been gnawing at my mind. Anna Egbert, more than anyone, had been pushing hard for a search of the tunnels since I had first mentioned them, and I had wondered why. This case might not be nearly so complicated as many of us had thought. Dallas might simply have gone into the tunnels to play Dungeons & Dragons, suffered an epileptic seizure, and died for lack of help. The cremation note and the corkboard might have been merely a part of the game. One thing I knew: it was imperative to search those tunnels.

At about 3 A.M., when I was a little more than one-third of the way through the phone messages, I received a call from the desk. I had left word that I didn't want to be interrupted except in an emergency.

'Mr. Dear, just a few minutes ago a lady was seen trying to look into your window. Another guest saw this and reported it to us.'

'Could the woman looking in the window have been a guest?'

'I don't think so. The man who saw her said she went down to the parking lot and drove off in a small car.'

'A Vega?'

'He couldn't tell what kind of car it was.'

'Did he give a physical description of the woman?'

'He said she was husky. Heavyset. In her twenties.'

'Well,' I said, after getting the name of the guest, 'I thank you. Please let me know if this woman is seen again.'

I was able to obtain enough details from the helpful man to know that my mystery woman had turned up again. Most of the time such weird behavior, so intriguing to the logical mind, ends up being explained by a single word: crackpot. There are a lot of them in this world, and a disproportionate number gravitate to a sensational investigation. Nevertheless, I was scarcely playing hard to reach – I welcomed information, in fact – and I wondered why this lady didn't just come forward to meet me. Certainly I was not going to drop anything else to pursue her identity.

Since the rhythm of my phone calls had been interrupted, I decided to open the lone letter I'd received since my arrival just over two days before. Like so much of this case, the letter was simply incredible. It was handwritten on Best Western stationery and was unsigned.

Dear Mr. Dear:

Has anyone looked into the Human Rights Organization? I understand it is the opposite of the Gay Organization & rather against the Gay Organization. Karen Coleman said Dallas was a member of the Organization & that she had dropped him off at a meeting or party about 1 month ago at the Torres Apt's on the North side of West Michigan Ave. about the 600 block. She knew he had been to at least 2 meetings & received literature from them.

What if this 16 year old decided to change his mind about being gay & decided to talk to the Human Rights Organization about the *under age activities*?

Did anyone question Karen about his discussing any indecision about his sexuality? The way she talked they discussed about everything. If she dropped him off at a Human Rights Org. Meeting wouldn't they discuss his reason for attending? Did he discuss being undecided or looking at both sides of the question? Has anyone questioned Karen or other straight girls to see if he was also experimenting with hetrosexuality.

Can't you check with the Human Rights Organization & find out exactly when & where they had meetings in E. Lansing? Talk to some of the people organizing the meetings. Dallas always spoke out in groups. He always had something to contribute. He always got to know someone.

None of the literature from the Human Rights Organization or the Gays were found in his room. Also the large poster of the Gay Balleranies that both Karen & I remembered was not with all the other posters left.

The room just was not done by Dallas. I do not believe he would be capable of that much organization even if he did try. People keep saying the things were in the drawers military style – Dallas never had any connection with the military. Did some of the people connected with him have military background? I had never seen sock put into a drawer standing on end & I'm sure he never has either. There were no momento's from Science Fiction Conventions, plays attended, etc. He always had that kind of stuff around.

Could this be a political disappearance? What would they do with him in that case? Would they be holding him somewhere? Would they sell him into white slavery? A 16 year old could pose a very dangerous threat to the Gay's Organization.

Everything about this letter was amazing, including the spelling. I analyzed it paragraph by paragraph.

Paragraph # 1: Yes, we had checked into the 'Human Rights Organization,' which was not a registered group on campus and did not go under that name. It was a collection of citizens who were basically interested in seeing that everyone got a fair shake. Most if not all the members were straight, but they were likely to support gay rights if the situation arose. Riddle had interviewed members of the group, who said that Dallas had a well-developed social conscience and was concerned with human-rights issues. This certainly fit the descriptions of gifted youngsters I had read about; very few high-IQ children start off as Dr. Strangelove. And yes, we had talked to Karen Coleman about attending those meetings, and her opinion as to Dallas's motives coincided with those of the group members.

Paragraph # 2: The 'Gay Organization' with which Dallas was associated, officially called Gays at MSU, might have a reason to dissociate itself from Dallas. He was indeed under age. Our investigation indicated that some faculty members belonged to Gays at MSU – a sticky situation, to say the least.

What impressed me about the first two paragraphs of the letter, indeed about its entire contents, was the tremendous amount of knowledge the writer had about the case. I felt I knew who had written this letter.

Paragraph # 3: According to Karen, Dallas had not questioned his sexual preferences. She did know he had experimented with sex with girl friends.

Paragraph # 4: We had done this. What interested me was how the letter-writer knew Dallas well enough to suggest it.

Paragraph # 5: The missing literature also puzzled me. Karen Coleman said she had removed nothing from the room, and I believed her. But I also believed that Dallas's personal effects were missing.

Paragraph # 6: We already knew who had straightened up the room, but what struck me again was the seemingly intimate knowledge the writer had about Dallas. I could not wave away what the writer said about the 'military style' of neatness. Couldn't someone else have come into that room after Karen Coleman?

Paragraph # 7: What can be said about these last remarkable lines? The writer of this letter had to know Dallas and was concerned enough about his fate to speculate on what it might be. Indeed, I concurred that the cause of gays would not be helped if members of their campus organization had been having affairs with the boy. I was quite certain that the words 'political disappearance' referred to a possible abduction by gays, but they could have another, more sinister meaning. For a moment visions of the CIA or the KGB danced in my head. The disappearance had certainly been handled smoothly, and there were enough bizarre twists and turns to the case to do credit to the most cunning cloak-and-dagger agency. And how had Dallas remained out of sight for so long? There had been not a hint of his whereabouts. In my mind and heart, though, a political disappearance involving a government agency just didn't jibe. It was a possibility not to be entirely discarded but to be put on a very distant back burner.

As I mentioned, I believed I knew who wrote this letter, but I was not going to spend even a minute confirming my hunch. Karen Coleman could probably identify the writer, and there were plenty of other means I could use. But if I nosed around trying to learn this information, other people who were considering coming forward, people who wanted to help but didn't want to become involved, would suspect that I couldn't be trusted. Informants had to be absolutely persuaded that whatever they told me would go no further. Most important, I wanted it known that the $5,000 reward would be paid, no questions asked, for the information that led us to Dallas.

The second of the three phone calls that I made that morning that proved valuable, if only by reemphasizing the strange paths I might have to pursue to bring this investigation to a successful conclusion, was in response to a message left by a well-known astrologer. Now, there must be sincere astrologers, and I believe that this individual was one of them, but I know for a fact that many are charlatans. (One of the most visible and respected astrologers once confessed to me that he was pulling a scam, gulling his well-to-do clients – many of them Hollywood personalities – into making investments determined by his astrological 'findings.' This man, a cynic if ever I met one, had nothing but contempt for the entertainers who put up their money because of his recommendations.) In addition, I am well aware that scientists have little but scorn for astrology. Nevertheless, Dallas was interested in such matters, so I was interested in what people in this field had to say.

'Mr. Dear,' the astrologer said, 'I'm glad you called. I've been following this case you have, and saw the picture of the corkboard in a newspaper. From studying the tacks as they're laid out on the corkboard and correlating their pattern with the stars, I can tell you that the boy will be returned alive on September twenty-seventh. I have no doubt of this.'

'What do you base this on?'

'I've been doing this sort of study for years. My reputation, as you'll learn if you check, is the very highest. I've had an excellent record of success.'

'What have you done in the past?'

'I'm not at liberty to discuss it, but I often handle delicate matters of a confidential nature.'

'Well, I appreciate your call.'

The date was very specific. Of course, I realized that someone seeking to enhance his or her reputation might make just such a prediction on the off chance that it would be right. A wrong prediction would go unnoticed or quickly be forgotten, but it would be jackpot time if September 27 turned out to be the day. And who knew? Maybe that configuration on the corkboard had been set up by Dallas so that an astrologer could explain it. After all, we suspected that Dallas was playing a game with us, matching his wits against ours, and the corkboard might indeed be a clue that only an astrologer could decipher.

I was doing a lot of things in this case I normally wouldn't even consider, but I felt that extraordinary methods were called for if I was to get inside the mind of this unusual boy and understand it. From what I had experienced, I could tell that Dallas had been crying out for help and attention, and/or that he just didn't care about his life. Certainly in his bizarre way he was seeking acceptance; this quest was a thread running through the pattern of everything I'd discovered about his life. I had been afraid out on those railroad tracks. No matter how little Dallas's life had meant to him, no matter how many drugs he had taken beforehand, I knew that when that train had borne down on him, he too had been frightened. Yet he had gone back to trestle again. Not all the money or awards in the world would get me back there. I knew that the boy for whom we searched was capable of going to remarkable lengths to capture attention, and despite his age he was a formidable opponent if indeed he was playing a game.

The third phone conversation I felt might prove helpful was with a top computer-systems designer with Union Carbide. He said he wanted to talk with me about Dungeons & Dragons.

'Go ahead and talk,' I said.

'Dungeons & Dragons is a highly complex game,' he said. 'Playing it on computers enhances the action, which is why I'm calling you. I understand that the boy you're looking for was a sort of *wunderkind* with computers.'

'You could say that,' I agreed.

'Well, I've played the game on Union Carbide's computers with other system designers across the country. It's really quite widespread. We play after hours, at night, and of course we have no authorization from the corporation. The game is even more of an adventure with computers. I wondered whether you'd checked the possibility that Dallas Egbert played the game in this fashion.'

'I haven't,' I said. 'But I will.'

'Well, it would have been natural for him to have done so. It's not just people from Union Carbide that I've played the game with. Employees of other companies plug into our computers and play along with us.'

It wasn't until several years later that I fully appreciated what this man was telling me. One company plugging into another's computers? Today, of course, we read about billions of dollars in computer thefts, about company secrets being pirated by computer operators, about children who are able to tap into even the most sensitive Pentagon information. Secrets that even the most resourceful and enterprising thief could never hope to acquire are now an open book for wizards not nearly as gifted as Dallas.

Damn, I thought to myself, I'm a private investigator, albeit a good one, not a computer whiz. I might be overmatched here. Out loud I said, 'You think Dallas could have designed a computer Dungeons & Dragons game?'

'I do.'

'What would it be like?'

'God knows. It would be a doozy.'

At 10 A.M. I made my next-to-last call of the marathon session: to a hobby store in East Lansing. From them I learned the name of a dungeon master. I called him.

'I'll pay you fifty dollars,' I said, 'if you'll play a game of Dungeons & Dragons with me. I want you to know I've read the books, but I've never played before. I want to play this afternoon.'

'I've got a date this afternoon.'

'This is more important.'

'Fifty dollars?'

'Sixty if the game is a good one.'

'I'd have to bring along a friend. The game is better if there's more than just one player.'

'I'll see you at two o'clock. Red Roof Inn, Room 211.'

'Fifty dollars?'

'Think big. Think of sixty. I want a really good game.'

Chapter 9

My dungeon master and his friend arrived promptly at 2 P.M., as agreed. I'd had only two hours' sleep, but I'd managed to shower and shave and put on fresh clothes and I felt wide awake. For reasons I can't explain, I tingled with anticipation and curiosity.

I didn't know what to expect from my dungeon master. Would he show up in a Merlin costume, with a funny pointed cap and stars emblazoned all around? Would he be dressed as some authority figure, an all-knowing wizard or a god? I knew he would have complete control over the circumstances of the fantasy adventure on which I was about to embark. I knew he would be absolutely fair, siding neither with me nor with the monsters I would face; he was an arbiter of the strictest impartiality, and his decisions were final. Would he come dressed in the robes of an eminent jurist?

He came dressed in sweater and jeans and scuffed tennis shoes. He might have been Jack Armstrong, so open, friendly, and Midwest-fresh did he seem. His friend, a good-looking Mexican-American sophomore who might have been an athlete, was named Louis. The three of us gravitated to the table and sat around it, and I explained again that I had never played Dungeons & Dragons.

'Have you read the Player's Manual?' the dungeon master asked.

'Yes.'

'Then let's begin.'

He asked me a few personal questions, including what

my favorite fantasy was, a subject I lied about. Then he asked me to roll dice of various shapes several times, wrote on a sheet of paper, and handed it to me when I was finished. It read:

Magic-User — Third Level

Strength	8	
Intelligence	17	
Wisdom	15	Cloak
Dexterity	14	Boots (low top)
Constitution	16	Scroll case
Charisma	13	
		Gold 39 pieces
Hit Points	6	
Armor Class	7	

Next came more questions. 'How many days' food do you want to carry?' the dungeon master asked.

'Seven.'

'Do you want waterskin or wineskin?'

'Waterskin.'

'Do you want any rope?'

'Yes.'

'Would you like a torch or a lantern?'

'I'd like a lantern.'

'Do you want a bag or a sack to carry things?'

'A bag.'

'What you've purchased has cost you twenty-eight of your thirty-nine gold pieces. Can you think of anything else you want?'

'Do I have a sword or a knife?'

'No. Because of your poor strength, you probably couldn't wield a sword.'

'I'll take a knife.'

'Which kind? A regular dagger, or a silver one? A silver one is good against werewolves, wererats, werebears, and so on. It costs thirty gold pieces. You don't have that many. Do you want to trade back some of your other equipment?'

'How much is the regular dagger?'

'Three gold pieces.'

'I'll take that one.'

'Roll this die,' the dungeon master said, handing me a many-sided blue cube. I rolled an 8. Next I rolled a 9. I was rolling to determine my magic-user's spells. He could Detect Magic, Charm a Person, and Create Continual Light (a second-level spell; the others are simpler, first-level spells).

'This is your last chance to buy anything,' the dungeon master said. He seemed like a cold sort to me – not frigid, or very unfriendly, just uninvolved. I could expect no favors from him. But I was beginning to glimpse some of the attractions of this latest college craze. Just answering the questions, learning who I was to be, started to make me forget where I really was and what my true identity was. Subtly and unconsciously, I was becoming my character.

'I think I've bought enough,' I said. What did I know?

'What kind of race do you want to be? An elf? A halfling? A dwarf? A human?'

'A human.' This was going to be tough enough without becoming something else that I wasn't.

'What name do you want?'

I thought it over for a moment. 'Tor,' I said. Tor sounded like strength. I knew the magic-user had very little strength – Dallas had very little strength, but he had wanted it. Maybe the name Tor would help me acquire it.

Louis already had a character he had played before. I

did not know his 'character sheet,' though later I saw it:

Fighter/Thief — Second Level

Strength 18
Intelligence 18
Wisdom 13
Dexterity 18+1
Constitution 18−1
Charisma 10

Hit pts. 13

Armor Class 6

Leather armor
with shield
Two-handed
sword (+ 1 magical)

Long bow with 24
arrows

Lantern
Rope
Food (14 days)
Wineskin
Waterskin
Bedroll
Boots (high top)
Cloak (many pockets)

Thieves' tools
Tinder box

Gold 11

Chance of Success:

Pick Pockets	35%
Open Locks	29%
Find/Remove Traps	25%
Move Silently	21%
Hide in Shadows	15%
Climb Walls	86%
Hear Noise	10%

Louis and I would go on the adventure together. I understood that he could be my valuable friend or might betray me in the most sinister fashion. I looked closely at him, trying to fathom his deepest motives. It was hopeless, of course. He was not the character he was playing, whom he called Dan. In truth, he was a college kid who had made it clear that he was missing an 'important' party to play this game. I could guess why the party was important, and told him he had to get his priorities straight. Sensibly, he didn't listen. I think he knew I was just jealous. Anyway, he soon gave the game his full attention, and I suspected he was now into whatever character he was playing. I let myself sink deeper into the role of magic-user.

The dungeon master talked in a noncommittal monotone. 'You two have just entered the town of Hann, which is on the northern edge of a body of water and is surrounded by rugged mountains. Northwest of the town, set in the mountains, is a tall, dark tower. You can smell the pungent odor of fish from the harbor. Dan fills Tor in on what is happening.'

'There's a nice tavern in town,' said Dan/Louis. 'It's not far from here. I'm thirsty. How about going there with me?'

'Okay.'

'I found a tunnel that leads from the tavern. We might want to explore it. But one important thing: don't, under any circumstances, make fun of the people of Hann.'

'I'm sure there's a reason for this.'

'As you head for the tavern,' the dungeon master said, 'several beggars, noticing that you are well-dressed travelers, run toward you asking for money. What do you do?'

'How many beggars are there?' Tor/I asked.

'There's a lot of confusion. You'd have a lot of trouble counting them all. They're tugging at your clothes.'

'I pull a gold piece out of my pocket,' said Dan, 'and throw it as far away as I can.'

'Some of the beggars run away and fight over the gold piece,' said the dungeon master. 'The rest are still in your way. While this is happening, you hear a commotion coming from down the street. A man carrying a box is being chased by several guards. What do you do now?'

'We duck into the tavern,' said Dan.

'It's several blocks away,' said the dungeon master.

'I'm interested in the box,' Tor/I said. 'I'd like to take it.'

'You're not a thief, are you?' asked Dan.

'I'm an adventurer. I want to know what's in the box.'

'Fine. You stay here. I'm going to the tavern.'

'While you're arguing,' the dungeon master said, 'the man bursts through the crowd of beggars. If you want that box, now's your chance.'

'I intend to take that chance.'

'Roll to see if you succeed,' said the dungeon master, handing me a die. I rolled an 18, the maximum being 20.

'You have the box,' said the dungeon master. 'What do you do with it?'

'I hide it under my cloak and walk away from the mob, toward the tavern.'

'One of the guards sees you,' said the dungeon master, 'and orders you to stop.'

'I run toward the tavern. At least I know there's a tunnel there.'

'You overtake Dan as you head for the tavern. Do you acknowledge his presence?'

'I tell him I've got the box.'

'I run with him,' said Dan, 'and show him where to go.'

'You reach the tavern,' said the dungeon master. 'But six guards are on your trail, just twenty feet behind. You make it inside, but it's midafternoon and the place is nearly deserted.'

'I point to a curtain,' Dan said. 'I throw a gold piece to the bartender and duck behind the curtain into a booth.'

'Are you following Dan?' the dungeon master asked me.

'Yes.'

'Inside the booth a wooden table and two benches are set up next to a stone wall,' said the dungeon master. 'There's a candle on the table and two candles on the wall.'

'I push the table aside,' explained Dan, 'and this reveals the entrance to the tunnel. I motion Tor to go in. I intend to follow and close up the entrance after I'm in.'

'I'm going into the tunnel,' Tor said.

'While Tor is entering the tunnel, you hear the guards yelling at the bartender, demanding to know where you've gone. The bartender says he doesn't know. Giving him the gold piece has bought his silence.' The dungeon master handed the ten-sided die to Dan to determine whether he could shut the entrance to the tunnel without being heard. He rolled a 7 the first time and a 3 the second time, giving him a total of 73.

'That's not good enough,' said the dungeon master. 'The guards have heard you.' The dungeon master rolled the die himself. He did not tell us what number came up. 'You hear the curtain being pulled open, and one of the guards yells that no one is here. Another replies that the other booths need to be checked.'

'I urge Tor to crawl down the passageway,' said Dan.

'The tunnel,' agreed the dungeon master, 'is just large enough to crawl through. After ten feet it opens into a room.'

'When I get into the room,' said Dan, 'I try to light my lantern.'

'What do you do, Tor?' the dungeon master asked.

'I wait to see if Dan's lantern lights.'

'The lantern lights,' said the dungeon master.

'Can I see Tor's face clearly?' Dan asked.

The dungeon master nodded.

'I turn to Tor,' said Dan, 'and ask him what the hell he's doing, getting the guards on our trail. They cut the hands off thieves in this town. You're a real jerk, Tor, and dangerous besides. We could have been killed by that showboat stunt of yours.'

'That's the chance you take for teaming up with me,' Tor replied. 'I'm a risk-taker.'

The dungeon master intervened. 'While Dan is talking,

you see several crates piled up in a corner of the room. You notice also that there's a regular doorway, hewn out of rock, that leads out of the room. One of the crates is open and you can see it's filled with straw.'

'When do we look at what I stole?' Tor asked.

'Nothing's worth the trouble you put us through to get it,' grumbled Dan.

'The box Tor stole,' said the dungeon master, 'is the size of a cigar box and made of rosewood. It has a large silver lock built into it. Do you have a key?' he asked sarcastically. It was clear he knew that Tor had no such key.

'No key,' said Tor.

'Let me see if I can jimmy that open,' offered Dan.

'Make a roll,' said the dungeon master.

Dan rolled a 27.

'It's open,' said the dungeon master. 'Inside you see a medallion resting on velvet lining. On the medallion's face are three curved lines. Is either of you going to touch it?'

'I'll pick it up by the chain,' said Tor. 'I don't want to touch the medallion itself.'

'Nothing happens,' replied the dungeon master.

'Isn't that medallion pretty?' said Dan. 'I'll take it off your hands if you don't want it.'

'That's okay with me,' Tor agreed. He realized that fine medallions like this one were very rare, and might contain deadly poisons.

'I put the medallion on,' said Dan. 'Does it make me invisible?'

'No,' said the dungeon master.

'Do I feel stronger?'

'No.'

'Am I quicker on my feet?'

'No.'

'Does the medallion do anything when I rub it?' Dan rubbed the medallion.

'A table appears, covered with food and wine.'

'I'm hungry,' Tor said. 'I'm going to eat.'

'I don't know.' Dan was nervous. 'Last time I was here I got ambushed. I think we ought to keep moving along. Bring some wine with us and let's be on our way.'

'I'm going to enjoy my food,' said Tor. 'I've only got a seven-day supply of food. I don't know how long I'll be in this god-awful place. I'll eat this food and conserve my own.'

'You'll be the death of me yet,' complained Dan. But he sat down and nibbled tentatively, keeping his eye on that door.

'Wind gushes through the door,' said the dungeon master, 'blowing out all the light.'

'I draw my sword,' said Dan, 'and back away from the table, up against the wall.'

'I stuff food into my pocket,' declared Tor. 'I can tell that Dan is afraid of that cold air, but I'm not.'

'A blinding flash of light illuminates the room,' said the dungeon master. 'For a moment neither of you can see. As your sight returns, you hear the voice of an old man telling you to return what you've stolen or it won't go well with you.'

'I was on my way to return it,' explained Dan. 'Just stopped here for a bite to eat.'

'The voice informs you that it will overlook this transgression if you will do something for it,' said the dungeon master.

'Who the hell are you?' Tor shouted at the voice. 'You're just a goddamn voice to me.'

'The voice,' said the dungeon master, 'as you can now tell, belongs to a gray-bearded old man. He says that no knave and lowly apprentice are going to defy him, the mighty Avatar of the Black Tower. The old man laughs at you. He says that if you bring him the Ring of Karn, he will spare your lives. He laughs once again and disappears, and in his hands is the medallion.'

'I don't know about Dan,' Tor said, 'but I think we'd better look for that Ring of Karn.'

'You've gotten me into more trouble,' Dan whined.

'Me? You're the one who rubbed that damn medallion.'

'I wonder why the wizard won't go get the Ring of Karn himself.'

'You've got two ways you can go,' said the dungeon master. 'You can crawl back the way you came, or you can go through that door.'

'I'm going through the door,' Tor said. 'I'm curious about what we'll find.'

'You go first,' urged Dan.

'You've got weapons,' Tor pointed out. 'You go first.'

'I'm not going first,' said Dan. 'You can use your magic.'

'Give me a few pieces of gold,' Tor said. 'I get paid for taking chances.' Tor knew his money supply was low. This was a way to raise some badly needed cash.

'Aw, what the hell,' agreed Dan. 'You're too puny to fight. I don't want to be stuck here alone. I'll give you two pieces of gold.'

'Make it four.'

'Three.'

'A deal.'

'Mark it off on your sheets,' the dungeon master said. 'Keep careful track of how much money you have. Now . . . the tunnel you're travelling through after you go past the door leads down, and you can see for a distance of twenty feet. The tunnel also twists as it wends downward, and in these spots you can only see for five feet. The air is getting staler the further you travel, and you can almost taste the odor of rotting trash. You hear rats rustling in the sewage. The passageway opens up into a large sewer that goes both to the right and to the left. Now, Dan, make a roll to see whether you're moving silently.'

Dan rolled 34. Unbeknownst to me, Dan wasn't concerned with walking silently; he wanted to pick my pocket. And he succeeded: he took his three gold pieces back, plus one other. If Dan had not made a lucky roll, the dungeon master would have told me of his thievery and I could have retaliated. As it was, I didn't know I'd lost my money.

'In each direction,' said the dungeon master, 'you can see piles of trash, and in periodic places lights are attached to the ceiling. You can occasionally glimpse movement in the piles of trash. They actually are in motion. One of the piles not only moves but has a squeaking noise emanating from it. What do you do?'

'I draw my sword,' said Dan. 'I've had experience with how dangerous this place is.'

'What happened to you?' Tor asked.

'A black marketeer came at me with a torch and nearly killed me.'

'We've got to go right or left,' Tor said. 'I vote for the right, the direction of the noise.' Tor figured that the squeaking noise was just rats.

'Let's go,' agreed Dan. 'Are my eyes adjusting?' he asked the dungeon master.

'Not if the lantern is kept on. Of course, if the lantern is put out, Tor can't see.'

'The lantern's staying on,' Tor declared.

'The passageway is wide and tall enough so you can walk side by side,' said the dungeon master. He rolled the die, telling neither Tor nor Dan the reason. Then Tor made a roll. It was a 6.

'Up ahead are five dog-sized rats,' explained the dungeon master. 'They are coming toward you, but you've seen them. They haven't caught you by surprise.'

'I attack the rats with my sword,' said Dan. He rolled the twenty-sided die and got a 12.

'You hit one,' said the dungeon master. 'You needed to roll at least a ten. How much damage did you do?' Dan rolled a six-sided die.

'I did five points.'

'That rat's dead,' said the dungeon master. 'Dan is fighting two more rats. Tor, two others have attacked you.'

'I pull out my dagger,' declared Tor.

'While you're pulling out your dagger,' said the dungeon master, 'both rats bite you.' He rolled the die twice, once for each rat. The total was five points. 'How many hit points do you have left?'

'I started with six,' Tor answered, examining his sheet of paper. 'I have only one left.' Tor thought what an idiot he'd been not to use his magic.

'Dan,' said the dungeon master, 'luckily, no rats have bitten you. Roll for initiative.' Dan rolled a 5, the dungeon master a 4. 'You've won,' said the dungeon master. 'The two of you get to attack first.'

'I hurl a magic missile,' said Tor.

'Roll how much damage you did,' said the dungeon master. Tor did four points of damage. 'You killed one rat,' said the dungeon master, 'and the other has backed away.'

Dan rolled the twenty-sided die. A 14. A hit. He rolled again to see how much damage he'd done: six points.

'You cleaved right through one of them,' said the dungeon master. 'The other rat turned and ran.'

'One rat left,' said Dan. 'Do you want to kill him, Tor, or should I?'

'I yell at the rat,' replied Tor, 'and move toward him menacingly while drawing my dagger all the way out.'

'The rat turns and runs,' said the dungeon master.

Tor realized that he was in pretty bad shape. He had only one hit point left. Lose all your hit points and you're dead. Kaput. Finito. Poof. Out of the adventure. Tor was going to have to do more thinking and less doing.

'Do you both continue?' the dungeon master asked.

'Yes,' Dan and Tor replied.

'You come upon a portcullis,' said the dungeon master. 'The portcullis is old and rusty and some of the grating has been knocked out. You can probably step through it if you want.'

Tor and Dan agreed to go through.

The dungeon master continued. 'On the other side the sewer goes to the left and continues forward. Two different ways. Which way do you go?'

'We're not going back to the top,' Dan said. 'Those guards will arrest us. Good going, Tor. What a loser you are. All you stole was that medallion, and the Avatar has that. I honestly think I'd be better off without you.'

'Screw you,' Tor replied.

'I don't think you see the big picture,' said Dan with a sneer. 'Yours is the worm's-eye view. You're down to one hit point. You're bleeding profusely. I think you want to make a deal.'

'What kind of deal?'

'What do you have to offer? You need protection. I'll provide it, for a price.'

Tor could tell that Dan was a low type, but it was easy to see that he did offer protection. 'How many pieces of gold do you want?' Tor asked. Tor hated Dan, a greed machine if ever there was one.

'Five pieces,' said Dan.

'Get lost,' said Tor. 'Take three or leave it.'

'No deal. I hope that rat comes back and eats you. What an epitaph: Here Lies Tor, Eaten by a Rat.'

'Well, at least I won't have submitted to your blackmail.' Even Tor, who had hardly been playing a textbook game, could see flaws in his reasoning. He felt bad enough about the way things had been going, but the slimy Dan had to rub it in.

'You're about the sorriest magic-user I've ever had the misfortune of running across. You have all this magic that you never use. You steal right under the noses of an entire battalion of guards. You stuff your face with food when your life is in danger. You fiddle with a dagger and get chewed up by rats. You're five feet four, skinny as a rail, and you run around like King Kong.'

'Can I cast a spell?' Tor whispered to the dungeon master, so Dan couldn't hear. 'To charm him into protecting me simply because he wants to, not because he intends to rob me blind?'

'I'll tell you if it works,' the dungeon master said in a low voice. Then, in a normal voice, 'You two still haven't decided what direction you're going to go in. Tor, which way do you want to go?'

'Left.'

'Dan, is left all right with you?'

'Fine.'

'Dan, as you turn the corner, make a roll.'

Dan did not realize that this roll was to determine whether Tor's spell affected him. He rolled a 3. The dungeon master winked at Tor. The spell had taken hold.

'Actually,' said Dan, 'you're not a bad guy, Tor. You're just a greenhorn. I need to develop the milk of human kindness. The more I think of it, the more I see what a really fine fellow you are.'

This was more like it, Tor thought. But Tor was feeling dizzy. He needed to sit down, rest, eat more of that food he'd taken from the table. The spell he'd cast, not to mention the beating he'd absorbed from those rats, had taken more out of him than he'd thought. 'Let's take a break and eat,' he suggested.

'Let's go on a little farther, my friend,' Dan replied. My friend! This devious creep had previously had nothing but ridicule for Tor, heaping insult upon insult, a constant rain of abuse that undoubtedly had been deserved. 'We can find a safer place, my comrade,' he continued, 'where you can relax and enjoy your repast.'

'All right,' the dungeon master said, 'you're heading down that sewer which led off to your left. Up ahead is a door on your left. Beyond the door, straight ahead, is a carrion crawler, a creature that feeds on the dead. The carrion crawler has many legs, like a centipede, and is nine feet long. The beast is three feet high and has tentacles coming out of its face. It looks like it is feeding on an arm that is not quite human.'

'I put away my sword,' said Dan, 'and pull out my bow and arrow. I'm going to try to kill the carrion crawler.'

'Roll the die,' the dungeon master ordered.

Dan rolled a 9.

'You were so far off that the carrion crawler didn't even notice,' the dungeon master said.

Dan rolled again. Another miss. But the carrion crawler had seen Tor and Dan and was charging toward them.

Again Dan rolled, and this time it was a hit. 'You got him in a shoulder,' the dungeon master said, 'but he's still coming.'

Tor could see that carrion crawler coming. The creature was hideous; it seemed almost as large as a train as it rushed toward Dan and Tor.

'The carrion crawler is five feet away,' the dungeon master said. His voice was without inflection, without emotion. He didn't care. That beast wasn't charging at *him*.

'I drop my bow,' said Dan, 'and draw my sword.' He rolled the die, swung, and missed.

'The carrion crawler swings a tentacle at Dan but misses,' the dungeon master explained. 'You get a whiff of the creature. It's nauseating, and you're afraid you'll gag. The stench is something straight out of the bowels of hell. Acidy, pungent with chemicals. The carrion crawler has been living in slime and putrid water. Now that the beast is almost on top of you, you can see the damage your arrow inflicted. Black pus oozes from the wound.'

'I swing at it again with my sword,' Dan said. 'It's a hit!'

'You chopped off several tentacles and buried your sword in its face,' said the dungeon master. 'A tremble runs through the carrion crawler's body. It emits a blood-curdling scream and strikes Dan with several of its tentacles. Dan, make a roll versus paralysis. You need to roll thirteen or higher.'

A 13!

'You're still with us, Dan,' the dungeon master said. 'What are you doing, Tor?'

'I'm feeling weak,' Tor said.

'Very understandable, my buddy,' sympathized Dan, who would surely have bitten Tor's head off if not for that blessed spell. 'But maybe you should lend some assistance, my dear pal. In the meantime, I swing again at the carrion crawler.'

'A hit!' the dungeon master said. 'The creature dies.'

'I wish you wouldn't put me through such a dangerous experience,' Tor said. 'You're supposed to protect me.' Dan was exhausted. He had red marks on his arms where the tentacles had lashed him.

'Sorry I didn't handle it better, my treasured friend.'

'Try to shape up, will you?'

'I'll do my best, most glorious companion.'

The dungeon master leaned over and whispered in Tor's ear. 'That spell you cast won't last forever,' he said. 'Maybe you should ease up a bit. Dan will remember how you treated him. Watch out when Dan starts looking confused. It will mean he's coming out of the spell.'

But by that time, Tor figured, he'd have his strength back.

'I think we ought to examine that arm the carrion crawler was gnawing,' Tor said. 'It may give us a clue as to what lies ahead.'

'It belongs to an orc,' Dan said, looking over the arm and then seeing the rest of the body lying up ahead in the sewer. 'Orcs are the foulest of creatures. Ugly. Mean. Dirty. Smelly. Terrible tempers. A gorilla, without the social graces of a gorilla. Their language would make a tavern wench blush. They always put themselves at the service of cruel and evil leaders. Carrion crawlers seem like Cub Scouts compared to an orc.'

'Why don't you lead the way?' Tor asked Dan. 'I'll be following behind.' Way behind, Tor thought.

'Whatever you say, old pal,' agreed Dan.

'You find a pouch at the side of the dead orc's body,' said the dungeon master. 'Inside are five copper pieces, two silver pieces, two rubies and a pearl, and a potion.'

'Is there a book next to the orc?' Dan asked.

'No,' said the dungeon master. 'But you do see a pair of boots dangling from his belt that are too small for him to wear.'

'Can I wear them?'

'Yes.'

'I put the pouch and its treasure into one of my pockets,' said Dan. 'I put the boots in another pocket.'

'Wait a minute,' complained Tor. 'We're partners in this. Share and share alike.'

'We'll split it when we find a place to rest,' Dan explained. 'There's not time for that now. These dead bodies will surely attract a lot of attention.'

This made sense to Tor.

'Do you want to go through the door or straight ahead?' the dungeon master asked. 'The door is a foot or so off the sewer floor. It appears to be a normal wooden door.'

'Does the door open inward or outward?' Tor asked.

'Inward,' the dungeon master said, 'from left to right.'

'I'll stand at the right of the door,' Dan said. 'Tor, you stand at the left. I'll push the door open with my sword. You, staunch companion, shine that lantern you graciously took from me into the room.'

Tor wondered if the spell was beginning to wear off. That 'graciously' business had a ring of sarcasm to it.

The dungeon master made a roll. 'From what you can see,' he said, 'the room is empty.'

'How big is the room?' Tor asked.

'Twenty feet by twenty feet.'

'I shine the lantern around the room,' Tor said.

'In the far right corner,' intoned the dungeon master, 'you can see an opening leading to the right. Against the far wall you discover a pile of clothing and spears that appear to be of orcish origin. What do you do?'

'Why don't you check out those clothes and spears?' Tor asked.

'Why don't you?' Dan replied.

Damn! Tor thought. *The spell is wearing off*. 'Well,' he said, 'close the door behind you. I don't want anything coming out of that sewer into this room.'

'As you approach the door, you feel a hot gust of wind that blows the door shut and makes a loud noise,' the dungeon master said to Dan.

'I'm going to search for traps,' Dan declared.

'You search the room thoroughly,' said the dungeon master, 'and find no traps.'

'We'll split the spears between us,' Tor suggested. 'I don't think either of us wants the clothing. It's flea-ridden and has a disgusting odor. I'll wedge that door shut with one of the spears.'

'We both need rest,' Dan said. 'Why not here?'

'The smell is terrible,' Tor complained.

'We may not find anything better.'

'That's true enough.'

'You sleep first,' Dan said. 'I'll guard that opening in the far right corner. I'll wake you in four hours.'

Tor wasn't sure he could trust Dan, but what choice did he have? He was wounded from the skirmish with the rats, and exhausted. He decided that he would have to sleep first, but he demanded to stay right next to Dan. Tor wanted at least the *possibility* of being awakened if his fellow adventurer decided to pull something. This agreed upon, Tor went to sleep, and Dan, his sword drawn, guarded the room, and especially that opening in the far right corner.

'Two hours have passed,' the dungeon master stated. 'Dan, make a roll.' He did so. 'That's not high enough,' the dungeon master said. 'Dan, you fall asleep also. Hours go by, and you sleep soundly. But then you're awakened by dark figures with rough, cruel hands. You've been surrounded by orcs. Do you struggle?'

'No,' said Tor. 'I've regained a lot of strength, but I want to gain back a little more. I'll make my move later.'

'How many orcs are there?' Dan asked.

'You can see four or five,' said the dungeon master, 'but there are more in the shadows.'

'I stand up,' said Tor, 'holding the tip of my dagger against my thigh. I look into the eyes of the chief orc.'

'He grins, then comes straight at you with a rope drawn. He intends to tie you up.'

'I charge at him,' Dan said, 'swinging my sword.'

Dan rolled the die.

'You knocked the chief orc aside,' the dungeon master said. 'But Tor is bound and gagged and being carried out of the room. Dan, four or five orcs are circling around you, and there are others behind these.'

'Well, I'm angry,' said Dan belligerently. 'These orcs are no good, and I'm going to fight them. They can't do this to me. I charge them too.'

'Roll,' said the dungeon master, unimpressed by this macho outburst.

'A four,' groaned a suddenly subdued Dan.

'You're clubbed on the head,' said the dungeon master, 'and fade into unconsciousness.'

'I decide to continue to play the waiting game,' said Tor. 'They're using ropes to bind us. That means at least they don't intend to kill us right away. Their purpose is to incapacitate.'

'The two of you are carried through that opening in the wall, around a corner, to a ladder that goes through a hole in the floor. You feel an updraft of steamy air coming through the hole. You are dropped through this hole to waiting hands and are carried out of that room into another. The temperature is getting higher, and your lungs taste sulfur and smoke. In this next room you see several orcs forging weapons in a furnace. You're carried out of that room, past the working orcs, who don't even take notice of you, and into a passageway that is dry and cool. You go a long distance in this passageway, the only diversion being listening to the orcs chatter. You are getting deeper and deeper into a maze of great complexity. Suddenly the chattering stops. A knife is put to Tor's throat. It is clear that the orcs want Tor to be quiet. Dan is apparently still unconscious, so this precaution is unnecessary with him, but enough time has elapsed now to see if he has awakened.'

Dan rolled that strange-looking die. An 18. 'Great to be back in the land of the living,' Dan said.

This is the land of the living? Tor thought. Bound up by characters who give new definition to the word *ugly* and whose intentions make those of the Nazis seem pure in comparison, and carried through a nightmarish maze with temperature extremes that first boiled, then froze – if this is the land of the living, how much worse can its opposite be?

'Up ahead,' said the dungeon master, 'you see a red glow that grows in size as you get nearer. The temperature rises with each step taken by your captors.'

'I pretend to be still knocked out,' said Dan. 'I want the element of surprise on my side if the time comes.'

The dungeon master continued. 'You come to a portion of the wall where there is a crack just large enough to wedge through. The heat at this point is terrific. The orcs, on tiptoes, are as still as death.'

'Now!' shouted Dan. 'Now is the time I make my move! The orcs clearly are distracted by whatever has plunged them into silence, and what passes for their minds can't be concentrated on us with this heat bearing in on them. I start to struggle violently.'

'The orcs who are carrying you start to run. From behind the crack you hear a mighty rumble, like a hundred volcanoes erupting at once, and the very ground underneath you trembles, as if in the grip of a fearsome earthquake. A voice that beats like thunder roars forth awesomely: "You orcs have disturbed my sleep for the last time!" '

'A dragon!' moaned Dan.

'Now's the time to make your move, huh?' said Tor.

'With a dragon nearly on top of us!' Dragons are the most fearsome creatures of all. Monsters don't come any tougher, meaner, or deadlier.

'You look behind you, toward the crack, as the orcs run,' the dungeon master calmly related, 'and you see flames shooting toward you. The passageway is engulfed in wave after wave of fire, mowing down everything in its path. Several orcs go down, consumed by the holocaust. Dan, you are severely burned, left lying on the floor. Your leather armor has melted and is sticking to your body, but you're alive, if you want to call it that. Tor, fortunately, because you weren't struggling, you avoided being hurt. The orcs carrying you were able to speed just out of reach of the flames. The dragon figures he's torched everyone, and ceases his attack. As the heat begins to subside, the cooling effect causes cracks to appear in the tunnel. You sense the start of a massive cave-in. Several orcs sneak back, pick up Dan, and as quickly and quietly as possible carry him to where Tor is being held.'

'Orcs are the most rotten of the rotten,' Dan said. 'They don't care about me. It must be that their asses will be grass if they don't get us to wherever they're supposed to go.'

'So you're still alive,' Tor said to Dan. 'Are you going to try something else insane? Jesus, waking up a dragon!' This was really nasty. Dan was near death, and the best Tor could offer was abuse.

'Ohhhhhh,' replied Dan.

Wonderful, thought Tor. And I was counting on *him* for protection?

'You travel further,' said the dungeon master, 'to a stairway that leads even deeper into the ground.'

'I hope you remember how to get out of here,' Dan said to Tor. 'I've been knocked out, and now I'm too injured to pay attention.' He spoke these words one at a time, with the greatest difficulty.

'What good are you, anyway?' Tor asked.

'Ohhhhhh,' moaned Dan.

'At the bottom of the stairs you travel again through a maze of passageways and tunnels,' continued the dungeon master. 'The orcs obviously know where they're going. They make not the slightest hesitation at intersections. All of a sudden the passageway widens, and the floor is constructed of black marble. You see orc sentries in full regalia, standing at attention, as you pass by. In front of you are large black double doors made of oak, and they open silently as you approach.'

'Ohhhhhh,' Dan moaned again.

'Shut up,' whispered Tor fiercely.

'The orcs carry you into a magnificent throne room. Along the walls of this incredible treasure trove are statues depicting legendary orc heroes of the past, creatures of unsurpassed evil. The two of you are placed in front of the throne, which is raised above the floor. The ropes that bind you are removed, and you are forced to kneel.'

'Ohhhhhh.'

Dan's conversation was beginning to grate on Tor.

'I know it hurts terribly,' said the dungeon master, who seemed not at all concerned by this fact. 'Now, perched on the throne is the chief orc – more hideous than the others, if that is possible; arrogant; a creature that many times over has proved through vile deeds that he deserves his high station.'

'Do you still have that Detect Magic spell?' Dan whispered to Tor, the words tortured and raspy, spoken with enormous difficulty.

'Yes,' Tor whispered back. 'Armed and ready to go.'

'The chief orc leans over on his throne,' stated the dungeon master, 'and growls that he wants the medallion. This fellow is clearly not someone to be trifled with. He has methods that would turn the Sphinx into a blabbermouth. As he leans back on his throne, you see a light bounce off a ring he is wearing.'

'The ring's our one way of getting out,' Dan whispered with what seemed his last breath.

'I use my Detect Magic to determine whether the chief orc is wearing the Ring of Karn,' said Tor.

'Now that you've cast the spell,' said the dungeon master, 'you catch glimpses of the lives of the previous wearers of the Ring of Karn, for that indeed is what it is. For just a moment you have an inkling of the awesome power of the Ring.'

'I'll make a deal with you,' Tor said to the chief orc. 'My friend and I are simply profiteers, looking for adventure and treasure. The medallion is of no real value to us, but apparently it is to you. We'll swap the medallion for our lives and safety, plus a trinket to make all this agony we've gone through seem worthwhile.'

'The orc wants to know why he shouldn't just kill you and take the medallion,' said the dungeon master.

'I've hidden it,' Tor lied, 'where no orc could find it.'

'Your audacity intrigues the orc, and he inquires what trinket you speak of.'

'I look around the room,' Tor said. 'My eyes linger for many moments on numerous objects. I look at the chief orc and what he is wearing. Again my eyes sweep the room. Again they return to the chief orc. I seem undecided.'

'The chief orc grows impatient,' stated the dungeon master. 'He wants an answer to his question.'

'I'll take that ring on your finger,' Tor said to the orc.

'The orc, stupid as only orcs can be, is not aware of the

great value of the Ring of Karn and removes the Ring and tosses it to you. As it flies through the air, surprise and pain appear on his hideous face. His powerful body withers before your eyes, disintegrates into a pile of ooze and bones and armor. You hear cries of alarm from behind. The undying one has died. The Ring of Karn bounces twice on the black marble floor, dribbles to a halt at your feet.'

'Pick it up,' Dan rasped.

'I have it!' Tor cried.

'The Ring is cold in your hand,' the dungeon master continued, 'as the scene fades before your eyes. You feel a wisp of wind blowing right through your bodies, and suddenly both of you are atop the Black Tower. Right before you is the Avatar, and over this old man's shoulder you can see in the far distance the winking lights of the town of Hann. The Avatar congratulates you on having acquired the Ring of Karn. Then he asks you to give it to him.'

'Hand it over,' Dan said, his voice barely audible through the pain. 'You don't argue with a wizard.'

'You mean I went through this hell for nothing?' said Tor.

'Give it to him, damn you!'

Tor was a magic-user, and the Ring of Karn was the most powerful magic he'd ever possessed. Tor was not going to hand over that Ring without at least first trying it on.

'I put on the Ring,' Tor said.

'The Avatar is unbelievably old,' explained the dungeon master. 'Only by tremendous effort is he even able to stand. You can see the delicate outlines of bones pushing against his ancient skin. This Ring of Karn is very important to him, his last hope. Dejected, he turns to walk away.'

'Hold on a minute, old man,' Tor said to the Avatar.

'The Avatar stops to listen,' said the dungeon master.

'Maybe we can make a trade,' said Tor. Despite the horrendous dangers Tor and Dan had gone through to satisfy the old man, the Avatar was basically a force for good, and Tor was willing to help him if there was something in it for Tor too. 'I'll give you the Ring of Karn,' he continued, 'if I can become your apprentice. I want to learn all you know.'

'The Avatar agrees to your condition.'

'I take off the Ring and hand it to him.'

'The Avatar puts on the Ring and transforms into a sixteen-year-old. He grins impishly and disappears, but both of you are returned to perfect health. Dan finds a very fine sword in his sheath. At Tor's feet is a scroll containing a new and powerful spell. That's it,' the dungeon master said. 'I thank you, gentlemen, for a very interesting game.'

'What do you mean, "that's it?"?' Tor said.

'That's it.'

'Our asses are out in the middle of nowhere, and the game's over?'

'Yes.' He started to gather up papers and leave.

'I can't just be stranded,' Tor said.

'Well, maybe on another day you can try to find your way back.'

'With Dan?'

'He's there with you, isn't he?'

'Past those dragons and orcs and rats?'

'Why not?'

That's right, Tor thought. *Why not?*

Tor was going to say that he wanted someone more competent than Dan along with him the next time, someone who didn't wake up sleeping dragons and steal gold pieces. God knows that getting back, to wherever 'back' was, would probably be more hazardous than the journey they had already completed.

Tor looked up to complain about Dan, appeal to the dungeon master's innate sense of fairness, but he found himself seated alone at a bare table. The motel room was empty, and darkness had fallen on East Lansing.

Chapter 10

Sunday, September 2, began with breakfast – poached eggs, bacon, hash browns, milk, orange juice – at a restaurant near the Red Roof Inn. My first casualty during an investigation is always a decent diet, and this was the first really substantial meal I'd had since arriving in Michigan. Getting to the restaurant without a lot of company had posed a problem, because a determined knot of reporters was camped in the lobby. When I passed through to pick up messages, I perfunctorily brushed aside questions, promising news later in the day, and managed to escape without being followed – an accomplishment that soon would become a difficult challenge. I'd told Frank Lambert to meet me at the restaurant, but he was late arriving so I went ahead and ordered without him.

Lambert, whom I hadn't seen at all the previous day because of my lengthy Dungeons & Dragons game, came to my table just as I was finishing my meal. He'd had that Friday-night meeting with a student, and all day Saturday to poke around for information. As usual, I was impatient, eager to walk out and solve this case, but it seemed I was going to have to wait on Lambert. I watched with amazement as he ordered enough food for five people.

I drummed my fingers on the Formica table. I chewed my mustache. 'Don't let me rush you,' I said.

'We've got another wrinkle in the case,' he stated.

'Just what we need,' I replied.

'There's another private investigator looking into the

disappearance. Everywhere I go, he's been there first.'

'Does he look like a professional, or is he a sleazebag?'

'I haven't seen him. Haven't been able to catch up with him. But from what I gather, he's a professional.'

'Is he local or out-of-town?'

'Out-of-state.'

'Where?'

'Chicago or New York.'

'They're a long way apart.'

'Well, that's the best I've been able to do.'

'Where is he staying?'

'I don't know. The people he talked with say he's good with the questions, skimpy with answers.'

'Where has he shown up?'

'The gay places.'

'I think he's on the right track.' Lambert's food had arrived and he was taking his time eating.

'Do you have his name?'

'Don Gillitzer.'

'Did he flash a badge or an investigator's license?'

'No. That seems strange to me.'

It did to me too. Showing credentials helps when you're trying to elicit information.

'Who's hired Gillitzer?'

'I talked to five or six people he interviewed. He never said who he was working for. One guy asked him flat out. He just evaded the question.'

'Maybe he's looking for the reward.' This would not have been an unusual occurrence. Many private investigators supplement their income by collecting rewards on cases. They are modern-day bounty hunters, and usually create more trouble than good; it's an instance of too many cooks spoiling the broth. The reward in this case was not that high, but there were obvious other benefits for any investigator who solved a case as well publicized as this one: a vastly increased clientele, eager to retain the services of the person who cracked the Egbert disappearance; favorable publicity that no amount of money could buy; instant celebrity. Attorney F. Lee Bailey, for instance, needed the Sam Sheppard murder trial to vault to fame and fortune; as brilliant a lawyer as Bailey is, he could never have attained his vaunted stature without the Sheppard coup. Likewise for lawyer Marvin Mitchelson with his palimony suit against Lee Marvin.

I wanted to get hold of Gillitzer, and quickly. He could scare off a lot of people we had been carefully cultivating. While Lambert proceeded determinedly and steadily through that mountainous mound of food, I thought about how I would reach Gillitzer. At the same time I leafed through the messages that I'd picked up at the motel's front desk. I figured I was due for a break, and I got one: Don Gillitzer had called. He'd left a number where I could reach him.

Lambert ordered more toast.

'Damn,' I said.

'Look, I can talk while I'm eating.'

'What else have you learned?' I asked.

'Not much of immediate benefit. Over the long run, maybe I've accomplished a lot. Like you told me to do, I'm putting on a lot of pressure. I'm letting everybody know we're here, and that we're not giving up, not leaving until Dallas is found. I'm letting it be known in no uncertain terms that anyone involved in this disappearance could be in tons of trouble. Time is running out. All we want is the boy, and if somebody turns him over, we're not interested in being vindictive. But if we have to find him – and we will – they don't know what trouble is. I leave this message everywhere: bars, pool halls, game arcades, campus hangouts, gay hangouts. I'm leaving threats, but the threats are real. People can't help but know that we mean business, that time is running out for any deals to be cut.'

'That's good,' I said. And it was. If others besides Dallas were involved, and I believed that there were others, they had to be frightened into the open. We had to apply relentless pressure. To put it as plainly as I can, I wanted to scare people. Unrelenting fear, balanced with the carrot of hope, can crack some of the hardest heads.

'Today I want more of the same,' I said to Lambert, who had finished his main courses and was looking over the dessert menu. 'You get the word out everywhere: there'll be trouble like no one's ever seen if we have to find Dallas; we forget it if we get him back. You and I know that if the crime is hideous enough, we won't forget it, but we don't have to mention that. Also, we have no right to speak for the police.'

Lambert ordered strawberry shortcake. I headed for a phone booth near the restaurant's rest rooms and dialed Gillitzer's number. A man answered and I asked for the private investigator, identifying myself when Gillitzer came on the line.

'I need to talk to you in private,' he said.

'Name the place.'

He gave the name and address of a bar in downtown Lansing and suggested 1 P.M., and I said I would be there and hung up. I had a reason for being abrupt: I didn't want him to be able to 'read' me, in any way to be able to size me up or get an idea of what I knew about him. He could be just about anybody, representing practically anything. The possibilities were too numerous to ponder. Gillitzer might be an investigator brought in by gays who were worried about the case, to speed Dallas's release from other gays. Responsible homosexuals – the vast majority – might have retained Gillitzer to protect them against a potentially scandalous situation. Or Gillitzer might be involved in the abduction, and want to make a deal or scare me off. It's happened before. I knew for sure that I wasn't going to be frightened away. Or Gillitzer could simply be a crackpot, of which two types exist: the dangerous and the merely annoying.

I told Lambert where I would be at one o'clock. He was still eating.

'Nice place,' he said. I could tell he didn't think it was.

'You've been there?'

'A gay place. Classless, or democratic, if you want to describe it that way. Rich and poor alike. Pool table. Pinball machine. Dark. Secluded booths. It's a very rough place – plenty of dope there. It's not an establishment where straights want to be.'

I knew what Lambert meant. I realized that I might be considered an enemy. Plenty had been written about me since my arrival in East Lansing, and my men had been highly visible in the gay community. It would not be difficult for homosexuals to believe that I was trying to pin Dallas's disappearance on one or more of them. What I was doing, of course, was following the evidence wherever it led, but certain gays, knowing about vendettas of the past, might not look at it that way. For protection, I intended to carry a .380 automatic tucked under my belt near the pit of my back (where people seldom check when frisking) and a knife concealed in my boot.

I made sure I entered the bar right at one o'clock, but I hesitated just inside the door for perhaps ten seconds to allow my eyes to adjust to the dark. Then I looked around. Three men were seated at the bar, two others were at a table, and at the extreme rear of the establishment was a lone fellow sitting with his back to the wall. I walked straight toward him, keeping my eyes on his hands.

'Are you Don?' I asked when I reached the table.

'Bill Dear?' He stood up to shake hands. He was two inches taller than I am, a good six feet five, with a fine athletic build. He was perhaps twenty-eight years old, had black hair, and was dressed tastefully and expensively in a preppie sort of way. Many women would consider this handsome man a head-turner.

'Don,' I said when we were seated at the table, 'I understand you're looking for Dallas Egbert.'

'I guess you want to know why,' he said. 'Let me tell you a little about myself. I currently live in New York City, where I'm a private investigator.'

I looked at Gillitzer even more closely. He could have been an ad for the All-American, red-blooded young executive that big corporations want us to believe works for them. He certainly didn't resemble any New York City private detective I'd ever known. I don't want to portray a stereotype, and certainly I've met only a tiny fraction of the Big Apple's private investigators, but the ones I have dealt with have possessed at least two of the following characteristics: a physical appearance best described as dumpy; a physical condition highlighted by chronic coughing that speaks of chain-smoking strong cigars; shifty, darting eyes; rapid, furtive hand movements; clothing, including trench coat, out of a Raymond Chandler novel; hollow eyes sunken in an unshaven face; language that's supposed to be street-smart but is somehow off-key; wrinkled shirts (obviously slept in); mud-spattered shoes; and a hangover. Always a hangover.

'I'm going to be up front with you,' Gillitzer continued. 'I'm gay. I've read everything I can find about Dallas, and you should know that I've become infatuated with him. I've heard this can happen, but it's never happened to me before. I suppose it's not much different from falling in love with a movie star. Anyway, when I saw a picture of Dallas, I knew I had to meet him. That's why I flew in from New York.'

'Then you're not working for anyone?'

'Just for myself.'

'You're paying your own way?'

'Yes. Completely.'

'Well,' I said, 'you asked to meet me privately. I know you've been questioning people we've already contacted, and I'm fairly certain that the reason you asked for this meeting wasn't to tell me about an infatuation.'

'That was part of it. What I really want is to join forces with you. Work for you, if you will. Oh, I don't expect pay, and I'd be very discreet. But overall I think you're much more capable and better equipped to find Dallas than I am. I know of your reputation and believe it's deserved. I'd like to be part of the team that finds him.'

'What do you expect in return?'

'One thing only: I want to meet him. Nothing else. Just meeting him, if only for a moment, would mean a great deal to me.'

Gillitzer impressed me as bright, sincere, and, most important, honest. I did not find it unusual that someone had become fascinated with a person he had never met. I know men my age who still can imagine nothing more fulfilling than meeting Doris Day, whom they fantasized about as youngsters. Granted, they do not fly a third of the way across a continent on the off chance of such an encounter, but I felt that it was just a question of the degree of commitment. I felt strongly that Gillitzer was as he depicted himself. Certainly, if he assisted in finding Dallas, he had every right to meet the boy.

'When did you arrive in East Lansing?' I asked.

'Two days ago.'

'Where are you staying?'

'Different places. I could stay in touch with you.'

'What have you learned so far?'

'Dallas has spent time in this very bar. I've talked with people who remember him. I don't have to tell you, he was a super, superintelligent person. From what I gather, he really didn't have any close friends. He was seeking acceptance, someone to care about him. I hope it's not too late.'

Gillitzer spoke with such emotion that I thought he might be describing himself. 'It sounds as if you know what you're talking about,' I said.

'My adolescence was not unlike his.'

'How is that?'

'I'm not going to talk about it, but please believe that I understand a little of what he's suffered. Not with the same intensity – I don't delude myself on that. He must be so brilliant. So sensitive. Yes, I understand a little, but I can never understand it all.'

'What else have you learned?'

'Not anything that's really specific. Mainly that Dallas was a loner. That worries me more than anything. I don't see how he could have learned to take care of himself.'

'What do you think has happened to him?'

'Who can tell? I don't think he's a suicide. Forced to make a guess, I'd say someone is holding him.'

'Who? Why?'

'Who, I obviously don't know, but he could have been picked up and held. It could be ugly. He might be passed from one individual to another, one group to another. Why? For purposes of sex, most likely. It happens with straights also, you know. I fear this is a possibility because usually I can get a fix on a case when it involves my milieu, the gay community, but in this instance I'm getting nothing.'

'What do you suggest?'

'Here is why I think I might be a big help to you. I think I have to go deeper underground, to places where you would never pass muster. Bathhouses, for instance. They make you *prove* you're gay before they let you in.'

'Prove it?'

'Usually a tryst with the manager.'

'No thanks.'

'I know. I don't like it either. But I could do it. That's the point. For Dallas, I could do it. You never could.'

This might be true enough. Gillitzer could probably submerge himself in the gay community as I or my men couldn't. And it was clear that I could use additional help; already I had considered contacting my office for more men. The Egberts really couldn't afford what they were already getting, but much of it would be on me.

'All right,' I said. 'I think it might work out if you find out what you can for me. Before I leave, though, I'd like to know whether you're familiar with the Dungeons & Dragons aspect of this case.'

'I've read about Dallas playing the game. I haven't found anyone who admits playing it with him. It's the sort of recreation I can see would appeal to Dallas – a mental fantasy game. I'm sure he would be good at it. I've played it myself, and it's complex and challenging. Perfect for Dallas. The only trouble is, he might become addicted to the game.'

'I know what you mean,' I said. That single game I had played in my motel room provided an inkling of how Dungeons & Dragons could grip a person. I had concentrated so hard on evading dangers, trying to gather fortune, and simply staying alive that for long periods I actually forgot where I was and became a magic-user in the perilous maze. My mind pictured the maze as the dungeon master described it, and it seemed as if my temperature rose as the air became moist and steamy. My body hurt after those big rats attacked me. Once, when I got up to go to the bathroom, I developed a limp. Very shortly after I began the game, I was no longer in that motel room; I had escaped to another place, another world, another time.

People who have studied Dungeons & Dragons often contend that the game is particularly appealing to individuals who find it difficult to deal with their real surroundings. Gary Gillette, president of the Michigan State University Simulation Society, put it a different way: 'It's a throwback to a simpler time, a simple way of life. It's easier than knocking heads in the real world. I don't want to say all people who play Dungeons & Dragons are incapable of dealing with reality. It's not true. But people who take it too seriously are. Alternate reality is popular because reality is not very popular.'

Reality was not, could not be, very attractive for Dallas. Searching for an activity that permitted him to escape from an existence he found increasingly unbearable was as inevitable for him as looking for water would be for a man dying of thirst. Predictably, once he found a way out, however temporary, he would want and need more and more of his 'fix,' like a junkie craves the needle, until the game was using him, not the other, healthy way around. At this moment he might be playing out the ultimate Dungeons & Dragons game, and that was frightening.

Suddenly I realized that maybe I should be *hoping* that Dallas was playing an advanced, dangerous, far-out version of Dungeons & Dragons. If the game had failed him, what was the alternative? How could he be certain of escape? The answer stuck like a knife point in my brain.

And in spite of what I had said to Riddle, Lambert, and Hock in Texas, I was continuing to have doubts about suicide. One single, gigantic, incapable-of-being-ignored fact screamed at the top of its lungs: this was the nineteenth day Dallas had been missing. I didn't care how bright the boy was, nineteen days was a long time to be away without the slightest trace.

I left Gillitzer in the bar and stopped at a convenience store to use the pay telephone. When I got through to the Red Roof Inn, the desk clerk gave me the usual banter about reporters crowding the lobby and callers jamming the switchboard – the manager, I was told, was beginning to weigh the benefits of increased occupancy against the disruption taking place at his establishment.

'Are any of those messages marked urgent?' I asked. The fact that someone said the call was urgent didn't make it so, but it was my chief barometer for judging. Another of those psychics might believe that what he or she had to say was urgent.

'There are five or six. I've set them aside.'

'Give me those, please.' I was going to have to start being much more available to the press, but I wasn't ready for that yet. It was better not to make an appearance to pick up the messages.

Two of the calls were indeed from psychics, and the out-of-town variety at that, so I decided to give my credit card a rest and dialed one of the local numbers.

'Hello,' greeted a cheery voice.

'This is Bill Dear. You called.'

'Uh, right.' There was a hesitation. 'Just a moment.' The voice had gone from cheerful to dark and secretive. 'All right,' it said. 'I needed to move to a room where I could be alone.'

'Go ahead. I'm at your service. Why did you call?'

'I'll give you my name, but you mustn't reveal it.'

'Agreed.'

'You can't identify me by description, or in any other way.'

'Okay.'

'I don't want anyone in the world to know I've talked with you.'

'That's fine.'

'Mr. Dear, I believe I can trust you. You wouldn't have been in business so long otherwise.'

'You can trust me. I keep my word.'

'Well, I think we should meet. I have information about Dallas.'

'How about right away?'

'That would be good. I think I've waited too long to speak up.'

I'd heard that before. Nineteen days had passed. If this man had anything important to tell me, he was right, he had waited too long. I asked him to name a place and he mentioned a bar in East Lansing. I told him I'd be waiting for him.

The bar was a college hangout, with a juke box, pinball machine, and television set. Beer seemed to be the only beverage being served. I ordered a schooner so I wouldn't look even more out of place and took a table in a corner. My caller wouldn't have any trouble recognizing me.

Bars outrank anywhere else as a spot where informants elect to meet. They think a bar will be dark and they might go unrecognized. They also believe that bars are places where many customers have problems, and therefore they'll be in a sympathetic atmosphere. Most important, they are assured of being able to have a drink, which can be a courage-builder. What they have to say may be difficult or even incriminating, and drinking can dull the mind and senses and make an unpleasant task less distasteful.

My informant wore dress slacks, sports shirt, and sports jacket, the kind with patches on the elbows. He had a tan you'd associate more with California than with Michigan, and I imagined he had a Datsun 280-Z parked outside. He spotted me and nodded, but before coming over he ordered a *pitcher* of beer. This might be good.

'Mr. Dear, I'm going to be a senior this semester. I can't afford to get into trouble now,' he began.

'Anything you tell me will be treated confidentially. You're here to help me and I appreciate it. I was threatened with jail once, and was willing to go, for refusing to reveal confidential information. If I get the wrong kind of reputation, I might as well fold up my tent and go out of business.'

My college senior took a big swallow of beer. He had a ballpoint pen in his hand and was doodling on a napkin. He still hadn't looked into my eyes. 'Well,' he said, 'I thought you should know that I was one of those who played Dungeons & Dragons in the steam tunnels with Dallas.'

My mind raced back to some of those first phone calls I'd made from the Red Roof Inn. A young woman who said she was a senior had talked of playing Dungeons & Dragons in that underground maze. She hadn't played the game with Dallas, but she had promised to try to find someone who had. Maybe this fellow was the result of her efforts. In any event, I was very eager to hear what he had to say. He was the first person who had actually played the game with Dallas to come forward. 'How well did you know him?' I asked.

'He wasn't in any way a friend. He was just someone I played D & D with. He was a good player and was invited into our game. We considered ourselves very advanced players and looked for others who fit that mold.'

'Who invited him into the game?'

'I don't know. He just showed up one day. Look, I've got a reason for talking to you. It's because. . . .'

'It's because you fear Dallas may have been hurt in the

tunnels,' I said. 'You're afraid he might be dead down there.'

'Right. But –'

'Just let me ask the questions. I appreciate your coming to me. Be assured that I share your fears about Dallas and the tunnels, and will do everything I can in that regard. Now, can you give me the names of other members of your group?'

'I won't do that. They could get in trouble. I will tell you that I've talked with them about Dallas, and they know nothing about his disappearance. You have to understand how they feel. They can't tell you anything more than I can, and, quite honestly, they risk expulsion if what they did becomes known publicly. We weren't what the administration would consider good little boys and girls down there.'

'Girls were part of your group?'

'Half were girls. Dungeons & Dragons isn't an arm-wrestling contest, it's a *mental* game. The women in our group were very imaginative. It got tough in the tunnels, of course, but it wasn't the sort of tough that required lifting heavy boxes or duking it out with John Wayne types. The women could handle the conditions as well as any guy.'

'How many played in your group?'

'Eight. That includes the dungeon master.'

'I'd really like his name.'

'Hers. And I can't give it to you. She'd be in more trouble than any of us. She spent more time down there than any of us. She had to go down in the tunnels in advance so she'd know the setting and be able to lay surprises for us.'

'Tell me about the surprises.'

'Just being down there was a surprise. You could get lost very easily. And the conditions were terrible – so hot you thought your brain would boil. But I know what you mean. The DM would hide treasures, which all of us had chipped in to buy, and the person who found them could keep them. And there'd be niches you could reach into. You might come up with a handful of decaying calf's liver, or soggy spaghetti representing an orc's brain, or something equally unappetizing. Of course, you might find a treasure also. The DM really didn't have to set traps. There were plenty of those already.'

'Were there many other groups playing D & D in the tunnels?'

'Absolutely. Those tunnels go forever, and you'd think you'd never run into anyone down there, but we did. People who dressed for the game – I mean, they wore costumes of the characters they were portraying.'

I knew that this took place at other schools. At the University of Texas in Austin, for example, players held what they called combat practice, dressing in medieval attire and arming themselves with rattan replicas of ancient weapons.

'What did you do when you bumped into other D & D groups in the tunnels?' I asked.

'We just tried to get past them. Not interrupt whatever action they were into, at the same time trying not to be deflected too much ourselves. Just getting around them could be a big problem. In most places those tunnels aren't that wide.'

'How many times did Dallas play with your group?'

'Three. We asked him not to come back.'

'Why?'

'He seemed to be on drugs. And he wasn't mature. Oh, he was a brilliant player, but he'd do silly things. Like a child. And then when we learned how young he was, we got scared that we'd be held to blame for anything he did. And we were afraid, because he was so young and inexperienced, that he might inadvertently let it slip to the wrong people what we were doing. It was just a lot of things, Mr. Dear. He didn't fit in. There was an even bigger gap between us than the actual years. He was a little kid always trying to be helpful, but he just succeeded in being annoying.'

'So you told him not to come back.'

'The DM did. Really, she didn't want to hurt his feelings, but it was the best thing all around. He could have been hurt down there.'

The best thing? I wondered. It was another rejection. Another example of not being accepted. *Alienation* was a word psychiatrists later enjoyed using when describing Dallas. I don't imagine that getting thrown out of an advanced Dungeons & Dragons game lessened the alienation. But I could see no fault in what the students had done. They could not be expected to understand the nuances of dealing with a gifted child.

'When was the last time you played the game with Dallas?' I asked.

'In late July.'

'Less than a month before he disappeared?'

'Right.'

'Where did you enter the tunnels when you were playing the game? At what spot on campus?'

'We used three different entry points. From one of the dormitories, from in front of the administration building, and from the old power plant.'

'You just go into the tunnels from a dormitory?'

'No problem.'

'So you could get into the dormitory from the tunnels.'

'Yes.'

'What dorm is this?'

'I really don't want to say, Mr. Dear.'

'From in front of the administration building. Terrific.'

'We thought it was funny.'

'Right. And the old power plant.' I pictured that corkboard.

'The easiest of all. There's no one around there.'

'Describe what sticks in your mind about Dallas.'

'You could tell he was immature, and this could mislead you. You wouldn't expect him to make sound decisions in the game, and some of the things he did would seem far-out, but then they'd work out. He was brilliant. Very creative. And he would take more chances than you'd think a magic-user would.'

'Anything else?'

'It's funny – the girls seemed to want to take care of him, protect him. One of them called him "cuddly," as if he were a baby. He was a perfect candidate to be mothered.'

'Do you know whether Dallas was in the tunnels at times other than when you were with him?'

'He said he was. And I could believe him. He was pretty sure-footed down there.'

'Do you know whether the tunnels are being used for drug transactions?'

'You hear a lot about that around campus. I don't know. I do know drugs are *used* down there.'

'You've seen a picture of the corkboard found in Dallas's room, haven't you?'

'I guess everyone's seen it.'

'Could it be connected with a game of Dungeons & Dragons?'

'I thought it could be the layout of a game.'

'Look at this.' I handed him the aerial photograph Frank Lambert had taken of the power plant, and also a picture of the corkboard.

'They look identical,' he said. 'Almost drawn to scale. I'd bet that if those other tacks mean anything, they're also positioned to scale.'

'I bet you'd win that bet. Let me ask you this: When you were playing Dungeons & Dragons with Dallas, did you have any idea how bright he was? I know you're aware of the fact now, from all the newspaper stories, but did you know it then?'

'It makes me feel like a fool, but no, I really had no idea. He certainly didn't tell us. I always realized he was good at the game, but I guess I never really thought about what that meant. He just seemed like a pain in the ass, wanting to be so helpful and all.'

'Have you heard of anyone being hurt in the tunnels while playing the game?'

'No. And that's sort of a miracle by itself. The reason we chose the tunnels is that they are dangerous. Of course, if someone did get hurt, he wouldn't advertise it.'

'How about getting lost? Ever hear of anyone getting lost?'

'No. But it wouldn't take any big screw-up for it to happen. Our DM was always very careful. She trailed string behind her. When the adventure was over, we just had to follow the string back to the starting point. Without precautions you could get lost down there, and I mean permanently.'

'Are there other places near campus where the game is played?'

'You mean dangerous places?'

'Right. Like the woods at night.'

'Not that I know of. The tunnels are perfect for the game. It's hard to imagine something more true to it. I think if you checked, you'd find that MSU isn't the only place where this occurs.'

I already had checked. At Southern Methodist

University and at the California Institute of Technology, students also played the game in tunnels beneath the campus. It was a seven-day-a-week vocation for some students at the University of Iowa.

'We've talked to a lot of students at MSU,' I said. 'We've heard reports about unsolved rapes and robberies. Do you think the tunnels could be used to gain entrance or exit for these purposes?'

'I believe the tunnels are used for a lot of reasons. We go into them to have fun. What others do, I don't know. But sure, it's possible. If we could get into a dorm through the tunnels, so could someone else.'

'Why do I get the feeling around campus that I'm being stone-walled? I can understand a reluctance to talk with someone who even resembles a cop, but surely the situation is serious enough now that students should be coming forward. You came forward.'

'I almost didn't. I could be in serious trouble if what I told you leads back to me. I think the trouble is Dallas's age. *Sixteen* – just a child. If he was treated like everyone else, did the things everyone else does, no one is going to want to come forward and say, "Hey, I was his pal, and here's all the fun we had together." '

This was true. But why not anonymous information? Why couldn't someone call, tell us what we needed to know, and hang up? If people knew what had happened to Dallas or where he was, they must have strong reasons indeed for remaining silent. A game seemed preposterous, at least if others were involved. After this length of time, even the most obtuse person could see that the game was no fun anymore. So, scratch a game being played with others.

Yet others seemed to be involved. Peggy Hogan had said that she might know people who had information. She was Riddle's project, and I was eager for Riddle to return from Louisville and apply some pressure in that direction. Again my mind turned to the possibility that a game had begun and then had turned into something entirely new.

'I'd like you to stay in touch,' I said to my informant. 'Just look around, if you will. Check with other D & D players. If you learn anything, let me know.'

'I will. And I have your promise on the other?'

'Of course. Your identity will never go further than me.'

Driving back to the Red Roof Inn, I knew I would have to face the reporters, and this time I intended to use the session to my advantage. I was going to have to pretend to be hot, which wouldn't be difficult. I was hot. It was time to shake things up.

The questions and answers lasted forty-five minutes, but the important part for me came right at the beginning. I asked for quiet and started talking. 'I have just been given some further information which confirms that Dallas Egbert was playing Dungeons & Dragons in the tunnels beneath the campus. This information is absolutely unimpeachable. The university says it's impossible even to get into those tunnels. It is possible. It is in fact easy. And Dallas went into those tunnels. Mrs. Egbert, I might add, told me that Dallas went into the tunnels. I do not know why the university is taking the position that access to these tunnels is impossible, but I know the school is wrong. I've told my clients I will do everything I can to find their son, but my investigation cannot proceed in a professional manner until we are given free rein to search these tunnels. I'm not speaking for the campus police, but I do know that they feel the tunnels need to be checked. No sincere person could possibly believe otherwise. Why, I ask, would responsible school officials deny us access to these tunnels? Surely it's not to keep their own students from knowing about their existence – the students already know. The knowledge is so widespread that many students use the tunnels to travel between buildings on cold wintry days. They keep warm this way. So what is it that MSU administrators don't want the public to know? The public, I might point out, owns this institution. Surely it's the public who is being deceived, not the students. I have suspicions about why the school pretends ignorance, but it is not a good idea at the moment to sling mud. What's at stake here is a boy's life. A very exceptional boy. Everything else except finding the boy is immaterial.'

Most of the questions following this calculated outburst were about whether I thought Dallas was in the tunnels and whether he was dead or alive. How could I answer these? I reiterated that lead after lead pointed to the tunnels and it certainly was morally obligatory for us to search them.

When I finally got to my room, I had a message to call Dick Riddle in Louisville. He said that he and Hock had not spotted Dallas at the science-fiction convention, but that the next day, Monday, Labor Day, was the big finale, and if he was going to be there, that would be the time. Riddle wanted to know how I was doing.

'Trying to force bureaucrats to move, to light a fire under their rear ends,' I said.

'Then it still points to the tunnels?' he said.

'I don't know where it points, Dick.'

'Well, I'd rather have my job than yours. If you like colorful, weird characters, this is the place to be. I can't think of anything much worse than trying to get bureaucrats to admit they've fouled up.'

I flipped through the thick stack of messages I'd brought up from the desk. A lot of requests from radio interviewers. Newspapers. Calls from overseas, including

French national television. I intended to return them all. I wanted to talk to the media about why Michigan State University didn't want us down in those tunnels. Of course, there were other calls; most of them would be from well-wishers or cranks, and there might even be a few that were important. I intended to answer all of these calls too.

But first I needed to get something to eat. I was tired, but not from the long hours. I was used to them. Anyone in the private-investigation business can tell stories about endless stakeouts and the deadly dull drudgery of it all, when life is not one brilliant Sherlock Holmes-type deduction after another but a contest to determine whether you can break a world record for staying awake. No, I was tired not from the long hours but from the feeling that I was getting nowhere. If I had a hot lead, something I could race out to follow up – if I could get the feeling I was active, *doing something* – it would be better, even if the lead finally dead-ended. The best lead I had was those tunnels, and I risked arrest if I went into them without the university's authorization. I knew that that technicality would not deter me for long.

I called Frank Lambert's room and was both pleased and disappointed when he answered – pleased because I wanted company, disappointed because if he hadn't been in, he might have been busy on an important tip.

'I know you can't possibly be hungry,' I said, 'but I thought you might like to go to a nice restaurant with me. It would be a better atmosphere for you to tell me all the good things you've accomplished today.'

'Why do you think I'm not hungry?'

'You ate a month's worth of food for breakfast. I won't ask you to sacrifice and eat more, just so I won't feel guilty dining alone.'

'I won't feel guilty. I'm starved.'

'That's nice of you to say, but I know you're just thinking of my feelings. Meet me downstairs at the car. At least you can come along.'

'Dammit, Bill, I'm telling you –'

'Meet me at the car.'

One of my friends at the front desk had given me the name of the best restaurant in East Lansing, and I wasn't even out of the motel parking lot before I realized that the place would have a number of unexpected guests. Right on our tail were three cars, the several-years-old, compact kind that reporters drive. The reporters were doing what I would do if our situations were reversed. Following the investigator, presumably the one who knew the most about the case, might lead them to a scoop. In the days that followed they became much more expert at the art of tailing, but this evening a blind man might have spotted them. For a moment I felt guilty about my choice of restaurants; the reporters probably couldn't afford a meal there, and I could hear the editors responsible for expense accounts screaming, 'You paid *what?!*' These accountants might understand the expenditure if the reporters learned anything, but I knew that tonight they would discover nothing more interesting than that Frank Lambert has a world-class appetite.

The steak was simply excellent, the salad bar outstanding. Even the most diehard Texan, fanatically loyal to Lone Star steaks, would tip his ten-gallon Stetson to this Michigan restaurant. Lambert, hardly a gourmet, said it was the finest meal he'd ever had. I don't know whether the reporters enjoyed their meals. I imagine they simply blotted the unpleasant expense-account review out of their minds. Each one sat at his or her own table; I thought it incredible that they apparently believed I hadn't seen them.

Lambert had done everything I could have expected.

Forsaking the Joe College image, he had approached individuals and members of groups on campus as Lambert the Tough Private Investigator, promising mercy if information was forthcoming and the wrath of a vengeful, inflexible, impossible-to-control legal system if we had to crack the case ourselves. Lambert had painted me as an avenging angel who had never failed on a missing-person case, and as someone who was absolutely ruthless with those who wrongly refused to come forward with vital information. He had done just the right thing.

When the waiter brought the check, I whispered to him that I wanted the tabs of the three reporters too. I told him not to say anything to them until I had paid, and to ignore their efforts to settle up and be ready to leave when I was. This accomplished, Lambert and I strolled out. I nodded to each reporter as we went.

'What now?' Lambert asked when we were in the car.

'More phone calls,' I said dejectedly. 'There are a lot of people out there who don't realize that their sleep will be interrupted tonight.'

Chapter 11

The phone just wasn't going to stop ringing. I tried to plug my ears with a pillow, and when that didn't work, I pulled the covers over my head and curled into the fetal position. Still the telephone shrilled on. I rolled over onto my knees and put the top of my head on the bed's mattress, each hand pressing a pillow to an ear. Each ring of that phone jarred like an electrical shock into the migraine that I was in the middle of having.

Then I woke up.

It wasn't a dream at all; the phone really was ringing, and I had the great-grandfather of all headaches. I would have looked like a fool, if anyone had been there to see, as I untangled myself from the bedsheets and very gingerly tried not to break my neck while easing out of that ridiculous position. I knew the call had to be important; those excellent people on the front desk had been very supportive of my needs, and nothing less than a full-scale emergency would prompt them to wake me up. I caught a glimpse of my alarm clock before picking up the receiver – 6 A.M. I'd been asleep ninety minutes.

'That woman's back again,' the desk clerk said. 'She's been spotted on the outside balcony, trying to look into your room. I think she's still out there somewhere. Do you want me to call the police?'

'No. Let me handle it.'

I hurried into a pair of pants, reached for my gun, and went to the door next to a window that opened onto the balcony, which circled the motel like a walkway. I put my ear to the door but could hear nothing. I pulled the curtain open just a fraction to see whether I could spot anyone outside. There was no way of knowing what to expect. This was the third time the woman had drawn attention by acting suspiciously around my room. I was aware that my campaign of threats might have produced an effect opposite to the one I intended. Someone who was desperate enough might just try to kill me.

I opened the door quietly with my left hand, switched my gun quickly to the right hand as I stepped onto the balcony, and pointed it rapidly to the left and then to the right. She was visible for just over a second. In the parking lot, maybe ten feet from the Vega she was about to jump into. Barefoot, I ran along the balcony to the stairs which led to the ground level, but I was too late. The Vega was pulling away, and I couldn't even get the tag number. It was still dark in East Lansing, and my mysterious visitor was wisely driving with her lights off. I considered chasing her, but it clearly would be fruitless. My car keys were still in the motel room, and she'd be long gone by the time I retrieved them.

But I'd gotten a look at her, and I wouldn't forget. Heavyset – not fat, heavyset. A big woman. Young. Short hair. I hadn't seen her face, but if I ran into her again, I would recognize her.

I started to think hard when I got back into my room. Who was this woman? Someone who intended to fire through my window? There was really no telling who had been aroused by our apparently ubiquitous presence in East Lansing. Could she be an informant? If so, why all the mystery?

I cursed when I realized that there would be no sleep for me this day either. I was dead tired but at the same time too on edge to go back to bed. I drink coffee maybe once a year, but this morning I rang the front desk and asked if someone could bring some to my room. I learned that even most of the reporters weren't awake. Only two were in the lobby.

I thought about my mystery woman and whether I should spend this Labor Day, September 3, trying to track her down. I could cruise the streets of East Lansing, looking for a red Vega. The chances of finding her were pretty good, but it might take a couple of days. I could rent a van and use it for surveillance, employing my videotape equipment to film her activities. I have a video truck with one-way glass in Texas; I could have it driven to Michigan in twenty hours. The van has curtained windows, a bed, and a sound detector that will awaken the investigator to any comings and goings at the place he's watching. It also has a police monitor, sound-recording equipment, and a screen on which to watch the person under surveillance. If I found the red Vega, I could slap a magnetic device underneath it, and all we would have to do was follow the signal to know where the woman was at all times. The video van has a two-way radio, walkie-talkies, and a telephone too. The question was whether I should get someone to drive it to East Lansing, whether the expense was justified – assuming, of course, that I found the red Vega.

I drank coffee, trying for an artificial alertness, and wondered how I could most fruitfully spend this holiday. Looking for the woman was one idea, and if Lambert looked for her in another car, it would take half as long; but even if I found her, I might have nothing more than another oddball. What was important in this case? The tunnels. Those damnable tunnels.

I wondered whether Gillitzer had accomplished anything yet. Or Hock and Riddle, on this crucial last day in Louisville. I wished they were back; they could be driving the streets of East Lansing, looking for the Vega.

Alone, I paced in my room, gulping coffee and filled

with restlessness and a powerful yen to be out and about. I wanted to move mountains. Or at least slam my fist into a wall. This investigation was so frustrating – it led everywhere and nowhere.

What to do? Use the press, of course. I was going to rave about those tunnels again, and I was not going to stop until I got what I wanted. Continuing to stir up the media was hardly a full day's work, however. Besides, I thought I'd done a fairly good job of it the night before, and not just during that impromptu news conference in the lobby. To each and every newsperson whose call I had answered I emphasized the importance of getting into those tunnels.

The one other conversation I had had that might prove helpful had been with Ralph Hoffman, an expert on Braille. Hoffman said that he had seen the photograph of the corkboard and thought it could be a map, or possibly even a message, in Braille. The message could be read, he said, as 'And for it you braved.'

Braille. I let that thought turn around in my mind. Those tunnels were pitch black, according to Lambert. You might be as sightless as a blind man down there. Maybe you could use Braille to feel your way about in them. Or maybe the corkboard actually was a map in Braille, a double clue pointing to the tunnels: one clue, the map itself; the second, for blind people, to emphasize that the hiding place (or whatever it was) was dark.

'And for it you braved.' If there was any meaning to this, the key word had to be *it*. What was the 'it' for which Dallas braved? Attention? Notoriety? A cry for help? Could the 'it' be the mere thrill of adventure? He had lain under trains; could what he was doing now be even more dangerous? Dallas believed in reincarnation; might not the 'it' have something to do with his belief in another, better life?

Whatever the answer was, my talk with Hoffman was

an additional example, if any more could conceivably be needed, that pointed to the tunnels. *The tunnels*. I wondered if the people who had forbidden us access to the tunnels were enjoying their Labor Day. I knew Mr. and Mrs. Egbert weren't.

I was stumped. Maybe some fresh thinking was needed here. I thought it over, then called a friend of mine in Dallas, Joanne Reeves, a person with a mind I respected. What I needed was a clear brain with an emotional distance from the investigation, to give me an opinion on what had probably happened to Dallas and what lines of the case would be most productive to pursue.

'I'm sorry to wake you so early in the morning,' I said when Joanne answered the phone. It was 7:30 A.M.

'I've been awake for an hour,' she replied cheerfully. 'Reading about you, as a matter of fact. That case you're on sounds just fascinating. Have you solved it yet?'

'Don't be a wise guy. I called to ask for your help.'

'Help? On what? The missing genius?'

'Yes.'

'Well, I don't see what help I can be. But I'll try. I really hope you find that poor little boy.'

'Just let me tell you what I know. Then give me your opinion.'

'I'm no detective, Bill. I don't know anything about these things.'

'You're smart. You can give me your impressions. Just listen, please. I want to tell you everything I know about this case.'

And I did. I tried not to leave anything out. I expected her to laugh derisively when I told her about trestling, or about how I'd actually lost my identity while playing Dungeons & Dragons, but I wouldn't have known she was on the other end if I hadn't occasionally heard her breathing. It took quite a while, perhaps two hours, but I brought Joanne right up to the moment of that third visit from my mystery woman with the red Vega.

'What do you think happened to Dallas?' I said. 'That's the help you can give me – your opinion. Maybe you see something I don't.'

'What you've told me is just incredible, Bill. I don't see how I can help.'

'Try. You like mystery novels. Treat this like fiction, which it ought to be, and tell me what you think happened.'

'All right. Do you trust Peggy Hogan?'

'I've never met her. She's Riddle's project. He says he has no reason to mistrust her.'

'Well, if you eliminate what she has to say, I'll bet Dallas is in the tunnels. I'll bet he went down there and killed himself. Everything except Peggy Hogan points that way to me.'

'Joanne, I love you.' I really felt that way. The people who were running Michigan State University were intellectuals and certainly far better qualified in the thinking department than I am, and I'd been afraid that maybe I just wasn't seeing clearly with this obsession I had with the tunnels.

'I don't see how I've helped,' Joanne said.

'You've made me believe in my sanity,' I replied.

'I hope I'm wrong about Dallas, Bill.'

'Me too. I hope we're both wrong.'

'Well, I'll be praying for him and you.'

My appetite was whetted. I respected Joanne's opinion, but she was a lay person. Why not get the opinion of a law-enforcement officer I respected? I knew just the man. He was a senior detective, a twenty-year veteran of the Dade County Sheriff's Department, a man I'd known personally and professionally for years. His specialties were kidnapping and murder.

'Bill!' he said when he heard my voice. 'You're all over the papers down here – a real glamor boy. Us real detectives get no glory at all.'

'I told you to join me in private practice. Listen,' I went on, 'I'm sorry to bother you on Labor Day, but . . .'

'Don't give me that. Tell me why you called. I expect you want an opinion on that case that's making all the headlines.'

Once again I laid out all the facts as I knew them. My friend in Miami was a professional, one of the very best, and I had no doubt that I could count on him for a cool, hard-headed analysis. If I was wrong, he would tell me.

'What do you think?' I asked when I had finished.

'Let me question you as I would a witness,' he said.

'Fine.' Actually, by answering questions, I might be able to see the shortcomings in my investigation.

'From what I've gathered,' my friend said, 'you've checked with students at the university.'

'As many as I can.'

'You've talked to a number of professors?'

'Those who will talk to us. Some won't cooperate.'

'You've talked to school administrators?'

'Yes. But they're not cooperating the way they should.'

'You've interviewed his past roommates?'

'Yes. Some Dallas didn't get along with. He was young, and his habits could be irritating.'

'Have you been able to locate many of his friends and acquaintances?'

'Some. But I'm not sure Dallas had many friends.'

'How about acquaintances?'

'Every one we could find. Talked to them at length.'

'Have you checked the boy's background? And I mean going way back.'

'I've gone back to the age of ten. I think I've learned a lot about the family history. I've covered Dallas's habits and morals, his drug involvement. I even uncovered a homosexual problem he had in the Cub Scouts. The organization tried to keep the incident as quiet as possible, just asked him to drop out. I learned this the hard way, since the family didn't tell me. What it involved was Dallas making a pass at another Cub Scout.' I'd learned this from a Dayton reporter.

'What about organizations the boy belonged to?'

'I've covered them all. He was a member of some; others, he just attended meetings.'

'What activities did he have other than school?'

'Science fiction. Computers – he worked with computers a lot. Drugs. The trestling I told you about. Dungeons & Dragons.'

'All right,' my friend said. 'You've done a ground search and an aerial search of the campus and its environs. You've checked the boy's room carefully. And his clothes. You've had the handwriting analyzed. You've covered friends, organizations, and events. Family, background, habits, social life, school functions, teachers, and administrators. Computer experts and game-players. Let me commend you for playing Dungeons & Dragons – I don't know if I'd have thought of it.'

'Know your adversary,' I said.

'I agree. Bill, I think you've done everything you can. There's only one thing left to do.'

'Tell me.'

'You know it as well as I do.'

'Tell me anyway.'

'You can't go any further, and you know it, until you resolve the question of the tunnels one way or another. There, I've said it. If you stick your neck out and get it chopped off, you can say you're not the only person who thought it was the way to proceed.'

I breathed a sigh of relief. 'What do you think happened?' I asked. 'I know you don't like to make guesses, but tell me what you think.'

'You have to look at a number of possibilities. One, that the boy has committed suicide. Probably he did it in the tunnels. Most of what I've heard points to suicide. Two, the boy might have been injured in the tunnels while playing Dungeons & Dragons. He could have been alone or with others. If others were along, he was probably injured so seriously that there was no hope that he'd live. Better to leave him there than risk getting exposed. Students wouldn't feel this way, I think, but a professor, with his or her entire career at stake, might. Three, someone is holding him against his will, either for purposes of sex or because he can make drugs. I would suspect he's been murdered by now, if that's the case.'

I hoped my friend was wrong on this point.

'Four,' he continued, 'he could be a runaway. I don't think this is very probable. Most runaways don't stay so completely out of touch for very long. And you say he disappeared right before his final exams – that's a usual time for a student to take off, but not this boy; he would have no trouble with exams. Runaways don't burn all their bridges if another possibility exists. No, I think if this boy were going to run away, he would do it after the exams. Five, he could have witnessed something, probably in those tunnels, that he shouldn't have seen – maybe a drug deal going down. Unless the drug dealers up there are a lot more inept than they are here, they're using those tunnels. What a perfect place. The people who should know, the custodians, say they're inaccessible. No one will ever look in a place that's inaccessible. Hell, they *can't* look.'

I could hear the disgust in his voice, but he went on rationally outlining possibilities.

'Six, he might have been picked up by a gay man, someone he'd known before. The man might be so fascinated and stimulated by Dallas and his superintelligence that he can't let him go. You told me about this Gillitzer who came from New York and is willing to work just on the chance of meeting the boy. Another guy might want much more. You know how rich people will buy a stolen painting, one they can never hope to show to anyone, just so they can look at it themselves. Somebody might consider Dallas just such a treasure. Anyway, that's it. Six possibilities I see. I'm sure you've considered all of them.'

'You didn't mention that Dallas might be playing a game with us.'

'A *game*? It's not likely. Not after all this time.'

'Rules may not apply to this boy.'

'Look for what you want. Follow your instincts. But I'd wager dollars against doughnuts that no game is involved here.'

'What do you make of this woman who keeps nosing around my motel room?'

'If he's being held, she may have some answers for you. She comes at odd hours, as if she's deathly afraid of being seen. The way she approaches it, I'd think she's building up her courage. She gets close to making contact, then something spooks her. Of course, she could just be a crazy. I don't have to tell you about those.'

He certainly didn't. 'Well,' I said to my friend, 'I really appreciate your time. You know how it is to get so close to a case that you doubt that you're seeing clearly. I know you've helped me.'

'You're doing all you can. Keep after it. I wish I was there with you. I could dig my teeth into that case. You can't imagine how little inspiration there is checking out another mob murder. Anyway, good luck, Bill.'

I considered calling another police detective I knew, but there really wasn't any reason to – I knew what needed to be done. My two friends, whose experience and knowledge I respected, had told me what was needed. I'd known it all along. It was the tunnels, and with or without authorization, I was going into them.

I imagine that all along the thought had been hiding somewhere in my mind, but it seemed to come all of a sudden. Why not *today*? Why not just walk out of this motel and onto the campus and down into the tunnels, right now? I didn't expect to be caught. If I was, the danger lay in having my private investigator's license lifted, and thus my means of livelihood taken away, but I could put up a hell of a fight if faced with that. Legally I might be wrong, but I had no doubt that I was morally right.

I opened my curtains and saw a fine, sparkling day of bright northern sunshine and fresh air so clear it glittered. When I'd last talked to my office, I had learned that Texas was in the middle of another heat wave. September, and a heat wave. I wanted to step onto the balcony and fill my lungs with this good Michigan air. I called the desk instead.

'Are our friends still down there?' I asked.

'Not so many as usual. I think they've made a deal. They share anything they learn in the lobby.'

'How about messages?'

'If anything, they're coming in even faster.'

'Dallas hasn't called, has he?'

'No.' The clerk laughed. 'I don't have anything here that's marked urgent.'

'I'll be gone for a while. I'd appreciate if you don't tell anyone.'

'Right.'

'I'm really grateful for all you and the others have done.'

'Just have Dallas give me his autograph when this is over. And I want yours too.'

I put on jeans, a sports shirt, a sports jacket, and tennis shoes. I hoped I looked like a professor out for a stroll. My only baggage was a small flashlight, hidden under my jacket, and a Swiss knife with a screwdriver, knife, file, scissors, corkscrew, bottle opener, and assorted other devices. It is handy for picking locks, unscrewing bolts from doors, and prying open locked boxes.

I went out on the balcony, walked to the back, and swung over the side to the pavement. I walked across a road to a cornfield and stood there for a few minutes to see whether I'd been noticed. I hadn't. Then, in a roundabout way (I could have been going anywhere if I'd been asked), I made it back to my car. I drove out the back exit of the motel parking lot.

I wanted to enter the tunnels from the old power plant. I parked my car a block away, and I don't believe anyone noticed me as I made my approach; the campus appeared virtually deserted. A side door of the plant was unlocked, and the entire building seemed empty. I opened the door, slipped inside, and soon was walking downstairs. My stomach felt as it had when I'd played hide-and-seek as a boy; butterflies fluttering, tension making me extra alert. No, it wasn't hide-and-seek I was remembering; it was that Dungeons & Dragons game. But the feeling was much more immediate and real. Entering the dungeons *in real life* definitely raised the adventure level several notches. I imagined it could be raised several more if additional dangers were mixed in for spice.

The power plant was clean and very dry. Enough light came through the windows to produce a just-before-twilight effect. I had no idea how to get into the tunnels, whether through an opening in the floor or through a door, so the best I could do was launch a careful search. It soon became apparent that there wasn't any way to get in through the floor, so I concentrated on opening doors. Each one I looked through simply led to another room or to storage closets. But after about ten minutes I hit the jackpot.

The door was just like every other door, except it led into a long, squarish corridor a little over six feet high and five feet wide. The corridor was very dark – I could see only a few feet into it. There was no telling how far back it went, but I could see a light bulb attached to the ceiling. I was pretty certain other light bulbs would extend along the corridor.

I had been peering into the darkness, but now I checked outside and found a light switch. When I looked down the corridor again, I could see perhaps forty feet. It was a straight shot back that far; after that I couldn't tell. I turned the light off, stepped inside, and closed the door behind me. I didn't want any light to seep through the crack under the door, and also I didn't believe that Dallas had traveled along this corridor with the light burning.

My vision was now exactly at zero. I could probably feel my way along the wall, but there was no purpose to it, and surely that was not the method Dallas had used. I turned on my pocket flashlight, the magic-user's lantern, and started forward cautiously. I wasn't really expecting anything, but I wanted to be ready for everything.

Right away the heat closed in. A dry heat, like the desert's – not unbearable, but I remembered what Lambert had said and prepared for it to get worse. I traveled perhaps forty feet (the flashlight was inadequate for the task) and came to a big round opening; the start of the tunnels. I flashed my light through the opening and the beam penetrated perhaps ten feet, but I couldn't tell whether the tunnel ended just beyond the reach of the light or stretched on forever. I stepped back and shined the light in a circle. To the left and right were other round openings, identical to the one in front of me. I could hear my dungeon master asking, 'Which tunnel do you want to enter? Or will you turn around and go back?'

I chose to go left. There was no reason for the decision; it just seemed as good as any. The height at this beginning point was less than in the corridor, and so was the width. The first thing I did was crack my head on an iron pipe.

The temperature was much higher now, and I decided to leave my jacket behind. The going was slowed to a snail's pace after I received that blow to the head, and I walked in a crouch. Then I stepped in a puddle of stagnant water. I'd been watching for pipes on the ceiling and to see in which direction the tunnel led, but I could tell I was going to have to keep my eyes on the floor also. I could feel the wetness soaking into my tennis shoe, and knew my foot would soon be smelly and miserable.

Just like this tunnel. The heat was clammy now, like a swamp's, and seemed to rise with each tentative step I took. A hundred and fifteen degrees, I guessed, and I hadn't gotten to the good part yet. But the worst was the darkness. It was simply absolute. The darkness wrapped itself around me, disorienting me, depriving me of my most valuable sense. I can think of very few phenomena more frightening than total darkness. Not without reason does the Bible speak of it in terms of the ultimate horror, God's rejection.

But being in the tunnel really was similar to that game of Dungeons & Dragons I had played in my motel room. For me that game had been exciting enough, because my imagination is a good one. But maybe if I had played the game more, I would have wanted more. These tunnels were practically guaranteed to set your imagination racing, but *you didn't need an imagination down here.*

'*Sssssssssssssss!*'

The sound shot right in front of my face. My body snapped rigid. I think my heart stopped. It was so sudden, so loud, so close, and so totally unexpected that later I thought the phrase 'nearly scared to death' applied to how I felt. 'I don't believe this!' I said aloud.

The noise, like a thousand snakes hissing in unison, had come from the floor, and I shined my light downward. There I saw a pressure-control device that lets off excess steam so the pipes won't explode. When the pressure of the steam builds to a dangerous point, the control device releases a rush of steam and thus lowers the pressure.

Well, I thought, the university was right not to want students down here. The steam had singed my face; a few more feet and it might have scalded off my features. If I'd had any doubts that Dallas could have been hurt down here, they were eliminated. I was sure that pressure-control devices were scattered throughout these tunnels, and each one was potentially deadly to those who dared to trespass. And I imagined that the fearful rush of steam could occur in a multitude of places, not just in the one I had happened across.

The authorities' mistake was in pretending that the tunnels were inaccessible. I had walked in with nary a how-do-you-do, and I wasn't even familiar with the campus. I had been told that students used the tunnels to walk from building to building to keep warm on cold days. I was sure that they traveled only in the sections that could be lighted, and doubted that this practice could be very widespread. But these easily accessible tunnels were a disaster waiting to happen. Maybe it already had happened.

I continued to creep forward through the tunnel. The

progress was slow and agonizing, and the wet, slimy heat soaked my body with sweat the way a clammy, out-of-kilter steam bath might. I'd judged I'd traveled a hundred feet when I came to another intersection, and again I had a choice: go straight ahead, turn right then left, or retrace my steps and get out of here.

I went left. I had accomplished much of what I'd intended – that is, satisfying myself that the tunnels could easily be entered and getting an idea of what Dallas had faced – but since I was down here, I figured I might as well see what other wonders awaited. When I'd first committed myself to entering the tunnels, I'd thought there was a chance, albeit a slim one, that I might actually find Dallas. Now the possibility of that was virtually nil for this excursion. But no law said that if he had been hurt, he had to make it *deep* into the tunnels before it happened. (Often when people are searching a wooded area for a body, they find it not in the middle of the woods but on the very edge. Sometimes I have wondered how it could be possible that an individual *didn't* see the well-traveled road that would have meant safety and life.) If Dallas had entered the tunnels with suicide in mind, however, and had left that corkboard as a map to his resting place, he probably would have come well prepared to reach his destination, and I was not going to find it during my spur-of-the-moment excursion. In addition, I was not going to proceed a long way farther. If Dallas's body was nearby, I believed, I'd know it. After twenty days, that body would have an odor that would turn a vulture to vegetarianism.

'And for it you braved' came into my mind as I crept along the new tunnel. I really wanted to know what 'it' would mean to Dallas. Knowing might not bring me an iota closer to solving the case, but everything about this boy fascinated me. Like Gillitzer, I so wanted the chance to meet him. He was worth the game. If anyone ever had been mishandled, treated wrongly, it was this unusual boy. Not many people on this planet were more deserving of another chance, either.

I'd traveled perhaps ten feet in this tunnel, which was different from the previous one only in that it was hotter (the deeper you went into the maze, it seemed, the higher the temperature got), when I encountered my second auditory surprise. Voices. I froze stone still and listened. I heard them again. I couldn't make out the words of the conversation, but that there were humans besides myself in these tunnels was unmistakable.

I went faster, physically and mentally. It crossed my mind that perhaps I'd heard Dallas. Maybe supplies were being delivered to him by an accomplice; possibly he still was playing his macabre game. How could anyone be sure? If Dallas had access to outside information, he surely knew that the hunt for him had been on in earnest for some time. He had boasted to his acquaintances that he could elude any search, and now would be the time to prove his contention.

Just a moment's reflection, though, told me that the odds were very long indeed that I'd heard Dallas. Perhaps the voices had been those of other Dungeons & Dragons players. Labor Day would be as safe a time as any to get into the tunnels. Yes, the voices most likely came from D & D players, although they could have come from university maintenance personnel. Or from some of those drug dealers, who would be remiss if they hadn't discovered a use for these 'inaccessible' tunnels.

I wanted to cry out, alert whoever it was of my presence, establish a dialogue until we could locate one another. But I didn't dare. I wasn't carrying a gun with me, but I expected that a drug dealer would be. If only I could be sure that these were D & D players or maintenance people. I'd take my chances, even with the latter. I needed numerous pieces of information about the tunnels.

The voices were still audible, but it was impossible to tell how far away they were. I imagined that sound could travel a long way through those corridors. All I could do was try to track the noise as quickly and silently as I could, get close enough without being detected, and determine whether I should make myself known.

The predictable thing happened. My right shoe caught in a hole gouged out of the concrete floor, and I crashed to my hands and knees amid the clatter of fallen flashlight. '*Damn, damn!*' I said, not loudly enough to be heard – but that damage had already been done. Sprawled on the floor, I could hear nothing but my own pained breathing.

The head of the flashlight had been jarred loose, the skin was scraped off my right hand, and both knees of my jeans were ripped open, but I was going to survive. For a moment I was so angry that I wondered whether I wanted to. To make matters worse, I leaned my right hand against the wall of the tunnel for balance, and it came back dripping with slime. The walls were caked with what seemed a decade's accumulation of ooze.

I got the flashlight working and went on, at a slower pace and more cautiously. I told myself that the owners of those voices faced the same obstacles that I did – dangerous footing, complete darkness, terrific heat – but I knew that I was probably deluding myself. It was much more likely that they'd had experience in the tunnels, knew what to watch out for, and had come much better prepared. Surely their lighting arrangement was superior to my small, hand-held flashlight.

But I might find them. Who could tell? Scuffing the floor with my shoes to avoid another stumble, left hand pointing ahead in a sort of salute to avoid overhead pipes, right hand spraying the flashlight's beam, I inched forward to an uncertain destination. My knees and right hand stung. My entire body was washed in sweat. I had traveled perhaps another twenty yards when I felt something scurry over my left foot. A rat, I guessed. It struck me as uncanny how close conditions in these tunnels were to the scenes described by my dungeon master back in the Red Roof Inn. He had assured me that he had never played the game in the tunnels, and I believed him. Well, it was going to take more than a rat to frighten me, after the steam from that pressure-control device. *Of course*, I thought, as the parallel became apparent: the steam and the dragon. The steam was the most dangerous aspect of the tunnels, striking suddenly and with finality. The dragon was the most feared creature in Dungeons & Dragons, breathing fire and incinerating anyone in its path.

I went ten yards more . . . twenty . . . thirty. I listened for the sound of human voices, but they had vanished as suddenly as they had appeared. I reached yet another intersection. Straight ahead, left, right, or back from where I came? I had only a one-in-three chance of choosing the tunnel the voices had come from, and less than that, probably, of catching up to them. I had seen a map of these tunnels; there were *8.5 miles* of them. What was needed was not a single man blundering blindly through a mystifying maze, but many men, searching from different directions in a professional manner, clothed and equipped with as much foresight as, say, Edmund Hillary had used before climbing Mount Everest. We needed drawings of the tunnels. Better lighting. Where overhead lights existed, they should be turned on; where they didn't exist, portable lighting equipment had to be available. We would have to take safety precautions against that release of steam.

I thought it was just common sense to head back. I'd learned what I needed to, and exploring further was not likely to be beneficial. It might even be foolhardy. I was confident that I could find my way back to the power plant, since I had carefully noted the several turns I'd taken, but going deeper into the maze might make the job difficult. The heat might disorient me, play tricks on my mind; I knew that under conditions like these, a person could be close to collapsing without realizing it.

A return trip always seems shorter. Getting out of those tunnels was hardly a pleasant holiday stroll, but the time in passage seemed cut by two-thirds. The darkness was as total as before – night or day, it would always be black down there – but it wasn't so uncomfortable, so frightening, as it had been before my mind adjusted. I've been told (I don't know if it's true) that humans are the only inhabitants of the planet who can and do live anywhere on Earth, so adaptable are we. It wasn't an appetizing thought, but I guessed that survival was possible in these tunnels.

When I opened the door leading from the corridor to the power plant, I was careful to listen for sounds of activity. I didn't need to be found and charged with trespassing. That could be disastrous. The entire issue could become my actions, not the urgency of finding Dallas. But the power plant was as deserted as it had been when I entered, like an obsolete relic a space traveler might encounter on some long-abandoned planet.

Outside the light was dusky; it would soon be night. I thought it amazing that *six hours* had passed. Time races by when you're having fun, but that was scarcely how I'd describe my stint in the tunnels. I figured that I must have been so absorbed by the experience that I'd completely lost track of time, and once again I thought of hide-and-seek. While I was playing that game when I was a boy, time lost all meaning to me.

Trying to maintain some semblance of dignity as I hurried to the car, I took stock of my appearance. I looked as if I might have crawled out of a coal bin. Sweat mingled with the dust, soot, and slime of the tunnels could have been the makeup for the Creature from the Black Lagoon. And I was emotionally drained too. I knew what Dallas had felt when he returned late at night from an underground session of Dungeons & Dragons.

I'd left my sports jacket in the tunnel. Remarkable – how could I have missed it? I'd spread it right across the floor when the heat became stifling, and my method of walking had not included picking up my feet. In fact my feet seldom left the floor as I scraped along. Well, I certainly wasn't going back to get the jacket.

A stop in a gas-station rest room removed a bit of the grime, which seemed to have caked even inside my clothes, but I was still something little children and maybe even adults would run from. It was going to be drive-in-the-back-way, climb-over-the-balcony time again at the Red Roof Inn. I really did have sympathy for that motel manager. He didn't need my kind in his previously sedate, family-oriented establishment.

I must have resembled a poorly attired Phantom of the Opera racing along the balcony and then quick-stepping inside my room. I made straight for the telephone, called the front desk, and told the operator not to worry about any calls during the next five minutes that mentioned a strange character on the balcony. After five minutes, I said, I'd appreciate the same alertness the staff had shown before.

I took a long, hot, soothing bath. I think that several times I dozed off. My knees were scraped worse than I'd thought, but the hot water, which stung at first, seemed as curative as a spa's. I stayed in the tub until my fingers wrinkled and for a long time after that. The robe I wore after toweling off was as fresh and dry and soft as down.

I called the front desk again. 'Any messages marked urgent?' I asked.

'Plenty of messages. None urgent. A few callers from newspapers said urgent, but I imagine you wouldn't think so.'

'Anything from Louisville?'

'You mean Mr. Riddle? Yes, he called this afternoon.'

'I'll be down in a few minutes,' I said. 'I'll pick up the messages then.'

'There's a crowd here.'

'Good.'

I called the Holiday Inn in Louisville where Riddle and Hock were staying and asked for Riddle's room.

'Is this Mr. Dear?' the operator said.

'Yes, it is.'

'Mr. Riddle said to tell you he's gone to the Grand Ball.'

'The Grand Ball?'

'That's the concluding event of the big science-fiction convention. Mr. Riddle said that he and Mr. Hock would be joining you tomorrow.'

The Grand Ball. I was supposedly the boss of this lash-up, and while I hung out in seedy bars and life-threatening steam tunnels, Riddle and Hock were tripping the light fantastic. With my luck, I thought, they would have found Dallas.

What was I thinking? I hoped they *had* found Dallas. I shook myself hard and told myself to start reasoning straight. The important thing was that the boy be found, not that I do it. The thought that had passed through my head was unnerving. This was not a contest between me and Dallas, but a very serious undertaking that could well involve his life. I asked myself, If someone else could produce the youngster this instant, *would you be happy*? I decided that yes, I would. I cared very much about his safety. But that insensitive thought lingered in my mind, and try as I did, it couldn't be exorcised.

I put on a fresh change of clothes and headed down to the lobby. I made sure my messages were safely in hand before I raised my arm and asked for silence. Again I talked about how a search of the tunnels was *sine qua non* if the investigation was to proceed. I reiterated that the tunnels were easily accessible and that I could prove the fact to anyone who doubted. I said I had new information demonstrating beyond doubt that the tunnels were even more dangerous than I had originally believed. On this occasion I made a flat-out plea for the reporters to raise the issue in their stories.

'What were you doing today?' someone asked as I beat a retreat toward my room. The media crowd was obviously disappointed by my brief appearance, but what could I say? That I was baffled? I couldn't tell them that, not until a real search expedition came up empty in those tunnels. And perhaps not even then. I had other lines out in the water; maybe one of the fish would bite.

'Trying to retrace Dallas's steps,' I said, and then I was gone.

There was a message from Gillitzer. 'What have you learned?' I asked when I heard his voice.

'Nothing. Just like before, nothing. And that worries me a lot.'

'Maybe the gay angle is the wrong one.'

'It's the *way* I learn nothing. I can tell which people should know if anything's going on. When I mention Dallas, however casually, a curtain of silence, wariness, drops right between me and whoever I'm talking with.'

'So you think there are people who know?'
'There's something.'
'Stay after it,' I said. 'I want you to know I appreciate your efforts.'
I turned to my inch-thick stack of messages and decided to return the calls in a top-to-bottom order. I dialed the first number and soon groaned.
'Hello,' the voice said. 'I'm a psychic, and I live in North Dakota. I see very clearly where . . .'

Chapter 12

I was well rested when Riddle and Hock came to my motel room door on Tuesday, September 4, to report what they'd learned at the science-fiction convention in Louisville. I'd actually gotten five hours of sleep after wading through the phone messages. I woke up at 10:30 A.M. and called downstairs to see whether anything required immediate attention before I showered and shaved. A number of newspaper stories had been left at the desk, and I asked for them to be brought up. The headlines give a good impression of the sort of interest this case was generating:

Missing Genius's Trail a Baffler
Did Genius Stay Near Campus? Troubled Boy, Bizarre Saga
Vanished Computer Genius May Have Left Bizarre Clue
Teen Genius Believed Dead
MSU's Young Genius Is Probably Dead, Investigators Believe
'Whiz Kid' Clues Lead Nowhere
Missing Youth Could Be on Adventure Game
Did MSU Student Die in 'Dungeon'?

These stories were only in Michigan and Ohio newspapers, and because frequent reports were going out over the national wires and the case was already being reported on network TV news, I felt that Michigan State University administrators would soon find the pressure intolerable and relent in their opposition to a thorough search of the tunnels. I also hoped that the pressure exerted by this kind of coverage would affect anyone who might be collaborating with Dallas or holding him against his will. There was no guarantee that Dallas was anywhere near East Lansing, so press coverage in all parts of the country could be important.

Riddle and Hock arrived at 1 P.M. We sat around the table and Riddle spread out a thick sheaf of notes he'd taken. He must have caught a glimpse of a notation that jogged his memory, because he chuckled to himself. 'You really should have been there, Bill,' he said.

'I heard about the Grand Ball. I hope this investigation didn't interfere with your social life.'

Riddle ignored the dig. 'I mean it,' he said. 'You should have been there. We've been to every planet in the universe.'

'Some weird people, eh?'

'The Grand Ball that you're moaning about was a costume ball,' explained Hock. 'Mainly people dressed as characters out of the "Star Trek" TV series. Lots of Captain Kirks and Mr. Spocks. And characters from *Star Wars* – Luke Skywalker, Princess Leia, Darth Vader, plus a bunch of the characters from the barroom scene, half-animal, half-people.'

'Pretty weird,' I said.

'Those were the normal ones,' Riddle said. 'There was this one fellow in a silver flight suit so tight it looked like it was spray-painted on, and he wore knee-length riding boots like the Nazis. The top half of his suit was open to the bellybutton, and his torso was painted a neon blue. He wore one of those beanie caps with a helicopter blade on top, and carried a ray gun. He shot me with it once. It set off a pinwheel effect of sparks and a loud siren.'

'Well, he probably thought you were strange too.'

'Actually, he liked me. Said he was the Third Prophet of Agharta, sent to Earth from Uranus to spread the wisdom of Metratron. Something to do with the worship of trees and rocks. He offered Hock and me a ride back to East Lansing in his spaceship.'

'You should have taken him up on the offer.'

'Not really. If you'll pardon the pun, there were a lot of spaced-out people at this convention.'

'Well, give me good news. I need good news. Tell me you found Dallas, or at least that you know where he is.'

'We can't do that,' Hock said. 'But we've got information, impressions mostly, that we think will be very helpful. I know I won't soon forget what I witnessed.'

'Let's get on with it,' I said. 'We've really been hurting for manpower since you've been away. You especially, Riddle. You're going to have to get right on the Peggy Hogan matter.'

'Would you like us to go chronologically?' Riddle asked. He had his notes spread out in front of him.

'Yes.'

'As soon as we got to Louisville, we contacted Ben Ryan, the security manager for Galt House Hotel, and Roy Mittel, chief of security. Ryan is Mittel's supervisor. They'd been expecting us, and said we could have the run of the convention. They also said they'd keep their eyes open for Dallas. Of course we had photographs of Dallas, and copies were given to all of the security people plus the registration-desk personnel and the managers of the various exhibits and game rooms. If Dallas showed up, he'd be spotted.'

'How many people attended the convention?' I asked.

'Must have been a couple thousand. It's a big annual affair that draws top science-fiction writers as speakers. Anyway, Ryan and Mittel took us to Ken Amos, the convention chairman. He gave us press passes that allowed us complete freedom of movement. Amos was very helpful.'

'Everyone was,' Hock added. 'They knew about Dallas's disappearance, and treated it as if they'd lost one of their own. Renewed my faith in people. They were genuinely concerned.'

'We asked Amos how we could find any individuals or delegations from East Lansing,' Riddle said. He was able to give us the name of the MSU student heading the delegation, Stuart Stinson. He was checked in to Room 908 of Galt House, and we were lucky enough to catch him in on our first visit. He rounded up three other members of the MSU group. Carl Stemboll, Randall Farmer, and Marjorie Foster. All four of them were members not only of the Science Fiction Society but the Tolkien society at Michigan State.'

'How many of them knew Dallas?'

'All,' Riddle replied, 'but none could be considered a friend. They saw him at meetings but never socialized with him. They said Dallas was always high on drugs.'

'*Always?*'

'That was the word they used,' Hock said. 'Described him as in a fog. Half-asleep. Eyes dilated. Slurring his words.'

'He never contributed anything?' I asked.

'Once in a while he'd speak up,' Riddle said. 'But other students were alienated from him. They didn't encourage his participation, and I imagine he sensed this and didn't offer a great deal. It's a wonder he kept showing up at all. No one wanted him there.'

'Did they know his age?'

'No. They've read about it since the disappearance, but the information came as a surprise. The girl, Marjorie Foster, said his age explained a lot about Dallas that she couldn't understand before.'

James Dallas Egbert III (United Press International)

Sergeant Bill Wardwell of the Michigan State University campus police holds the pushpin-studded bulletin board found in Dallas Egbert's room. This was the perplexing clue for which William Dear had to find a meaning (United Press International)

Private detective William Dear in front of his country house near Dallas (Sunday People)

James and Anna Egbert pose with pictures of their missing son in an East Lansing motel room (United Press International)

A view of one part of the tunnels underneath the campus. Often the pipes were very hot, and Dear was once scalded by an unexpected jet of steam

The tunnels were a bewildering criss-cross of wires, cables, and pipes of all kinds

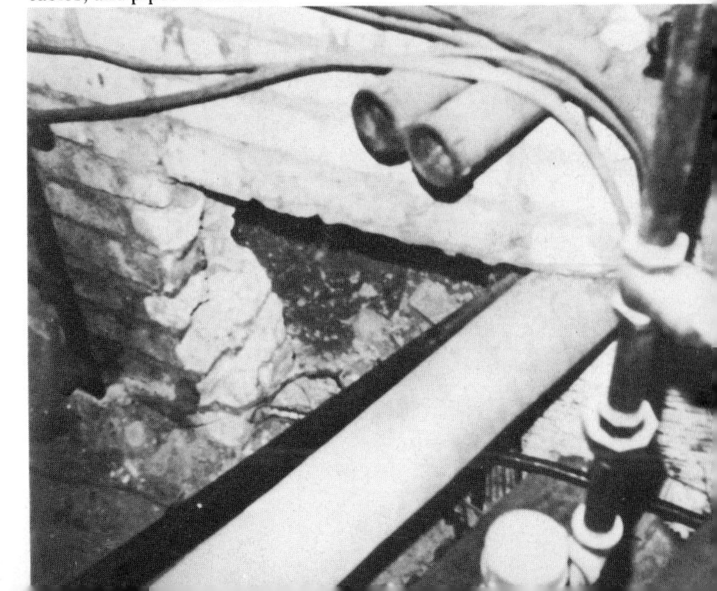

William Dear and his colleague Dick Riddle walk through one of the cleaner and more accessible parts of the tunnel (Photo by Pat Beck, *Detroit Free Press)*

'Another room contained a large dining table, with a papier-mâché figure at the head. One could have eaten off the table, it was so clean. In this grimy maze, that could only mean that someone had been here recently. But the entrance was so small that the table couldn't have been brought into the room. It was like a ship in a bottle'

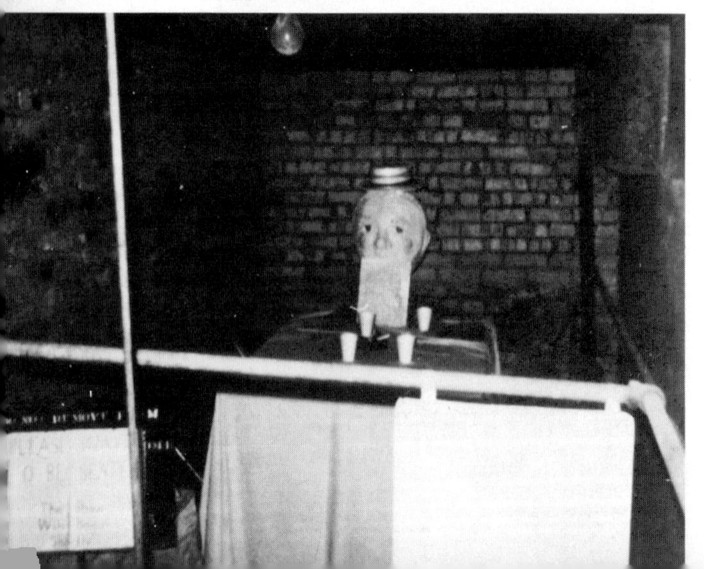

'Why didn't they tell him just to stop showing up?'

'He wasn't that obnoxious. Just terrifically stoned. Always by himself.'

'Did they know about his extraordinary intelligence?'

'Not really. They could tell he wasn't a dolt. I think they treated him like you might a drunk in a bar – you just don't want anything to do with him.'

'All four of them,' Hock said, 'believe that Dallas is dead. OD'd. They suggested we search out near Party Hollow, the clearing in the woods that campus groups use for a variety of purposes. Usually it's quiet at Party Hollow, a place to be alone and think. They believe Dallas might have gone out there and died.'

'We've looked out there,' I replied. 'Maybe not as carefully as we should have.'

'The Tolkien society people meet at Party Hollow once a year to celebrate the birth of Gandolf the Magician,' Riddle said. 'I understand they perform some sort of ritual.'

'Was Dallas a member of either the science-fiction group or the Tolkiens? I'm mixed up on that.'

'The science-fiction group,' Hock said. 'Not the Tolkiens.'

'The four we talked to from East Lansing,' added Riddle, 'seemed like pretty sensible kids to me. I don't believe they were lying to us. Their association with Dallas was always at arm's length.'

'Had Dallas talked about attending this convention?' I asked.

'Stuart Stinson said he had. He wanted to attend but didn't know if he had enough money. He didn't register to come as a delegate, which didn't mean he wouldn't show up. He could just come on his own and register late. He definitely wanted to be there. Stinson said it wouldn't surprise him if Dallas did come.'

'That it with the kids from Michigan State?'

'Yes. They said they'd keep an eye out for him. If he was going to get together with any group, it would probably be theirs.'

'So what next?'

'A lot of our time was spent pounding the convention floor, eyeballing people, trying not to make it obvious,' explained Hock. 'We crisscrossed our routes for maximum coverage, focusing our attention particularly on the game rooms, and especially the rooms featuring Dungeons & Dragons. You can't believe how popular that game is. People were packed around the tables where it was exhibited. On the periphery people sat at tables and played. There were staggered time schedules, like tee-off times in golf. A player got ninety minutes, and that was it. And they didn't want players signing up for more than one session.'

'What made an impression on me,' said Riddle, 'was the emotional and psychological involvement of the players. It was intense. I've seen Monopoly players who really get involved, but it's nothing compared to this game. Dungeons & Dragons players are absorbed by the character they've assumed. They give up their own personalities. Standing there watching a player, you can almost feel the concentration. I could see changes in some people's physical appearances.'

'I understand something of the game's hold,' I said. 'I'm a little ashamed to admit it.'

'I would say every player I saw was above average in intelligence. But let me give you an example of the concentration. One fellow seemed trapped in a dungeon at a dead end, with monsters coming up from behind to block any retreat and only a trap door available for possible escape. The player decided that his best chance was fighting the monsters. This battle went on for about fifteen minutes. Each time the character got hurt by the monsters, I swear this guy felt the pain. He winced. His face contorted in agony. Once he even let out a scream. I could see the determination in his eyes as he struggled to save himself. I've seen some fairly perilous real-life situations, Bill, as you know, but none of the people involved was any more caught up in the drama than this fellow was. When he finally won his battle, the guy was totally exhausted. He hadn't left his chair, but I'm telling you he might just as well have gone fifteen rounds with Larry Holmes.

'But there was more than exhaustion,' Riddle continued. 'The players were really proud whenever they overcame an obstacle or circumvented a barrier. It was like a terrific personal triumph. And the opposite was true when a player's character was killed: a devastating blow. I saw people whose characters had been killed pacing in circles around the room, chins on their chests, mumbling pitiably. They never got mad, like I've seen good chess players do, or cursed their opponents or their own stupidity; they just more or less went into shock and mourning. Of course it seemed silly to me, an outsider, but the game was a very serious matter for the players.'

'Most of these were college kids?'

'No,' said Hock. 'A lot of professional people. Advertising execs. Electrical engineers. Draftsmen. Salespeople. Attorneys. Computer programmers – plenty of computer programmers. Artists. Writers. One of the big-shot writers who talked at the convention played Dungeons & Dragons. What we have, I think, is people who can accomplish things in D & D that they could never hope to do in real life. The players are mainly creative, with good imaginations. I'm reminded of the meek, Caspar Milquetoast type who becomes a maniac when you put him behind the wheel of a car. Caspar has power now. The same with many D & D players – they're armed with considerable weaponry and/or other instruments of power, like magic spells and potions, and they have *carte blanche* authority to use them. The game is an outlet for their fantasies.'

'I'm sure,' added Riddle, 'there were people there who could have gotten to a point where they couldn't differentiate between the real and the unreal. And I imagine they could get a false sense of security. I wondered about Dallas in this regard. I wondered if he could have begun to believe he could do things he really couldn't. That might have gotten him hurt, or killed.'

'I'd think it's similar to a P.I. or police show on television,' I said.

'Right,' agreed Riddle. 'Someone watches those shows and thinks he can do the same thing. But here you're not watching, you're *doing*, at least in your imagination, and I think that could be a powerful force in your mind. Anyway, it was something to see.'

'Was there much drug use at the convention?' I asked.

'Some. None that we saw while the convention was open, but this changed when the exhibits shut down at ten o'clock. I think there's not necessarily any connection between drugs and Dungeons & Dragons. It does bring up a point, however. We know Dallas took drugs, and I find it frightening to think of what the combination of drugs and D & D might do to him. Again, that false sense of security – he might think his magic-user could do anything. Dungeons & Dragons advertises as a fantasy game; add Dallas's tremendously creative mind and the power of some drugs to distort reality, and you could very well have a recipe for disaster.'

'I know you didn't find Dallas,' I said. 'What's the next best thing you can tell me?'

'How about two people who might have seen him after

the August fifteenth disappearance?' Hock said.

'Might have?'

'They couldn't positively I.D. the picture we showed them, but they thought it could be him.'

'Tell me. I'm all ears.'

'It was our second day in Louisville,' Riddle said. 'We'd been buttonholing everybody we could to show our photograph of Dallas. It was remarkable how many people already knew about the case. And it wasn't just that they'd heard about it; they were *interested*. Anyway, there were these two professional people. After drawing a long string of blanks, we ran into them practically one after the other. Each in his mid-thirties, I'd guess. Henry Seduschak and Henry Wood. Seduschak is from San Gabriel, California, and Wood's home is in Hartford, Connecticut.'

'They weren't together?'

'No. We interviewed them separately. It just happened that we found them in the space of a few minutes. They'd just finished playing Dungeons & Dragons in a game room.'

'They were a long way from home.'

'Listen, people came from all over the country for this. Anyway, both Seduschak and Wood had attended a TSR convention at the University of Wisconsin at Parkside on August nineteenth. TSR, as you know, is the company that manufactures the Dungeons & Dragons game. Each thought they might have played a D & D game with Dallas. They couldn't be sure, but they said the photograph bore a definite resemblance to the boy who'd played with them.'

'How did they describe him?'

'Poorly dressed. Sloppy. Very quiet. A young kid. They called him that: "a young kid." They really had no cause to pay much attention to him.'

'How many people at this TSR convention?'
'Several thousand.'
'Did you check with TSR?'
'Yes,' Riddle said, 'I called the company in Lake Geneva. Wanted to see if Dallas had been registered at the convention. I talked to Joe Orlaskey, the convention coordinator, and asked him to check his registration list. He was most cooperative. He found a "James Eggberg," who gave his address as Number 28 Bryan Hall, here at Michigan State. Right about then I thought we might be on to something.'
'So you followed up on this Eggberg?'
'There's a James Engburg at Number 28. He's currently at his home in East St. Louis, Illinois. It's one of those coincidences that drive you crazy.'
'That doesn't mean that the boy Seduschak and Wood saw wasn't Dallas.'
'That's right.'
'Could Dallas have been playing D & D without having registered?'
'Sure. It wouldn't be that difficult to slip in. Or he could have used another name. They don't check for I.D.'
'Did you talk to others who attended the TSR convention?'
'All kinds of them. No one else could say he or she might have recognized Dallas.'
'Well, there's not much more you can do with this lead. If that was Dallas whom Wood and Seduschak saw, it means that he was a runaway, at least on August nineteenth.'
'Several times we were told that someone of Dallas's description had been seen in one of the game rooms of Galt House. We managed to track all of these people down. As you can see, we didn't bring Dallas back with us.'

'You didn't learn anything else in Louisville?'

'Not a thing. And from what I know of Dallas, he would have been there if he could. It was right up his alley.'

'I agree with Dick,' Hock said. 'If he's alive and just a runaway, I think he would have shown up. The only reason not to would be fear that all the publicity has made his face too recognizable.'

'He could have been in a costume at that Grand Ball.'

'I doubt it,' said Hock. 'To get in, you had to prove you were registered. I guess that was possible. But a costume ball doesn't seem like his cup of tea. Too frivolous. And he wasn't that sociable.'

'I couldn't agree more,' I said. 'Dallas would come for the D & D games and the more serious aspects of science fiction, but the Grand Ball wouldn't appeal to him.'

'That's the truth,' Hock agreed, shaking his head. 'I never believed in flying saucers before I attended that convention, but I swear that's the only way some of the delegates could have arrived.'

'You guys just never had fun as kids. Too strict an upbringing. Missed out on a lot of the fun of growing up.'

'*Kids?* Some of the people there were older than I am.'

'Well,' I said, 'I really am glad to have you guys back. Hock, I need you to start working on the schematics of this tunnel search.'

'The university has given its okay?'

'No, but operate as if it had. Start the arrangements. I'll worry about the permission. I want you to get a diagram of the tunnels from the campus police. Get our sizes – mine, yours, Riddle's, and Lambert's – and buy overalls for each of us. Lightweight ones – I can promise you that it will be hot down there. Buy some good flashlights or lanterns. Not the ninety-nine-cent variety that's on sale, *good* ones. I want baseball caps. The bills will keep dirt from falling into our eyes. Buy some good first-aid kits, in case anyone gets hurt down there.'

'I guess the tunnels are coming up real quick,' Hock said.

'I have a meeting with Captain Badgley and Dick Burnett tomorrow morning. I'm hoping we'll get the permission then.' Ferman Badgeley was chief of investigations for the MSU campus police; Burnett was the campus police chief. Burnett agreed that the tunnels needed to be searched, and he was working to obtain the needed permission from the university.

As I've said, I did not believe the school could continue to hold out. But I was under pressure myself – from the Egberts. I'd talked to them two nights before, and a letter from Anna Egbert had been delivered this morning. It read, in part: 'You sounded so discouraged last night, like you were just going to give up trying. Please use the dogs, try to get the FBI in on it, threaten whatever people with whatever you can, get any expert opinions you can.' Mrs. Egbert had certainly misunderstood my tone (which might indeed have sounded tired), and me, if she thought I was going to give up. I don't give up on cases, and certainly not on one that involved me so personally. But she was desperate for her son's safety and filled with grief and fear, and maybe this was her way of encouraging me.

The dogs she referred to were something I'd mentioned in relation to searching the woods around the campus. A few German shepherds could cover more ground in less time than a posse of fifty men on foot or horseback, but the investigation had persuaded me that dogs were unnecessary. Trying to get the FBI involved was a hopeless undertaking, since they would simply plead that they had no jurisdiction. We did not have sufficient evidence to show the likelihood that a kidnapping had occurred, which would have brought them running in a minute under conditions of the so-called Lindbergh Law. A ransom note would have done the trick, but we didn't have a ransom note. As a matter of fact, we didn't have anything.

As far as 'threatening' people went, I had an idea. I turned my attention to Dick Riddle. 'While Hock is seeing to preparations for the tunnels, I want you to get right over to see Peggy Hogan,' I said. 'See if she has contacted any of those informants she mentioned.'

'I'm on my way,' Riddle said.

He and Hock left, and I rang Frank Lambert's room. 'Meet me at the car,' I said. 'We're going back into the woods.'

'Going trestling again?' he asked.

'I may just push you underneath one of those trains,' I joked.

Lambert and I headed for the freeway, which was not where we wanted to go. As I expected, two cars, each driven by a reporter, followed. I got in the extreme left lane of the freeway and drove at the speed limit. I have taken numerous defensive-driving courses and have been a driving instructor for police officers. The reporters, I figured, would be no problem at all.

Traffic was light. I waited until just before our little caravan reached an exit sign, switched on my right blinker signal, and changed lanes. I applied my brakes, giving every indication that I was going to turn, but instead I continued straight ahead and gradually eased back into the left lane and brought my speed back up to 55 mph.

'The old lull-'em-to-sleep move,' Lambert remarked.

'Easy,' I said. I really didn't enjoy doing this with reporters. I wished I could be more cooperative. But the old saw that they had their job and I had mine did apply here, and I couldn't do mine, at least today, if they were along.

I counted three exits, humming along in that left lane as if I had miles to go. Just before the fourth exit, perhaps thirty yards from it, I cut the steering wheel sharply to the right, and as niftily as a dancer pirouetting I was off the freeway and on the ramp. I knew it would take several precious moments for the two behind me even to react to what I'd been planning for three exits, but even if they had been able to act instantaneously, I doubted whether they could have accomplished the maneuver, and I knew they wouldn't try.

What came next was frosting on the cake, and the surfacing of perversity. I drove back on the freeway, heading in the same direction. I knew the reporters would have exited at the next ramp and would be coming in the opposite direction. I waved and smiled as we zipped past each other.

'Never a dull moment,' Lambert said. 'You pay terrible, but at least there's some excitement.'

'I pay good,' I said. I was hurt.

'That's what the Army told me in Nam. I didn't believe them either.'

'You get good fringe benefits,' I said defensively.

'That's true,' Lambert replied thoughtfully. He was dressed as Joe College, and I suspected he was thinking of some girl friend he'd found.

We drove in a roundabout fashion to the edge of the woods near the MSU campus and got out. Party Hollow was east of Hagadorn Road and downstream from where we stood, and it took us thirty minutes of walking through the woods to find the place. It was perhaps thirty yards in diameter, a clearing in the middle of the forest. In the center, arranged in circular fashion, were signs that big bonfires had been built here: ashes, charred rocks and wood, the remains of seared newspapers. I could imagine a bonfire out in this remote spot. Had it risen eerily to the tops of the trees while strange rites were being performed, or had it been a pleasant campfire, with songs filling the air, hot dogs and marshmallows roasting, sweethearts cuddling in the crisp, cool night? There was a fallen tree upon which people could sit. I imagined that Dallas had come out here to think. He might have come at night too, when the fire roared, though surely not to munch hot dogs. I wondered if he had come out here to die, intentionally or by the accident of overdose.

What caught my attention right away – it was impossible to miss – was a clean white envelope perched upright in the circle where the bonfires had been set. It was addressed to 'Paul,' and not sealed. A note inside, handwritten in blue ink, read: 'We may be a little late. Start the fire if you arrive first.'

I felt that if Dallas had died out here, he would have been found by now. Party Hollow was obviously a place that had frequent visitors, and someone would have smelled him, if not seen him. In fact, *we* would probably have detected that terrible odor.

I guessed it was close to 5 P.M. Not too much time. But Lambert and I gave it our best shot. We conducted a crisscross perimeter search, venturing at most a couple hundred feet into the woods surrounding the clearing. I didn't expect to find anything, and we didn't. The corkboard and the cremation note (no matter who had written that) in no way pointed to such an easy solution, and these were the two tangible clues we had.

No longer interested in playing games with reporters, I drove Lambert to within two blocks of the Red Roof Inn and thought about that note addressed to 'Paul.' I knew it was the longest of shots, but did I have anything better to do until that meeting with Captain Badgley in the morning? The note indicated that a meeting was planned. It was almost surely something completely harmless, a college get-together under the stars on a bright, clear, early-September night. Yet it might be more. It was just conceivable that it had to do with Dallas, that the pressure we'd been applying had forced the hands of people who might be involved. Party Hollow would be a good place to meet at night.

I reached the clearing when only the barest glimmer of light was still available. Just minutes remained before this would be extinguished. Party Hollow was empty, and I moved close enough to see that the envelope was still in place. Then I retreated back into the woods.

It just did not make sense to hide myself on the ground. There was no way to tell from which direction the visitors would approach the clearing, and I didn't want everyone frightened nearly to death if someone stumbled over me. Besides, a view from up above would be better. The disadvantage was that I would be so far away (about twenty yards) that I wouldn't be able to hear.

I groped my way up the thickest, safest, sturdiest tree I could find and soon I was twenty-five feet in the air, perched on my haunches on a strong limb close enough to the trunk so I could steady myself. I was sure I would be invisible to anyone standing underneath the tree, and especially to anyone next to a bonfire. I removed my Zweiss binoculars, which I'd brought with me from the car – a very small, very expensive, quite excellent pair that can be folded into a package no bigger than three inches by three inches. They can be stuffed into a pants pocket.

The weather was just delightful, so different from the climate I was accustomed to in Texas. Staying up there wasn't bad at all, and I convinced myself that it was for a good purpose. Although it was unlikely that Dallas would walk into that clearing and thus into my arms, I might reasonably hope to witness a scene close to one he had lived through. But as the minutes turned into an hour, I couldn't help but reflect rather morosely on the ludicrous activities I'd engaged in during this investigation. Trestling. Playing Dungeons & Dragons. Entering the steam tunnels. And now here I was doing it again. The sounds of night creatures seemed to taunt me, and I had to brush away pests that used my arms and face as landing pads. The trees surrounding the clearing blotted out most light around where the bonfire would be built, and the area was as dark as a cave. It occurred to me that college students might consider midnight a good time for a meeting, and I knew that by then my leg joints would be crippled and my back twisted and locked.

I occupied myself by speculating about that note addressed to 'Paul.' The meeting might involve a drug transaction; if it did, I would weigh my chances of bursting in and demanding information about Dallas's activities and whereabouts. What was more likely, I thought, was some activity of the Tolkien society or some other group. Lambert and I had seen pentagrams, five-pointed stars encased in two circles, painted on trees surrounding the clearing. Between the two circles were magic symbols which, I was later told, were associated with the ancient Druidic religion and witchcraft, and were used as protection by a sorcerer against demons. Pentagrams had also been drawn into the ground, where a sorcerer could stand on them and be safe. I had discovered through my talks with students that witchcraft was in vogue at Michigan State University. I suspected that most of it was an excuse to get drunk or moderately high and was not to be taken too seriously.

I had convinced myself that midnight would be the hour, so it was with relief that I heard rustling through the underbrush off to my right after ninety minutes in my tree perch. I could hear voices but not individual words or sentences. I half-expected to witness some sort of lark, punctuated with giggling and laughing, but the voices, while youthful, seemed very serious indeed. I guessed there were four people. They had flashlights, and I could follow their movements by watching the beams from the flashlights, which cast a halolike glow similar to that of a car's headlights in rain.

They did light a bonfire, and it was really quite pretty when it reached and maintained its apex. It was bright orange against the black night, perhaps six feet high, manageable, but not so small that it could be intended just to warm hands or heat coffee.

There *were* four students, two boys and two girls, and there seemed to be nothing out-of-the-way or bizarre about their dress – no pointed wizard's hats or strange polka-dotted costumes. From what I could tell, which was hardly a great deal despite the light from the fire, they were dressed as thousands of other college students might be. They formed a diamond shape around the blaze, hunched much as I was, and if a single word could capture the atmosphere, that word would be *serious*. No one had lugged a case of beer out to Party Hollow, nor were there indications that a joint would soon be passed around. Conversation continued, but I had no idea what they were saying. I could only surmise by that impression of seriousness that it was not jocular or ribald.

Uncomfortable, harassed by insects, my bones aching, I hoped that they would soon get to whatever the purpose of this congregation was. After some thirty minutes, four others (again the sexes equal in numbers) arrived, but there were no loud how-do-you-do's. A nod of the head or a 'Hi, how are you?' was the most that transpired, I imagined. Well, get down to business, I thought. My ankles and especially my knees felt as if they were welded together.

The eight crouched around the fire, roughly two to a side, and then one of the girls, wearing a necklace (I could see it reflecting the sparkle of the flames), rose and faced the fire. Her only movement was a tilt of the head skyward. Then I heard her voice, fresh and clear and strong in the night, cry out, 'Great Gurdjieff, guide us to the goodness of God's goals!'

These were the only words I plainly understood during the entire evening. The students remained for forty-five minutes more, conversing in that same calm, reasoned, no-nonsense manner. They carefully extinguished the fire when they were finished and trekked back through the woods – to homework, I imagined, or overdue letters to family and friends. I came out of my tree (some might think I'd been out of it all along) believing that I'd never be able to stand straight again. My knee buckled on the first step I took after I was on the ground. I limped painfully to the bonfire site, but they had left nothing behind. Except for the warm ashes, there was little indication that anyone had been there at all. I sighed, and headed through the woods to my car. I doubted whether the group I had seen had anything to do with Dallas, but I was interested in how many such cults, and of what variety, existed on this and other campuses. There were probably many, and one we didn't even know about might have counted Dallas as a member. One of them might have the answers for which I searched.

I buzzed Riddle as soon as I was back in my room, which was around midnight. I supposed I should have been grateful, having earlier figured that I would still be in that tree at midnight, but I wasn't. I was angry and wild with frustration. It seemed to me that I wasn't getting anywhere. If Dallas was playing a game with me, he was winning. I wanted to be up and about, solving this case. I was filled with energy and had nowhere to expend it.

'Did you meet with Peggy Hogan?' I asked, my voice a decibel too loud.

'Saw her at her house.'

This was good news. 'Tell me how it went,' I said.

'Peggy was very nervous when I showed up,' Riddle began. 'It wasn't difficult to figure out that she didn't want to see me. Before I even started to speak, she said she hadn't been able to contact any of the people she'd hoped could help. She said newspapers had been trying to contact her about Dallas's membership in the Gay Council. I told her that I hadn't sicced the press on her, but that it wasn't surprising they'd been around. If I could find her, so could reporters.'

'What was your reaction to her saying she couldn't help?'

'I said I didn't believe her. She was crying. "I'm doing the best I can," she said. She said that the Gay Council had a meeting about the case and made the decision not to talk to the press, the police, or us until they could talk with a lawyer. I asked her why they needed a lawyer, and she said because Dallas was a minor. The council is afraid of lawsuits down the road.'

'Did she say she didn't want to talk to you anymore?'

'She didn't say it that way. She kept insisting that she just didn't know anything. I said it wouldn't help in any future lawsuit if it was known that she denied cooperation.'

'What about these people she said she couldn't contact?'

'I asked her for the names. I said *we'd* contact them. She didn't want to give me the names.'

'Oh, she didn't,' I said. My muscles tensed, and I could feel rage surging through my back and shoulders. A dark, angry cloud filled my mind. '*So she doesn't want to*,' I said sarcastically, and I could feel Riddle tense up on the other end of the telephone line. He'd witnessed my rages a few times before, and knew a dandy was on the way.

'I'm tired of this bullshit!' I shouted. 'It's gone too damn far, and we should have stopped it long ago! I don't care what it takes, I'm going to solve this case. If I have to walk over people, I will. I'm telling you, Riddle, here's what it is, a coverup. It doesn't matter who, or what the reasons. Professors. Gays. Students. Administration security. I'm going to find out the reasons, and God help anyone involved. I'm tired of kids telling me they don't know anything. Bullshit! They walked through walls with Dallas, let him do their homework for them, let him make drugs for them. Now nobody can help, huh? I'd like to wring a few necks. I wouldn't trade Dallas for this whole university. Protecting their own ass – that's what everyone is doing. So she doesn't *want* to give you the names? So disgusting, I swear, right now I'd like to resign from the human race.'

Riddle didn't say anything. He could tell I wasn't finished. 'The most basic decency is lacking here,' I went on. 'I think of the Egberts, just sick with worry, and somebody doesn't *want* to give us names. Damn! Dallas *lived* at this university, but he might just as well have been an occasional visitor for all people say they know about him. This look-out-for-its-own-skin university is the worst. This would never have happened if the place had done its job. Hell, I've heard educators moan about the quality of the students they're given to work with. They get a good quality, Dallas, and mess it up. A bum lying in a gutter would get more and better attention from the cop on the beat than Dallas got from this school. I'll laugh the next time I hear a professor yearn for good students! And the university – I don't see any lack of funds, but do you think one penny is being spent to find a child the school is responsible for in the first place? "We're the ones who lost your child, Mrs. Egbert. You gave him to us to look after, and we did such a good job that he's gone. You wanted us to educate him, Mrs. Egbert, and he learned a lot about homosexuality and drugs and trestling and Dungeons & Dragons. We did our best, Mrs. Egbert, but he's missing now, so you'd better spend a lot of money hiring good private detectives. Of course, we won't *cooperate* with the private detectives." Damn, Riddle, it's a hell of a nasty world!'

'Bill, I agree with you,' Riddle said calmly. 'I arrived here a week before you did, and I called my wife the first night and told her we wouldn't send our boy here even if it were free. I was angry with Peggy Hogan, too. I told her that for someone who claimed to be caring and concerned, she had a pretty strange way of behaving. She said that she considered Dallas her friend, and I said that friends were to be depended on. How could Dallas depend on her?'

I had cooled down some now. 'If she would cooperate, how much help do you think she could be?'

'I really don't think she knows that much. I think she's operating on the come-on that maybe she could learn something. Don't laugh, but the Gay Council is pretty straight. Sort of the establishment. I figure that if gays are involved with Dallas's disappearance, it won't be those who are out in the open, those who've obtained university recognition.'

'So you don't expect anything from her?'

'I really don't, Bill.'

I put down the receiver and drummed my fingers on the nightstand. I was still too upset, too disappointed, to start answering phone messages again. And too tired. What had we learned today? That we were further away from solving the case than we had been when the day had begun.

The truth was, though, that Mr. and Mrs. Egbert weren't sleeping. I gave myself another moment to feel sorry for myself, then picked up the receiver and dialed the first number. The next day – later that day, actually, since it was already morning – I wasn't going to stand for any stalling over searching those tunnels.

Chapter 13

I met Captain Ferman Badgley for the first time on September 5 at 9:30 A.M., in his office at campus police headquarters. Badgley, a tall, distinguished-looking man in his early forties with salt-and-pepper hair, had just returned from vacation to a hornets' swarm of national media attention. I had come to talk about searching the tunnels, but he had something else in mind. He got right to the point.

'Mr. Dear, I'm extremely upset that all these calls coming into our switchboard are being referred to you and your staff at the Red Roof Inn. This is our case. I've discussed this with Sergeants Lyons and Wardwell and told them how displeased I am.'

'I came to discuss a search of the tunnels,' I said. 'I think it's essential that we –'

'From now on, I'm running this investigation. Taking complete control of it.'

'That's fine. We all should be working toward the same goal: to find Dallas Egbert. Together we should have the manpower to instigate a thorough search. I've come to talk about that.'

'I want to talk about how the investigation is being handled. The calls have to go from the switchboard to our investigators.' Badgley was very upset. I don't know whether he realized that I too was steaming.

'Are you saying,' I asked, 'that we're not to receive any more calls?'

'I want all calls on the case channeled through this office.'

'I can't guarantee that, and you know it.'

'Well, that's the way it's going to be. Also, these press conferences you've been holding – there have been too many of them. From now on press conferences will be held through this office.'

So that's it, I thought. Maybe the publicity had embarrassed the university. 'Hold the press conferences wherever you want,' I said. 'Now let's get down to business.'

'I also don't like the inferences that this department isn't competent to handle an investigation.'

'What are you talking about? I've made no such inferences.' Dallas's mother had made derogatory remarks about the campus police, but I knew that the MSU police were understaffed for an investigation such as this one and that they were not likely to receive much cooperation from the university community.

'Let me sum up,' said Badgley. 'It seems to me that you've taken over this investigation. That's got to change. We're the ones responsible, and we're going to meet that responsibility. From now on the case is going to be handled with that in mind.'

'Get this, Badgley,' I replied, trying to keep my temper. 'I'll cooperate with you one hundred percent. But I'm working for Dr. and Mrs. Egbert, just like you're working for the university. The Egberts hired me, and they're paying me. I intend to find that boy. I don't have to obey university rules, like you do.'

Badgley seemed to me a good enough person. He was simply in a position, I believed, in which the desires of his employer did not mesh with the demands of this investigation. I didn't know whether he had received any instructions from school officials, but the administrators would of course prefer that all calls come to their police or so it seemed to me. They did not need for an outside investigator to learn about campus crimes such as rape and drug dealing. It wouldn't matter to these officials that informants would probably much rather come to me, a private citizen, than go to the campus police.

I sensed also that Badgley resented me and my men. This is not unusual for a police officer. The private investigator's life is often seen as glamorous, though in reality it can be quite different. On a professional level a P.I. does have more freedom than a cop does. He has money to employ in his investigation, and he is not constrained by bureaucracy. He does not have to get approval before he follows a case wherever it might lead. If I heard that Dallas had been spotted in California, for example, I could head west in a minute. Not so the policeman, who would need what often can seem like an act of God to get funds appropriated. On television, many private eyes are depicted as former cops, and with good reason; such is often the case in real life. A good policeman recognizes early on that he might be far more effective in private practice.

But Badgley seemed willing to compromise. 'As long as we're agreed,' he said. 'No press conferences of your own. We can hold them jointly, from these headquarters. The calls on the case come here.'

'I'll go you one better: I'll keep you updated on my calls that are made directly to me. You understand that I'll have to protect the confidentiality of certain calls. Now, about the tunnels. I assume we're going into them today.'

'I've got to check with the university. I'm not sure there's access to these tunnels.'

'There is.'

'Well, I don't know that. I'll talk with the responsible officials.'

Good grief, I thought. I had understood that the purpose of this meeting was to arrange the details of the search. I was prepared to lay all the facts I knew before Badgley, who, as a competent cop, would surely see that a search was the only sensible way to go. I had even had Hock purchase the equipment we needed. Now it turned out that Badgley hadn't even talked with the people whose approval we needed.

'You want me to go back and call Dr. and Mrs. Egbert,' I said, disbelief in my voice, 'and tell them that we still don't have the okay to search the tunnels? I can't stop *them* from calling a press conference, and I can practically promise that that's what they'll do if they find out the university is still dragging its feet.'

'You're going to have to give me a little time.'

'I don't know that I can. The press can't understand why we're not in those tunnels, either. What is the big deal here?'

'This has got to be handled through channels. I don't have authority to authorize this search.'

'I thought you were obtaining that authority.'

'I'll get back to you in a couple of hours. This is hitting me all at once. I can't move any faster.'

'I hope that something gets done real quick,' I said, getting up from my chair. 'The press sees the need for speedy action, even if the university doesn't, and I can't control them.'

'You're the one who unleashed them in the first place.'

'That's right,' I replied, and walked out of the room.

Riddle was waiting for me on the lawn outside the campus police headquarters. He could see that my mood hadn't measurably improved since that early-morning outburst prompted by the Peggy Hogan interview.

'Let's get out of here,' I said. 'I think I'm going to be sick.'

'Not good, huh?'

'Unbelievable. I'm still hearing that they're not sure the tunnels are accessible.'

'Not exactly blazing along, are we?'

Reporters were on the lawn. This had been the much-touted meeting that supposedly would culminate in the search of the tunnels. Damn, why did I give my word to Badgley? I thought. If this dragged on much longer, I knew I would be faced with a dilemma. I believe in keeping my word, but I had a commitment to the Egberts and, more important, a commitment to Dallas. It occurred to me that I could keep my word and my commitment, if the foot-dragging continued: I could call a *joint* news conference. Let Badgley explain why we weren't combing those tunnels.

'When are you going in?' a reporter asked.

I bit my lip. 'We'll have an announcement, probably late in the afternoon,' I answered. I hated what I'd just said. It sounded as if *I* were the one stalling. And as if I were a hypocrite, too. Time and again I'd stressed the urgency of the search, and now I was saying 'later.' Did it look as if I'd made a devil's deal with the university?

Some of the reporters were very alert. I'm thinking of Billy Bowles, with the *Detroit Free Press*, Bob France, of the *Dayton Journal Herald*, and Carol Morello, of the *Lansing State Journal*. There were others who had followed the case from the start and who also had suspicions about those tunnels and their use, and I didn't want them to think for an instant that I was backing down.

Riddle and I met with Hock and Lambert back in my room at the Red Roof Inn and discussed strategy. If the school continued to stall, we decided, we would make a big production of leaving, saying that the investigation simply couldn't continue when its most important avenue of inquiry was blocked. We hoped that the threat to pack up and go, plus a few spicy tidbits concerning the university's possible motivation, would bring a quick change of heart. Of course we had no intention of leaving. Wild horses couldn't drag me from this investigation, and I think my men felt the same way. If worse came to worst, we'd risk incurring trespassing charges, and whatever else the campus police could cook up, and search the tunnels without authorization.

While we waited for Badgley's call, we decided to take up a Detroit television station on its offer to fly us over the campus in its helicopter. While Riddle accompanied a reporter, a cameraman, and the pilot in the helicopter, Lambert, Hock, and I went up in my airplane to get a firsthand look at the campus from above. Riddle was going to study the old power plant and see if a pattern corresponding with the scattered tacks on the corkboard could be discerned from the air. I thought I might be able to get a clearer idea of the extent of those steam tunnels, which I figured tentacled out to almost every building on campus.

Right away I had to concentrate on what we were doing. My eyes were glued to the flight of the helicopter. Riddle had directed the chopper to hover about fifteen feet directly above the power plant's lone smokestack. I wondered what this was all about – the prosaic Riddle was hardly given to flights of fancy. It turned out that he wanted to look straight down the stack to see if Dallas had jumped down inside. 'It was pretty unlikely,' he said later, 'but if Dallas was playing a game, or what had been a game coupled with suicide, he might have chosen that place. We couldn't figure out anything the "gun" on the corkboard could represent except the old power plant. The cremation note, regardless of who wrote it, implied that it wasn't likely we would find the body. Well, I thought it wasn't likely that anyone would find a corpse in that smokestack. It's amazing – everybody in the helicopter thought it was a good idea.'

In the airplane I got an eyeful of the job we faced in searching the tunnels. This was no small school; we'd need as many search teams as we could put together. If that corkboard corresponded to the real terrain, the individual tacks must represent entrances and exits to the tunnels. At this time I knew only a few of the entrances, but I could tell that they corresponded to that pattern. Yet if this was the case, where did it lead us? A diagram of tunnel entrances? I would think that Dallas would play fair; the clues he left behind would be more specific than that. I imagined that if the corkboard did have meaning and we were bright enough to decipher it, we would go right to Dallas. The young genius would reason, perhaps correctly, that he was too bright for any collection of gumshoes.

But maybe I was underestimating myself, or overestimating Dallas. Maybe the corkboard simply meant nothing. Or maybe it was indeed a map of tunnel entrances but unrelated to his disappearance. The corkboard might have been Dallas's own guide for Dungeons & Dragons. The answer, it occurred to me, might be something much simpler, and for some reason I was making this case much more difficult than it really was.

I didn't think so.

When I got back to the Red Roof Inn, I first made sure that Riddle, Hock, and Lambert would be available to move on a moment's notice. It was just after 3 P.M. and there was no message that Captain Badgley had called. I guessed that he wasn't exactly grabbing lapels and shaking his bosses to expedite the search.

I hate inaction, and the bureaucratic chain of command – a feeling I imagine I share with many Americans. Often in a committee-operation it seems that no one has authority to act. Or everyone is passing the buck, covering their own behinds. I can't operate that way. I've worked since I was eleven years old, been on my own since age sixteen. At age seventeen, just out of high school, I joined the Florida Highway Patrol and became the youngest uniformed communications officer ever hired by that state. It wasn't that my parents, whom I love dearly, couldn't take care of me. I *wanted* to be on my own. The dream of working for myself was what brought me into the private-investigation business in the first place. I can make decisions. I have no patience whatever with sheaves of forms and labyrinthine chains of command intended mainly to protect those who designed them.

In this case, I felt, the moral prerogative should prevail: it was *right* to search those tunnels. I hoped I would make that decision if I were ever in Captain Badgley's position. Badgley – a good cop, I thought, judging from the citations on his office wall, who had to see the urgency of searching the tunnels – might find the freedom of decision-making invigorating. Being embarrassed, admitting wrong, was a price that one or both of us might have to pay if the prime consideration – finding Dallas – was to be satisfied. In the jargon of football, whoever was in charge was going to have to suck it up.

I started to doodle on motel stationery, absentmindedly writing down possible solutions. It was discouraging, twenty-two days after the disappearance, not even to know what kind of case I was dealing with. But as I doodled, my attention began to focus, and I grew more serious about the words in front of me. I tried to recall everything I knew about the case, to weigh what I knew against what I felt. I came up with the following:

Type of Case	*Likelihood*
Suicide	41%
Kidnap	28%
Runaway/hoax	21%
Murder	5%
Accidental death	3%
Other	2%

In short, this so-called high-powered detective still couldn't say there was even a fifty-percent likelihood that he was handling a certain type of disappearance. The possibility that Dallas was alive – kidnap or runaway/hoax – came to forty-nine percent. The possibility that he was dead – suicide, murder, accidental death – was also forty-nine percent. The 'other,' which I couldn't conceive of, made the majority percentage impossible. I wondered if these percentages were influenced by my frustrated subconscous. I certainly hadn't been aware of setting up a tie.

Badgley called just after four o'clock. 'We've got to talk,' he said. 'I'd like you to come to headquarters.'

This was hardly encouraging. His tone of voice was not what I would have expected from someone who was ready to pursue the proper course. Maybe he was the sort who liked to deliver good news in person.

'I'll be right over,' I said.

I thought of making him wait. The university had made *me* wait – and the Egberts, which was the real sin. A dose of the medicine I'd been swallowing might be in order. But my impatient nature made it impossible. I wanted to get over there, get this stalled investigation rolling again. I called Riddle. It was preposterous to imagine that Badgley's message would be that the tunnel search was forbidden, or that the school hadn't made up its mind yet, but much of the behavior I'd witnessed thus far had been unbelievable. If I was going to be danced around the tree again, I wanted Riddle to see it.

This time we went out through the front lobby. I hoped that every reporter in the state would follow us. I intended to call a press conference right on the steps of the police station if the stalling continued. I'd live up to the letter of my agreement with Badgley not to conduct a news conference on my own. Let him stand next to me. The press would love to hear him explain that the tunnels were inaccessible. I knew for a fact that one reporter had duplicated Lambert's and my forays, and I was willing to conduct a delegation straight over to one of those tunnel entrances.

When we reached the station and went inside, our friend Sergeant Larry Lyons, *in uniform*, was sitting behind a glass-enclosed reception desk. I looked at Riddle and raised my eyebrows. Lyons was a *detective* sergeant. Was he being taught a lesson because he'd cooperated with us?

'You get demoted for associating with us?' Riddle asked jokingly.

'Nah,' Lyons said. He smiled.

'Captain Badgley wants to see us,' I explained.

Lyons used an intercom to dial Badgley's office. Then he pressed a security-door release to permit us to enter the inner sanctum. 'He only wants to see you,' Lyons said to me.

Again I exchanged glances with Riddle. This seemed another unfavorable development. I went through the door and back to Badgley's office. I half-expected the news about the tunnel search to be negative. I had no idea that I was being set up.

'I've brought a lot of the equipment we'll need for the search,' I said to Badgley. 'My staff is ready. The press has been on me. How about going in this evening? No sense in waiting.'

'What did you learn from the airplane and helicopter rides today?' Badgley asked.

'That it's a big campus. Looks like we have a major search waiting for us. Look, Captain, when do we begin?'

'I'm working on it. I'm waiting for answers.'

'Waiting? I say, hell, we've waited long enough. This is just outrageous. I'm going to –'

'Cool your heels. Something should happen shortly. Let's sit and talk about that airplane of yours. A pretty handy machine. What kind is it?'

'A C-55 twin-engine Baron. Look, the press will –'

'Just wait, like you're going to. Now I told you, I expect a development shortly.'

Badgley was right. At this very moment a Michigan State Police lieutenant, Jim Baird, accompanied by a state police sergeant, was pushing his badge right up against the reception window for Larry Lyons to see and be impressed with. After Lyons pressed the button to release the security door, he glanced at Riddle and formed a silent, the crap-is-going-to-hit-the-fan whistle with his lips.

The first I saw of Lieutenant Baird and his friend was when they walked into Badgley's office without knocking. I was seated in a chair. Baird was a tall, big man, fairly young, who would have been nice-looking if he hadn't been taking himself so seriously. I'd been through these rites before. I stood up to show him that I was as tall as he was. The person sitting down, any veteran police officer can tell you, is at a definite disadvantage. The person towering above has a big intimidation advantage.

'My name is Jim Baird,' he said in a stern voice. 'State police. I need to talk with you.'

'Fine,' I said in a voice just as gruff.

'Is there a room we can use?' Baird asked Badgley.

I realized I was being subjected to the old change-rooms routine, as Maxwell Smart would say. Usually used to intimidate. The two state cops against the lone citizen, out of sight of the established law, Captain Ferman Badgley. Ten to one the room would be wired for sound. I was quite sure that these two hadn't come to discuss a search of the tunnels.

The new room was slightly larger than a closet, with space for a desk and two chairs. I wasn't going to sit down, and of course they weren't either, so we stood there nearly stomach-to-stomach, trying to convince one another we were hard types.

'It's been brought to our attention,' Baird said in his tough-guy voice, 'that you've been working this Dallas Egbert case but are not licensed in the state of Michigan.'

I reached back to my wallet and handed him my Texas license.

He looked at it. 'I never doubted you were licensed in Texas. We're talking about Michigan.'

'My office contacted the licensing division in Austin. We were informed that your licensing laws are patterned after ours. Section thirty-one says you can work for one employer and one employer only without being licensed in a particular state. I'm working for one employer.'

'We don't honor that in this state.'

'I also belong to the International Council of Investigators, ICV. I'm sure you know about it, Lieutenant Baird. I could call them, and with just that one call I could operate under their license. But I don't intend to. Your coming here after we've been working on this case for almost three weeks, without any offer of help or cooperation, strikes me as politically motivated. It seems strange that we've been able to work with Detectives Wardwell and

Lyons and others, with just one goal in mind – to find a missing boy – and your only concern is my license. I'll tell you what I'm going to do: I'm going to let *you* handle this case. *You* find Dallas Egbert. Since you're so concerned about my license, *you* try to clean up this mess. Explain to the press why the tunnels aren't being searched. Explain to Mrs. Egbert why it's important to avoid embarrassing important people, even at the price of her boy. And if you dare to tell the truth, I wish you good luck in explaining to your superiors why you humiliated the big shots who run this university.'

'Take it easy, Mr. Dear.' The gruffness was gone. 'We know you're a good investigator. We've checked, and your record speaks for itself. But I've got a job to do. You're not licensed in this state.'

'Fine. I'll get out.'

'You're not taking it easy. Look, we haven't had any complaints about you. If we –'

'You must have had a complaint. Why else would you be here?' It didn't take a master detective to figure where it had come from.

'As I was saying, if we don't get a complaint, I think you'll be all right. This is Wednesday. We won't be back in town until next Monday. If no one complains, I think you can keep operating as you have been until then.'

Baird had come in all huff, but now he was all puff.

'I hope we have this solved by Monday,' I said. 'It's possible, if we can get into those tunnels.'

'I wish you well in that area,' Baird said. I thought he might say more, but discretion prevailed. Instead he opted to say, 'This is a tough case, and I'm glad I'm not in your shoes.'

'Tell me,' I said, 'who filed the complaint?'

'I can't.'

That was all right. We shook hands, the two state cops

headed out of the building, and I went straight back to Badgley's office. 'About the tunnels,' I said. 'Are we going into them tonight?'

He had expected me to be off the case, not standing in his doorway. 'You're finished with the state police?' he said.

'Right. And ready for the tunnels.'

'If the search is conducted, and I'm not saying it will be, I'm going to conduct it my way. Everything will have to be approved by me.'

'I'm not your puppet,' I replied. 'I want that straight. But since I'm sure we want the same thing, I don't think we'll have a problem. When will you be ready to begin?'

'When I say so.'

'When will that be?'

'Approval needs to be obtained. I have to catch up on everything that's happened in this case.'

'You still don't have approval?'

'Not yet.'

'When will you get it?'

'I don't know.'

'What am I going to tell the press when I walk out of here?'

'You're not going to tell them anything. I'll do the talking from now on.'

'Okay,' I said, now blazing mad. 'I'm not going to make any excuses for you or the university. I'm through. I'm walking away from this. You tell the press why we're not looking for this boy. You tell the Egberts. I don't think you have any idea what trouble can be.'

I walked out fast, through the electric door, across the foyer, past reporters. I wanted to make this look good. The reporters were throwing questions at me. Riddle was half-trotting alongside, and I said in a loud voice, angrily, 'Tell Lambert to get the plane ready. I'm leaving.'

'You're not going into the tunnels?' I heard a reporter ask.

'Ask Badgley.'

'What was the meeting with the state police about?'

'Ask Badgley.'

'Is there trouble between you and Badgley?'

'Look, I have no comment.'

'Do we understand that you're going back to Texas?'

'No comment. Captain Badgley is the one to talk with. Find out from him what's happening. He can give you a story you'll love.'

We headed back for the Red Roof Inn. I was glad it was over, and wished I could have done this earlier. I felt that the ice had been broken. Even the most intransigent authority would have to take notice of what I expected would be a firestorm of unfavorable publicity. The story was capturing national and international publicity now. Nightly there were reports on the network news. The disappearance of Dallas Egbert had become a *cause célèbre*, but fortunately for the school, many of the tawdry details had not yet surfaced. They would show up now, unless there was some extra-quick action. I anticipated a very short wait. I'd sent Lambert to ready the airplane, but if I'd miscalculated, I could figure out a reason to postpone my departure. I was so sure of myself that I didn't bother to think what that reason might be.

I was right. 'Bill Dear,' I answered when the phone rang. I'd left specific instructions about whom I was willing to talk to.

'Mr. Dear, this is Chief Burnett over at the campus police. Understand you're leaving.'

'That's right.' I'd heard about Dick Burnett, but he hadn't been able to attend my meeting with Badgley, so I hadn't met him. He was chief of MSU's campus police, the top-ranking cop.

'I'd like to talk with you,' Burnett said.

'I'm sorry, Chief, but I don't think there's anything to talk about. It's your case. Captain Badgley made that clear.'

'That's not true. We need you, and we need you badly. You've done an excellent job so far, and you're closer to the case than anyone. Please come over. Give me a few minutes of your time. I think we can rectify all of this.'

I liked what Chief Burnett was saying, but more important, I liked the way he sounded. His tone of voice was sincere, and I sensed that here was a reasonable man. I'd figured that someone had better become reasonable soon, but Burnett's approach was not that of a man shoved up against a wall. Instead he sounded as if cooperation were his goal.

'What do you want to talk about?' I said.

'Finding Dallas Egbert.'

'Well, then I'll be right over.'

Dick Burnett was in his late fifties, had short gray hair, wore a conservative suit, and reminded me of my grandfather. I thought he might be president of this university, he was that elegant. He struck me as straightforward and concerned.

'I'm sorry I haven't gotten in touch with you sooner,' he said. He didn't offer an explanation.

Riddle, Burnett, Badgley, and I went to what looked like the campus police's main conference room and sat at a long conference table. Burnett opened the proceedings.

'The purpose of this meeting,' he said, 'is to resolve some problems that never should have arisen. I think Captain Badgley has something he wants to say first.'

'I want to apologize for my attitude when I met with you earlier,' Badgley said to me. 'I hope you'll try to understand that after coming back from a vacation and running into something like this, I was quite distraught. I think we can work together to get this case solved.' Badgley reached across the table and shook my hand.

'I think we all want the same thing,' I replied. 'To find Dallas Egbert.'

'I want it understood,' Burnett declared, 'that we're in charge of this case. We need to regain control of the investigation. The base of operations can't be your motel; it has to be police headquarters. The publicity can very easily get out of hand.'

'I have no problem with that,' I said.

Burnett continued. 'What I'm saying is that we shouldn't have let you take such complete control of the investigation. It was a mistake. I'm not blaming you, and according to what I know, what you've done has been first-rate.'

'I understand,' I said. 'But about the tunnels – a search has to be made of those tunnels.'

'That can be worked out, I assure you.'

'When? Some hazy date in the future isn't good enough.'

'Soon. Trust me. It will be soon. What I want from you is the promise that any releases to the press will be joint releases. We approve them together.'

'I have no difficulty with that either. As long as we're honest. I'm not going to lie to reporters.'

'Of course not,' said Badgley. 'Let's agree that we'll meet the press twice a day. Once in the morning, again in the afternoon. The press conferences should be held here.'

All this talk about the media convinced me that I'd handled this case properly, at least as far as getting into the tunnels went. I understood what Badgley and Burnett were saying. The campus police had not been able to find Dallas, though I certainly could not fault them for this; they simply weren't set up to handle such a case. Now they were concerned about their image, and about the image of the university. I didn't care one way or another about this.

'Two press conferences a day it is,' I agreed. 'Now – about the tunnels.'

'We can go in tomorrow,' Burnett said.

Hooray! I thought to myself. As with so many endeavors in life, success depended on getting the ear of the right person. If you're persistent enough (and I consider myself very persistent), in the end you locate the person with the key that clicks smoothly into place and opens the doors. Burnett was that person. Either he had the authority to okay the search or, more likely, he had known where to get it.

'What time do we go in?' I asked.

'I'd like you to coordinate this with Captain Badgley.'

'Fine.'

'I think,' said Badgley, 'we should go in the early evening. It might be cooler then. But it is important we do it tomorrow.'

'Right,' I said. What a turnabout this was – Badgley in a hurry.

'The campus will be crowded soon,' Badgley continued. 'Students are returning for the new semester. And there's a big football game here Saturday, just three days from now. We should go in as soon as we can.'

'Good thinking,' I said, hoping I didn't choke on the words. 'When do we get together to coordinate plans?'

'How about eight o'clock tomorrow morning?'

'I'll be here.'

'The press is out in the foyer now. Maybe we should talk to them tonight, show there's no friction between us. We can announce that we're going into the tunnels tomorrow.'

'I have a picture I'd like to distribute,' I said. 'I don't think anyone who sees the picture, recognizes Dallas, and has an idea where he is could possibly fail to volunteer to help.' I handed the glossy photo to Badgley. It had been sent to me by Mrs. Egbert, and I'd made fifty copies. I intended to give a copy to anyone who might get it reproduced in newspapers or shown on television. Even today, when I look at the picture, it makes me want to cry, and others who have seen it say that they are similarly affected. The photo was taken just two months before Dallas disappeared, and shows this little boy hugging a white teddy bear.

Badgley agreed, and we retired to the lobby to hold the press conference, which went smoothly enough. I'm sure Burnett and Badgley breathed more easily as they saw that I was going to stay within the guidelines they'd set down. I pulled no surprises, but *I* was surprised by what Badgley had to say. He revealed that the campus police had received anonymous calls from a woman who said she knew firsthand that Dallas had been playing Dungeons & Dragons in the tunnels. Badgley added that if Dallas was found in the tunnels, he would be found dead.

I agreed with this analysis, but I was upset by the news of the anonymous tip. I hadn't been told of it. Cooperation, I thought, was a two-way street. The campus police expected me to share all my information with them – and I certainly had more to share than they did – so I should be afforded the same courtesy. But now wasn't the time to complain. I didn't want anything to deflect Badgley's attention from the need for a tunnel search. I'd bring the matter up later, if I thought it made a difference in finding the boy.

That night I went to sleep at peace with myself. I expected quite an adventure on the morrow.

Chapter 14

We went into the Michigan State university steam tunnels at 6:45 P.M. on Thursday, September 6, just after night had fallen. It was a warm, clear, humid, early-autumn evening which reminded me of my Florida childhood and the times after dinner when we prepared to play hide-and-seek.

The idea, after we studied schematics of the great maze, was to cover as much of the eight and a half miles of tunnels as possible. A total of twelve searchers went in, entering the tunnels from widely spaced points in two-man teams. The division of manpower was democratic: four private investigators, four policemen, and four maintenance engineers. My partner was a maintenance engineer, Riddle's was a cop, and the four of us entered together from a central location roughly surrounded by the audiology and speech sciences department, the urban planning and landscape architecture department, the packaging department, and the engineering department. We walked through a door on the ground level of Wilson Road, down some steps that reminded me of a New York City subway entrance, and then through two doors that led into the maze.

We intended to split into two teams about one hundred feet into the tunnel, where it branched. Even though each team carried a map, it would be very easy to become hopelessly lost after this first turn. There seemed to be an infinite variety of turns. These tunnels, I thought, perfectly imitated a fantasy setting for Dungeons & Dragons. I could hear the dungeon master saying, 'Now you come to a fork. On the left is . . .'

Each team carried flashlights and a walkie-talkie so we could communicate with one another and with the aboveground command post, manned by Badgley, Burnett, and Wardwell. In addition, we carried chalk to mark the tunnel walls to help find our way back. Standard dress was coveralls over T-shirts and jeans. We knew we would have to crawl between pipes and around other obstructions, and we hoped that these clothes would provide protection against being burned or scraped. I'd had a foretaste of what awaited us, but most of the others, wiping perspiration from their faces, had no idea what humidity really was. Some thought it unnecessary to remove their jewelry and watches, which they were told to do because these could heat up like coals and scorch their skin.

A few overhead lights lit the way when we first entered, but we knew that this meager illumination wouldn't last. Several reporters and television cameramen ventured perhaps thirty feet into the tunnel with us, eager to get a sense of the atmosphere, plus a few pictures for the late news. I knew for a fact that these representatives of the media would acquire no insight at all into how rough it was going to become. Even so, and even with the occasional overhead lights, they needed strobe lights to record the first tentative steps that Riddle and I took.

We reached the fork in the tunnel and conditions immediately got worse. For one thing, we couldn't see; for another, within two steps the temperature shot up from seventy degrees to more than a hundred, and it was guaranteed to go higher.

'See you above,' Riddle said as he went off to the left. Almost instantly he became a shadowy blur.

I went right, followed by the maintenance engineer, whom I needlessly told to be careful. Only a total fool would attempt to make rapid progress here. Where we had entered, the tunnel had been tall enough to stand in, but now we had to walk hunched, with our eyeballs straining in their sockets just to peer straight ahead. The view below was okay, if we kept the flashlights trained on the floor, but that didn't keep me from kicking a metallic object which clattered ahead. I got down on hands and knees to inch forward and find it; a Strohs beer can. 'The tunnels are inaccessible,' I said, but if my partner caught the meaning, he didn't respond. 'Brutal damn hot,' he said instead, and he was right. We evidently were in one of the steamy, swamplike sections of the tunnels, not the dry-desert part that could fry your brain.

But the beer can focused my attention more clearly on the reason we were in these god-awful tunnels, and away from the extreme discomfort. Earlier in the day, while hammering out details of the search with Ferman Badgley, I'd learned of a letter which had just arrived at the *Lansing State Journal*. It was signed 'J.D.E. – MSU Student' and read as follows:

> There are so many problems in the world today, but that doesn't make communication impossible. Or does it? So many people want their Jesus, but He won't save His children until Satan has reached His peak of power. I will make the supreme sacrifice, perhaps being the one who breaks the camel's back. I will throw myself into the arms of Satan. He can use my mental power any way He wishes. Satan knows that He can't win in the end. In a real way I am helping to destroy Satan. The world is a harsh place. A man of intelligence and virtue isn't appreciated any more than a politician or a homosexual with a large penis these days. You may find this hard to understand, but sometimes I think God hasn't created a woman for me. In the tradition of romantics and heroes I love in a violent

way. This statement was written as explanation for my actions to the ordinary man.

The letter had been hand-printed, as Dallas was wont to do, and bore a Lansing postmark. If it was an 'explanation' for the boy's actions, it eluded me, but I hadn't really had time to study it. It smacked to me of a college prank in bad taste; the letter just didn't sound like Dallas, and several details didn't ring true. It was something to look into, however, if we came up empty in the tunnels. If that occurred, *anything* would be worth looking into. I didn't know where we'd go from here.

We groped deeper into the tunnels. Visibility was absolutely zero, and the temperature kept going in one direction: up. Even my feet were icky, squishy, inside my socks and boots, and I imagined that their smell was atrocious. The stench of the tunnels was like that of a stagnant, prehistoric, alligator-filled bayou, and my footwear was attacked not only by perspiration but by occasional puddles of water like the one I'd encountered on my previous journey into this netherworld. Seeing became even more difficult as salty sweat seeped into my eyes. I rubbed at it with the back of my left hand (my right hand held the flashlight), but I might as well have been applying lye soap to my eyes. My whole body was engulfed by a clammy steam bath, an effect that I guessed a fish would experience if it had no scales.

'It's obvious that kids come down here to play,' the maintenance engineer said from behind me.

'Helluva place to play,' I replied, coming to a stop and brushing sweat off my forehead with the sleeve of my coveralls. Coming to a stop didn't involve much at our slower-than-molasses pace.

'Just thought I'd tell you,' he said, 'that I know that what the school is saying is wrong. I come down here when I have to, and I mean *only* when I have to. When something breaks down. I've been through only a tiny portion of these tunnels, but there's evidence everywhere that the students have been here. I've heard them talking, but I've never run into any of them.'

'Run?'

'You know. Crawled. Creeped.'

'You ever stay down here for long?'

'I wouldn't be here now if I had. You're in for some surprises. It gets hotter than this, of course, but we'll also hit places where it's cool. Downright cold, in fact. Like having a fever and chills at the same time. This is a good place to catch pneumonia.'

I'd turned to talk to my partner, but although he was only a few feet away, seeing him was impossible. I thought of shining the flashlight in his face, but it did not seem the polite thing to do. *Polite?* What was I thinking of, in this cross between a catacomb and a swamp? I settled on aiming the flashlight at the floor, which didn't help either of us.

'Do you think Dallas came down here?' I asked.

'He could have.'

'Think he's here now?'

'Might be.'

'Any chance we'll find him alive?'

'No.'

I didn't want to hear this. He was probably right, of course, but I still wanted desperately to believe that Dallas was alive.

We started forward again through the darkness and soon came to another of those six-of-one, half-a-dozen-of-the-other choices, a fork in the road where neither way seemed particularly promising. I tried to put myself in Dallas's shoes, to figure which way he would have gone if he had traveled this route, but there was nothing to choose between. To paraphrase former Vice President Spiro Agnew, if you've seen one tunnel, you've seen them all. I took out the map and located our position. A right turn meant we would head toward Case Hall, where Dallas had lived; a left would point us toward the driver-training facility. We went right.

Nothing had come over the walkie-talkies yet. I imagined that Riddle and his partner were close to or underneath the football stadium. That's right, I thought, Riddle is near the football stadium. There are five teams besides mine underneath this school. It really isn't important that all we've found so far is a beer can.

Now the tunnel was even more confining, and I had to bend so low to maintain progress that I developed a fierce pain in my back. Bent over almost double, I nonetheless attempted to play the flashlight's beam around so that I wouldn't miss anything. Most of the walls were caked with slime, but in a clear area I caught a glimpse of what appeared to be writing. Closer examination revealed that someone had spray-painted thirteen names on the wall, and I took note of them. (Later I learned that thirteen was the designated number for a witch's coven, and that the MSU students who dabbled in witchcraft and black masses and such read books like *The Satanic Bible*, passed around helix-shaped Egyptian bracelets, and engaged in a variety of bizarre rites that were sure to drive their parents wild.) Other searchers, I would learn, also found spray-painted messages. One of these read 'This Way to Middle Earth' and had an arrow pointing toward the floor, which indicated the presence of Dungeons & Dragons players or members of the Tolkien society.

At times pipes got in the way, and we had to slither underneath or between them in the method GIs learn in boot camp when bullets are being fired over their heads. Two forks further on, while we were still traveling in the direction of Case Hall and the temperature was ever climbing (one searcher put it at 150 degrees, though the official figure was 130), I began to wish for one of those chilly spots my partner had mentioned. I didn't know when I was well off.

We came to an intersection and I was hit by a gush of air that I thought would quick-freeze me. Imagine stepping *instantly* from an overheated sauna into a deep freeze, and you know precisely what happened. I felt as if every drop of sweat on my body had turned to ice. Actually, the temperature drop was about seventy degrees, but since it occurred so suddenly, with a mighty, unexpected whoosh of air, it was like a blow to the central nervous system. I've heard, in fact, that the phenomenon is not very different from flash-freezing, and is caused by an accumulation of cross-drafts which build up in side tunnels connecting with the main ones.

Like a fool, I stood there for a moment. Maybe I just couldn't move. I could actually feel the sweat turning to ice. I got chills and began to shake, trembling as if in the grip of a fever. I took a step back into the welcoming embrace of that 130-degree heat and felt the ice (it wasn't really ice, of course) melt off my body.

'You're right,' I said to the maintenance engineer.

'How's that?'

'I don't think anyone could live down here for long.' I didn't want to admit it, but my hope of finding Dallas alive in the tunnels had almost vanished. He simply couldn't have survived. Occasionally we shouted 'Dallas! Dallas!' as we progressed, in case he lay injured and was able to respond, but the best I could wish for was that we had been wrong, that the boy hadn't decided to die, or to play an elaborate game of hide-and-seek, in these tunnels.

I felt a grip on my shoulders and turned to see what my partner wanted. But before I was all the way around, my back was clawed and the grip was gone. It had been a rat. He had simply transferred himself from a pipe to my shoulders, then hopped down, calm as can be.

The tunnels were filled with wonders. In places we found chutes in the ceiling, chutes perhaps ten feet long, which arrowed straight up to ground level. Manholes with see-through openings covered the chutes, and there were ladders a person could climb. Besides providing ready access to or egress from the tunnels, the chutes seemed an ideal vantage point for Peeping Toms. Also we found openings in the tunnel walls through which an individual could crawl to emerge into underground rooms. These rooms, which did not appear on our maps, were cooler than the tunnels, and it was conceivable that someone who was hiding out could survive in them for a considerable time.

Getting into the rooms was hard, dirty work, accomplished on hands and knees, but it was necessary because Dallas might have gophered into one of them to hide or to die. One room, about twenty by twenty feet, was littered with empty beer cans – a good spot for a party, if you wanted an unusual ambience. Another room, the *crème de la crème*, contained a large dining table with a papier-mâché figure at the head. One could have eaten off the table, it was so clean. In this grimy maze, that could only mean that someone had been here recently. But the entrance was so small that the table couldn't have been brought into the room. It was like a ship in a bottle, except that you could not break that table into pieces. I suppose it could be considered a monument to human ingenuity, like escaping from Alcatraz, but somehow I couldn't look at it that way. The fellow who had escaped from Alcatraz, admirable as his enterprise might be, had had nothing else with which to occupy himself. Presumably the students who had maneuvered that table into that room had had some homework they could have been doing.

Crawling through filth, conscious that we might get wedged in the tube, my partner and I went through one of these holes in the tunnel wall, breathing air that would have gagged a goat, scraping flesh off our legs and palms, ever in danger from particles of dirt that might lodge in our eyes. How would we have gotten them out? Certainly no hand was free to perform that delicate task. I thought I might choke for lack of oxygen, or go into some claustrophobic fit. For the first time I was angry with Dallas. If this indeed was a game, or if he had come down here to kill himself, it was an exhibition of thoughtlessness. Why drive *me* crazy? And the other searchers?

I suspected that there was something wrong with this thinking, but in the heat and the muck of the narrow tube my brain was filled with dark clouds and my heart, like Ishmael's, was in the midst of a rainy November. I started to cough. I'd never realized how your entire body moves when you cough: a sudden violent contraction and then a series of small tremors. I found out in this tubular prison. It was as if I were breathing in a sandstorm; grains of pebbles clogged my lungs, stuck in there, and I couldn't stop coughing. I was afraid that I might cause a landslide or a cave-in as my body bumped against those suffocating walls.

Blessed light! I don't know from where the light came, and no one should imagine that the room we came upon was well illuminated – it was more like a dungeon in a medieval jail, dim, gray, and forbidding – but we could see. Remarkably, even in this faint, eerie light, my eyes still required time to adjust. I had, I realized, emerged from a place in which there was *no* light.

The room was ten by twelve feet. On the sandy floor were a milk crate, two half-gallon milk cartons (one partially filled with milk gone sour), a carton filled with cheese-and-cracker wrappings and a few unopened packages, and a blanket. Perhaps this was where students had lunch. The room with the table, upon which was a sign that read 'Please be seated, the waitress will be with you in a moment,' was clearly where they went for coat-and-tie dinners.

But this room did not seem to be a joke. Why the blanket? It seemed to me that only one person had come here, and it looked as if that person had intended to stay a while. No one needed a blanket in the tunnels; he might in this cooler room, if he meant to spend time here. This could be just the place to which Dallas the Loner would have fled. A setup as elaborate as the room with the table probably would have been out-of-bounds for him, since groups generally shunned him. In that room – the Room with the Table that Couldn't Be There – it was possible to imagine infinite varieties of sinister occult gatherings. In the room where the maintenance engineer and I stood, I could more easily imagine a confused and frightened Dallas, crouching alone with his cheese-and-crackers and milk and blanket, hiding from a world that neither understood him nor wanted him.

Retracing your steps is generally not as difficult as making the journey in the first place, a point I've made earlier in this book. But not always. A psychological factor comes into play. If the original journey was so unpleasant, so unpalatable, that it grows in your mind, you never want to travel that route again. So it was with me. I never wanted to go through that tubelike tunnel again, choking, gasping for breath, powerless against a cave-in. What about encountering a rat in that tiny tube? There was no possibility of fighting one off. A rat could feast on my face and I wouldn't dare to lift a hand to defend myself. Once again I cursed Dallas. I was reminded of police officers I'd known who had investigated suicides. Not being completely untruthful, they'd say that people had the right to kill themselves, but they didn't have the right to make a mess that others had to clean up. But try as I might, I couldn't build up much of a head of steam against Dallas. Whatever his fate, it had been determined for him by others.

Almost anything – a shootout with desperate criminals, for example, or a vacation in the Ayotollah's Iran – seemed more appetizing than a return trip through that tube, except the alternative, which was staying where I was. I thought of crawling out backward, but quickly discarded the idea as absurd. In the end I thought about being at my condominium on the beach in Florida, cool water spraying my body, damsels in bikinis cavorting on the sand; locking out everything else, I slithered on my stomach like a snake through that wretched hole in the wall.

Obviously, I did not find nirvana at the other end. The maintenance engineer and I were back in those 130-degree tunnels, engulfed in darkness, moving like snails and crouching like apes. While we continued our search we found plenty of graffiti on the walls, as did the other search teams. Spray-painted, written in crayon or chalk, or merely finger-traced into the dust, the graffiti concentrated on three subjects; obscenity (and some was in truly bad taste, even to these jaded eyes,) drug use, and directions (probably for Dungeons & Dragons players). One artist of not inconsiderable talent had done a pencil-and-ink drawing of a train which might have been the old Empire Builder, which ran between Chicago and the West Coast.

We also found prophylactics, tennis-shoe prints on pipes (no sense at all to this), remnants of marijuana joints ('J. W. smoked here' written nearby), one boot, several jackets, and a whistle. In places the slime on the walls was green. I could hear a *drip, drip, drip* almost constantly, a Chinese water-torture to my brain, but I could never locate the noise. It was not difficult to figure out that sound carried a long distance in the tunnels. I could hear the steam rushing through the pipes, too, like an unseen, hurrying train – a phantom, I thought, with no substance.

At each intersection we checked our map by the flashlight's beam, trying to take the turn that led us closer to Case Hall. In readily agreeing to travel this route, I had remembered that Dallas had not been seen after his luncheon date with Karen Coleman in Case Hall. Perhaps he had never left the building, but had gone straight into the tunnels from the dorm.

This thought was on my mind as I crept through the heat and the dark when suddenly, quick as a trap sprung on a grizzly's paw, *Sssssssssssssss!* I leapt backward, cracking my head on the ceiling and almost falling on my spine at my partner's feet. My face felt as if had been attacked by a blowtorch, and my mind ceased to function.

'Pressure-control release,' the maintenance engineer said.

Thanks a lot, I thought. I had identified it much more quickly this go-round.

'It hurt me a lot when it happened to me,' he added.

Hurt *him* a lot? He hadn't been touched. My face felt as if the skin had been burned completely off.

I calmed down as quickly as I could. My partner had just been trying to be supportive, to say that he understood what I'd gone through; it had happened to him before. Though I was able to identify the cause of the shock, my mind was still reeling more than a minute after the event. And my body: it was like having a vibrator inside.

I gradually calmed down, and we continued. The

conditions grew nothing but worse. The oppressive heat sapped the mind and the spirit. I became debilitated. I would have thought my reaction to the heat would be to want to get out of it, but instead I experienced sleepiness, a weary acceptance, a languid, deadening calm that I had to fight determinedly. I was tempted to lie in one of those dank, putrid pools of water, covered with sweat, and simply nod off to sleep. We had to cope with physical exhaustion even to a greater degree than, say, a professional football player or boxer does. Such athletes are pumping adrenalin, and the blows they absorb, fearful as they are, hurt the most the next day. I know one of the stars of the Dallas Cowboys, who tells me that he feels the real pain when he wakes up the morning after a game, because the effect of the adrenalin protects him until then. Of course, adrenalin was the last thing we needed. We needed patience, persistence, concentration, the stamina to go a long distance (even though it was a short one).

Besides, no football player or boxer ever competed under such conditions. There were climate changes, and not just when we ran into one of those icy blasts of air. The stupefying heat could be both dry and wet, but no one should believe that one was preferable to the other. The dry heat fried the skin and the brain, while the wet heat parboiled them. The dry heat featured dust, whereas anyone who is into slime and stagnant water would prefer the wet.

In the dark our eyes simply could not function, no matter how 'accustomed' they became to the blackness, and I wished my nose could experience a similar malfunction. Think of snakes and alligators and swamps, and you understand the wet heat; or the tombs of pharaohs, and buildings so old and long unoccupied that they crumble to dust at the touch of a finger, or a musty mortuary, and you have the dry heat. Breathing was terribly difficult at all times, but in places the supercharged air scorched the membranes of my nostrils.

Hunger was no problem. Who wants to eat on the hottest day in history? Thirst was another matter. I would have paid a generous price for a drink of cool water, which I had foolishly neglected to bring. The other teams carried water and we had talked about needing it; inexplicably, I'd forgotten. So had my partner, but his job did not require assiduous planning and attention to detail. You're some supersleuth, I told myself.

Increasingly I found myself stopping and studying the map, to see how much farther we needed to go. At the beginning I had stopped only at intersections, but now I didn't require a legitimate excuse to take a break from our inch-by-inch search. I wonder now if being tired – I mean pass-out-and-sleep-for-two-days tired – is, like adrenalin, a deadener of pain, for although I didn't know it, I was injured, and the injury was growing worse by the moment.

I knew we were getting close to escaping this oven, and I had to caution myself not to be less careful. No law said that Dallas couldn't be hiding or lying dead near one of the tunnel entrances. I remembered the case of the Collyer brothers, many years before. Known as the Hermits of Harlem, they were rich recluses, who rarely left their fortresslike mansion. These rich whites lived in the largest black ghetto in the world, and in the course of some twenty years had made their home impenetrable with a mind-numbing collection of junk. Bales of newspapers and other useless items of garbage made it impossible to get inside or to move around if somehow anyone did get inside. There was even a Model-T Ford in the mansion, and the place was booby-trapped. When it became evident that the Collyer brothers had died in the house, it took a large contingent of police and firefighters *five days* to find the bodies. They were only a few feet from a main entrance to the home.

So I forced myself to creep forward, playing the beam of the flashlight on every square inch of walls, floor, and ceiling. Periodically we found graffiti and litter, but nothing I could point to and say, 'Hey, that proves Dallas was here,' or 'Look, a clue telling us he took the first turn north.'

Without the map it would have been impossible to tell how much ground we were covering. When this night was over, the maintenance engineer and I had gone about half a mile. So had each of the other five teams. Three miles of tunnels. There were eight and a half miles in all. We would have to come back – a fact we'd realized from the start but hadn't wanted to talk about. It was better to keep up our spirits and believe we'd find Dallas on the first trip. To be careful, to search every inch, we had to believe that the crucial clue, or Dallas himself, was just the next step away. Being meticulous was all-important, especially if this were a game. Any clues the young genius might have left would not be so obvious that a searcher would simply trip over them. But of course this same factor indicated that we would not succeed on our first foray.

The maintenance engineer and I were the last team out of the tunnels. We emerged at about 11 P.M., after four and a quarter hours underground, through unlocked double doors into the basement of Case Hall, where Dallas had lived – exactly the spot we had tried to hit by following the map. This by itself, I thought, was no minor accomplishment, given the bewildering number of turns, read by the beam of a flashlight by men whose brains were not 100 per cent functioning because of the oppressive heat.

It was quite dark in the basement, but after the tunnels

it was like emerging into a bright noonday sun. My eyes smarted in light I can best describe as very dim. What we did next was curious, and I can only call it the act of a compulsive person. *We searched the basement.* If we'd been in Mother Teresa's bedroom, we probably would have searched that. We'd grown accustomed to searching.

We then got out of Case Hall as fast as we could. We didn't want to scare some student half to death. After my first, much briefer excursion into the tunnels, I had resembled one of Genghis Khan's soldiers after thirty days of desert pillaging; I suspected I looked much less pretty now.

Outside, on the lawn, we radioed over the walkie-talkie and were told that a maintenance truck would pick us up. The temperature, in the middle sixties, felt just wonderful, and I breathed deeply this fine, clean air. Knowing that my newfound night vision couldn't last, I wanted to see as much as I could, and I concentrated (wisely, I believe) on the marvelous, shimmering heavens. Then I realized I'd been hurt. The snaps on my coveralls had become so heated in the tunnels that they had burned through my inner clothing, leaving angry red outlines on my chest. It was the equivalent of being branded; the marks of the coverall snaps were as precise and defined as any ranch's brand. They hurt like the devil, too. It seemed incredible that I hadn't been aware of the pain while I'd been in the tunnels.

We were driven to campus police headquarters, where we learned that everybody had been waiting for us; there had even been talk of sending a team in to find us. Searching for the searchers . . . I drank an ice-cold Coke and listened as each team talked of their experiences in the tunnels. Everyone spoke about the evidence that the tunnels – those inaccessible tunnels – had been extensively used, by students and perhaps others. Lieutenant Michael Rice, Lambert's partner, pointed out that 'several entrances have been discovered broken into in the past.' Maybe so. But why break in? You could just walk in and go wherever you wanted to go. Said another searcher, Sergeant Ted Glynn, 'One good thing that will come out of this is I'm sure the university will put some big money into security down there.' I sincerely hope that this happened; it probably was necessary after our search. But even if security was tightened, the doors were locked after many of the horses were stolen.

Most alarming was the fact that, as Carol Morello soon reported in the *Lansing State Journal*, 'the unlighted tunnels provide easy access to dormitories, the medical center and offices.' I've often let that roll around in my head. Jack the Ripper could have been loose at Michigan State University, and the students would have had virtually no protection from him. There had been unsolved rapes on the campus. Just as I believed that the Egberts were thinking of suing the school, so too it seemed that the rape victims had a case. I do not believe that many homeowners would purchase a residence where security could be breached by any maniac or felon who simply decided to walk through an unlocked door. Surely students in a dormitory have the same right to safety as any homeowner. But because those tunnels provided heat for the entire school, there probably wasn't a building on the MSU campus that was secure.

Just as shocking was the easy access to the medical center. Michigan State University is a large, rich, well-funded institution, yet parents had reason to worry that dangerous drugs could be stolen and sold or given away. Several thefts had indeed occurred at the medical center. The crimes had baffled the police. They didn't seem at all baffling to me.

I used to teach police courses, and one point I

emphasized was the desirability and necessity of locks. 'A lock will stop an honest person,' I liked to say, for its attention-getting value. The truth is that most people won't fiddle with a locked door. They figure that they are not meant to be on the other side, and let it go at that. But if a door is unlocked, many of us will look inside. Imagine a door leading into a bank vault; even citizens of high integrity might be tempted to scoop up some money. The urge is even stronger for someone with a drug habit, if he knows that what he craves is there for the taking. Of course, MSU needed security measures besides locks, especially around dormitories, medical facilities, and other 'sensitive' buildings, but these amounted to nothing more than reasonable precautions. Football was a big money-maker at MSU; I was willing to wager that people did not find it so easy to sneak into a football game.

After our discussion about what we'd found in the tunnels, we again studied the schematics of the maze and determined which sections of the underground campus we would search the next night. There had been no friction between team members, so the teams would remain the same; so would the time we intended to enter the tunnels: 6:45 P.M. There was no more talk about disrupting the football crowd or hurrying to finish because of the growing influx of students.

A big contingent from the media was present in the police-station lobby when we emerged from the conference room. Ferman Badgley answered most of the questions, and Riddle, Hock, Lambert, and I returned to the Red Roof Inn, cleaned up (a major undertaking), and then found an all-night diner that served bacon and eggs. Even the feisty, ever-ready-for-action Lambert confessed to being exhausted.

'Do you think Dallas is down there?' Hock asked.

'I think he's been down there,' I said. 'And since he disappeared.'

'But not now?' Riddle said.

'Not now. God knows where he is now.'

Chapter 15

I was alone in my room the next morning, September 7, at ten o'clock, thinking about Dungeons & Dragons, the tunnels, the corkboard map, and, for the thousandth time, about whether we were on the right track. I had almost eight hours to kill before going back into the tunnels. I no longer had enthusiasm for this prospect, though logic told me we hadn't even covered half of them. For some reason – an inexplicable mood change – I did not think we would find Dallas in that nightmarish maze, and I was trying to decide what track to follow next.

At that point the telephone rang. 'This is Western Union. We have a telegram for James Egbert. Dr. Egbert asked that we read it to you.'

Dallas's first name was James. For a moment I thought the telegram might be for him, then I realized it was for Dr. Egbert. It had been sent to him in Dayton and he'd wanted me to hear it. I told the Western Union operator to go ahead:

> I HAVE BEEN ALERTED TO THE STORY OF YOUR SON'S DISAPPEARANCE BECAUSE OF MY EXPERT KNOWLEDGE OF DUNGEONS AND DRAGONS AND OTHER FANTASY ROLE PLAYING GAMES. MYSELF AND MY ASSOCIATES WOULD LIKE TO OFFER OUR ASSISTANCE, AS WE SINCERELY BELIEVE WE ARE AUTHORITIES IN THIS FIELD. WILL FLY TO YOUR LOCATION IMMEDIATELY AT

OUR EXPENSE IF YOU ARE RECEPTIVE TO
OUR OFFER. WE ARE NOT OVERLY
CONCERNED WITH ANY REWARD OR
REIMBURSEMENT, BUT SINCERELY FEEL
WE COULD HELP. PLEASE CONTACT ME
IMMEDIATELY.
CLIFF PEROTTI
PLAYING BOARD PRODUCTS
PLEASANT HILL, CA

Why not? I thought. My own methods hadn't cracked the case, and it wouldn't hurt to talk to someone else. I found myself dialling Cliff Perotti's number in California.

When I got Perotti, I explained that Dr. Egbert had had his telegram forwarded to me. 'I'm the private investigator handling the Dallas Egbert disappearance.'

'I know who you are, Mr. Dear,' he replied. 'I'm an admirer of yours. I'm familiar with some of your investigations.'

'I see you're willing to offer your services. Let me get this straight. From your telegram you say you're an expert at Dungeons & Dragons. Is this correct?'

'It is.'

'Mr. Perotti, I need to know some things about you. I've had numerous offers of assistance. I can only use someone who might truly be able to help me understand what we're dealing with here. Publicity-seekers aren't wanted. But I'm willing to work with anyone whose motivation is sincere.'

'Oh, I'm sincere, Mr. Dear,' Perotti explained. 'I coauthored a book titled *The Spellcaster's Bible*. I'm an expert on Dungeons & Dragons and other games that involve fantasy role-playing.'

'Mr. Perotti, how old are you?' He sounded very young to me. Not immature. Just young.

'I'm nineteen, but I've been playing those games for years. Largely, that's been my whole life. I really am an expert. And I can relate to Dallas Egbert, not just because I'm young but because I'm fascinated with D & D. I know you have doubts about me at this point, but I assure you that we could work together well. I hope you accept. You must have tried to understand the game, and the mind of Dallas Egbert, and I think I can assist you to do both.'

'I don't know,' I said. 'I don't –'

'Mr. Dear, I run my own company. It's small but successful. I'm author of a published book.'

'We can't afford to pay you. Or any of your expenses.'

'I don't expect to be paid. I'll come at my own expense.'

'Why?'

'The case intrigues me. If this is a game of Dungeons & Dragons, it could be the best ever played. The Super Bowl of Dungeons & Dragons. I want to be part of it. And to tell you the truth, I see a lot of Dallas in myself.'

Gillitzer had said the same thing. I believed there were probably a lot of people who identified with Dallas in this quiet year, a year that closed out the 'Me Decade.' Dallas, who was ahead of his time as far as computers went, was a victim of the prevailing attitude. The care-for-your-neighbor sixties, with its rampant idealism, had turned into the look-out-for-yourself seventies, and except for Dallas's parents and a few scattered acquaintances, no one had tried to guide the boy's potential intelligently. I thought of James Dean and *Rebel Without a Cause*, a commentary on *my* generation, and believed that Dallas had experienced something of the same alienation.

'Well,' I said to Perotti, 'how do I know you won't be in the way? I don't have time to hold your hand, to babysit.'

'I'm a self-starter. I've told you, I have a young company. I don't mean to brag, but my intelligence quotient is quite high.'

I had to admit that Perotti might be able to help, for the reasons he had given. And I liked the way he sounded on the telephone: sincere, bright, and persistent. Still, I had to be careful.

'Mr. Perotti, some ground rules would have to be laid down before we can even begin.'

'I'll agree to anything you say.'

'Just hold your horses. Now, if you came, I'd be totally responsible for your actions. I could be sued. I've worked extremely hard to get where I am, and I have quite a bit to lose. It's impossible to describe how upset I'd be if that were endangered, which could happen if you barged in here like some rogue elephant. With that in mind, are you willing to come here, at your own expense, and put yourself completely under my direction?'

'Of course.'

'Mr. Perotti, I don't want you buying a pack of cigarettes without checking with me.'

'I don't smoke.'

'Good. But you get the idea. You don't do anything unless you first ask me.'

'Agreed.'

'You're not to pose as a private investigator. You'll identify yourself only as an expert on role-playing games. You're a consultant, no more. And don't expect to be privileged to any information I might have. The police are very touchy about this, and so am I.'

'Mr. Dear, I meant it when I said I'd do whatever you asked.'

'In your telegram you talk about associates. I don't want to hear about associates. You come alone. By yourself.'

'I'll be there as soon as I can get a flight.'

I hung up, thinking that if the tunnel search continued

to be disappointing, we probably would have to concentrate on what might be called the Dungeons & Dragons community. We'd had such little luck in this area because no one wanted to risk expulsion (or in the case of professors, termination) by admitting that they had played a real-life version of the game in the tunnels. Perotti might be able to infiltrate that community.

It was good to have a few moments to think. Fully clothed, I lay back down on the bed and stared at the ceiling, trying to make my mind go blank. I had to absorb what I'd learned in the tunnels the previous night. It would be easy enough simply to recall the hellish conditions and overlook whatever clues we might have uncovered. Certainly the most sensational of our discoveries was the room with the table set for four, the table that couldn't be there but was. What odd purpose had that room served? Something to do with occult rituals? A place to summon the devil? The devil would sure as hell be at home in the Michigan State netherworld of tunnels.

But I didn't *feel* Dallas in that room; he had been in the other room, the smaller one. I could picture him there. I'd known his fear and confusion, and the terrible sense of loneliness. He had crouched in that little underground room with his milk, cheese-and-crackers, and security blanket. What I didn't know was whether he had gone there to hide or to die. To hide, probably. Otherwise, why take the food?

This really was a remarkable little reverie. It was so clear to me. I was up above Dallas and to his front, looking right down on him. His shoulders were hunched, his chin was on his chest, his knees met his chin, and thick tears trickled down his cheeks. He was a very small boy anyway, but he appeared even tinier wound into a ball. I could have picked him up as I might pick up a kitten.

The waking dream was broken by the ringing telephone.

'Don Gillitzer, Bill.'

'What do you have?' I asked.

'I've been in bathhouses, private clubs, places you wouldn't believe. *I* don't believe some of them. I've been tested more than once. I was right when I said you wouldn't have passed muster.'

'I believed you. And I appreciate what you've done. But I need some good news. Give me some.'

'All I can tell you is that I think something is going on. It's scary, in fact. I try to be discreet, of course, but in the end the subject of Dallas Egbert has to come up. When it does, I've had several people just turn to stone. Faces harden. Teeth clench. No matter how friendly the person might have been with me, he suddenly grows cold, and I become a pariah.'

'Maybe they think we're trying to make the gay community a scapegoat.'

'It's much more than that. It's as though they possess dangerous knowledge and could be in big trouble. No, what I'm seeing is *personal* fright.'

'If we don't find Dallas in the tunnels, do you think there's a chance he's being held somewhere in the East Lansing area?'

'Bill, I think what started off as a game in the tunnels led to something much more serious.'

'Don't just leave it at that,' I said. '*Why* do you feel that way?'

'If Dallas was depressed, and if he went into the tunnels – and I believe both of these are true – then he decided to kill himself, I'd guess. It might have started out as a game, some excitement to relieve his depression, but when this failed, he turned to suicide. Somehow he botched the suicide. It happens. Confused, drugged-up, hurt, he must have come out of the tunnels. He could have been picked up by a chicken hawk, or gone to one for help.'

'A chicken hawk – an older man who uses young boys.'

'Right. Where else would he turn if he were superdepressed? I think he'd figure that a chicken hawk would help.'

'Say that did happen. What would follow?'

'Straights have plenty of rotten apples too.'

'I know that. Don't make me give my be-fair-to-everybody credentials.'

'Well, say he was depressed and on drugs. The man who held him might keep him on drugs in order to take sexual advantage of him. Bill, this sort of thing can happen. We don't like it any more than straights like sexual abuse of small children.'

'You base this guess on reactions to your probing. But wouldn't the older man go to great lengths to conceal what was happening? You say that several people have given you the cold shoulder when the subject comes up.'

'He might not. Dallas is a treasure. It could be like stealing a great painting. You want to show it to someone – it's not enough just to keep it for yourself.'

'I can agree that anyone with knowledge of this might want to keep his own part quiet. Especially if the knowledge turned into criminal involvement.'

'I know there are people out there with information. Nothing else explains the glacial hostility I encounter when Dallas Egbert is mentioned.'

I had a decision to make, and it was a tough one. Literally it could mean life or death. I decided to test my thoughts on Gillitzer. 'Let me talk for a minute,' I said. 'You listen. My first concern is to find Dallas alive. I'm wondering, if he is being held, what the effect of our constant pressure will be. Will we get the boy killed, or will it lead to his release? Will our deliberate effort to make possible informants uneasy – hell, to scare them to death – help bring them forward, or will it have the opposite effect? Maybe they'll start thinking that the chief witness should be silenced. And there's another aspect: if Dallas comes to his senses, assuming he's been drugged, and sees the fuss being made over him, might that not have a healthy effect? He could tell that people really do care, and this could encourage him to escape or get word to us in some way.'

'You're saying you have two choices,' Gillitzer said. 'Ease up, or turn the pressure up a couple more notches. The answer seems obvious to me.'

'Tell me.'

'Pressure. And more pressure. It's already there – the newspapers aren't going to go away. The police can't be reined in at this point. The press and the police are givens over which you have no control, and don't think there won't be others. Legitimate private investigators, but vigilante types too. These might stumble on something. You know better than anyone the role luck can play. Sure, you do the groundwork and you're more likely to be lucky, but flashes from the blue aren't that unusual either. The point is, others who come into this case, whether they're invited or not, aren't going to have the same concern for Dallas that you do. And for that reason they could be more dangerous to him.'

'I have to agree with you. I'd like you to continue what you've been doing, but take the gloves off. You don't have to be circumspect.'

'I can only help where the doors don't continually get slammed shut in my face.'

'You know what I need, and you know best how to get it. If the answers to Dallas's disappearance are in the gay community, I'm depending to a great extent on you to find them. I don't want you hurt. If you learn anything concrete, don't act on it. Come to me. I have the experience to handle situations that can get rough. But about taking the gloves off: if you run into someone whom you think is withholding information, and you don't think you're in any danger, open up on him. Tell him that this is no tea party. Tell him that he'll learn what real trouble is when the case is solved.'

'Okay,' Gillitzer agreed. 'I do think we might get a break pretty soon.'

'From now on, call me once a day, will you? In the morning. Call even if you don't have anything.'

After the talk with Gillitzer I buzzed the motel's front desk and asked about messages. For the past few days I'd let them accumulate, answering only those I thought might provide leads, and now I was just shocked by what the desk clerk said: 'There are hundreds and hundreds of them, Mr. Dear.'

I hadn't heard a complaint from anyone connected with the motel, yet it was clear that my business of detecting had superseded the Red Roof Inn's business of innkeeping. I think everyone connected with that motel was quietly cheering for us; the staff had become concerned about Dallas, as if he were a member of their immediate families. I reminded myself not to forget those presents from Nieman-Marcus when the case was concluded. Calls that should be getting through were getting through, and the ones I couldn't bother with were being held. Even though Captain Badgley's men were now handling calls previously routed to me from police headquarters, I thought the really important calls would still come to us. Hundreds and hundreds. It made me feel good about the American people. The same feelings I had about the missing boy were shared by countless others; the ones who called were merely the iceberg's tip.

There was one phone call I should make. I liked the Egberts, and I could empathize with them, but I hated to talk with them. I wished I could call them just once and say, 'Hey, I've got Dallas sitting right next to me. He's safe and he'll be home soon.' But to call and tell them I wasn't getting anywhere? One of the most dangerous jobs of police work is going out to a place like Central Park in New York City with the idea of getting mugged (hoping that your backups arrive in time to prevent serious injury or death), but I believe I would have preferred that assignment to having to tell the Egberts that there was still no end in sight to their ordeal.

'I read where you didn't find anything encouraging in the tunnels,' Anna Egbert said when I got through to Dayton. Usually I talked with her.

'Don't worry,' I replied. 'We're not giving up. We're going to find Dallas.'

'I thought he was in the tunnels,' she said. 'I think he *was* in there. But not anymore. This isn't a game.'

'I agree with you.' And it was good to hear what she had said. I'd come to the same conclusion, but I knew a mother would understand her son better than I ever could.

'I hate to see everything being brought out into the open,' she continued.

'I'm sorry,' I said. She was talking about homosexuality and drugs. It was too bad that these things had come out, but preventing it, given the attention the case had received, was impossible. 'There are piles and piles of messages here,' I continued, 'from all over the country, and from foreign nations too. People care. They're thinking of you and Jim, and especially of Dallas. They're praying for all of you. I think you should take great comfort from that.'

'But what are you going to do next? What *can* you do next?'

'We're going back into the tunnels this evening.'

'Dallas isn't there.'

'I believe you. Our intuitions tell us that's the case. But intuition can be wrong. There's good reason why judges and juries won't accept it as evidence. We have to go down there. We have to search the tunnels thoroughly.'

'Keep me informed of how you're doing,' Anna said.

'I will,' I replied. 'You just maintain your strength.'

'Find him soon, Bill.'

It was one o'clock by now, less than six hours before tunnel time, and I decided to ask Riddle and Hock if they wanted to have lunch. They would be resting in their rooms, on call in case there was something that needed to be done. There was no need to ask Lambert; he was always hungry.

'Almost anything I can think of,' I said when we were munching sandwiches, 'beats going back into those catacombs.'

'I've heard of people being hypnotized to stop smoking,' said Riddle, for whom such a course might be a good idea, 'and sometimes even the thought of cigarettes makes them sick. I feel the same way about the tunnels. I get sick just thinking about them.'

'I've never dreamed about hell before,' Hock agreed. 'I did last night. I was up on a cliff, looking down into it. The heat was terrific. I knew that it was the last place anyone ever wanted to be.'

'I kind of like the tunnels,' Lambert said. He was staring at his plate, chewing his ham-and-cheese sandwich. Slowly his head and eyes came up and met mine.

'You *like* them?' Lambert, for all his virtues, is not known for a wry sense of humor.

'Sure.' He took another bite of his sandwich.

A friend once told me that if you looked hard enough, you could find anything – a southerner who likes General Sherman, a black who admires the Ku Klux Klan, a public utility company that has a heart. I guess my friend was right. I looked at Lambert. He was trying to catch the attention of our waitress. Another sandwich?

'Why don't you ever get fat?' I asked.

'I exercise a lot.' He did indeed order another sandwich. 'I was out exercising this morning. Enjoying the campus. Football weekend, and all that.' He'd probably been walking with a girl friend. 'Called on some people I made friends with while I was playing Joe College. They had a piece of information about Dallas. Probably isn't important.' He was opening a packet of crackers to tide himself over until the second sandwich arrived.

'Well?'

'Dallas attended a campus theater production on August eleventh. *West Side Story*. He went with two guys named Larry Lopez and Paul Murphy. I understand they're students at MSU.'

This was four days before Dallas disappeared. Lambert was probably right, it wasn't important, but we weren't so overburdened with leads that we could afford to pass one up. 'Dick,' I said to Riddle, 'could you try to find that pair this afternoon? Go to the administration building, find out where they live?'

'It beats sitting around thinking about tonight.'

Indeed it did. I spent the afternoon in my room, sorting through that mountain of messages, answering any that seemed to show the slightest glimmer of promise. Most of them were calls from every sort of medium. The BBC wanted a transatlantic radio interview. I settled instead on a name and number in backwoods Vermont, not wanting to upset Badgley by giving a solo interview, and found myself talking to a psychic.

The tunnels that evening lived up to the billing my mind and experience had given them. If anything, they were worse. The night before the discomfort had been relieved, though slightly, by the hope that we might find the boy, by anticipation, and by a sense of newness. This night I couldn't be optimistic. The task was drudgery, pure and simple, and under horrendous conditions. The night before I had crawled on my belly through openings too small for a medium-sized dog and consoled myself that the other end might hold a clue to Dallas's whereabouts, or Dallas himself; but I didn't believe that anymore.

Whenever I think that Lambert is the sensible one, that it really wasn't as bad as I remember, I look at pictures of the openings we wriggled through and the holes we exited from. Even the surprise, the mystery on the other side, did not make it worthwhile. The thing was, we had to be just as careful the second night as we had been the first. We could not take shortcuts; tiny openings suitable for moles had to be explored. It is good to operate on Murphy's Law – that if something can go wrong, it will – or at least a variation of it: the one place you don't search is where what you're looking for will be. So we had to take the same care in East Lansing's version of Calcutta's Black Hole that second day of the search, even though most of us were without much hope.

In one sense, our determination to be thorough and precise probably paid dividends: any attempts to hurry would have been dangerous. There was a multitude of pipes to trip over or bang a head upon, plenty of slippery puddles of water serving to propel the unwary over backward. For a third time one of those pressure-release valves released pressure and scalded me. There didn't seem to be any way to avoid or anticipate these eruptions.

Once again we proved, if proof were still needed, that the tunnels led to virtually every building on campus. Want to get into a building that houses the offices of professors and thus the exams they are preparing? Use the tunnels. Interested in stealing a valuable piece of office equipment from an administrative building? Use the tunnels. Fascinated by the idea of terrorizing coeds? But the point is made.

It was after 11 P.M. when we emerged from the tunnels empty-handed. More than two-thirds of the search was complete. With relief I heard someone propose that the maintenance engineers could handle the rest, so that we detectives could get into 'more pressing' areas of the investigation the next day. As I went to sleep, again exhausted, I wondered what these more pressing areas were.

Chapter 16

'Get out of town. Get out of town, out of this state, do it right away.'

It was nine o'clock on September 8, and this was the first phone call the front desk had let through. The suggestion (for that is how it was meant to be taken) was prompted by nothing more than my standard method of beginning such conversations: 'This is Bill Dear.' The voice on the other end of the line was male, and the caller was trying to disguise his identity, perhaps with a handkerchief over the mouthpiece.

'Who is this?'

'I'd rather not tell you.'

'Be reasonable. I'm not getting out of town until this case is solved.'

'That's exactly what I'm talking about, Mr. Dear.' The tone of the voice was pleading. This was no thug making threats, but someone with a message he considered urgent. I reached over to the nightstand where my Panasonic tape recorder rested, picked up the rubber suction cup used to record conversations, and attached it to the mouthpiece of the phone. I'm not sure of the legality of this action, but it seemed to me that this might be a life-or-death matter for Dallas.

'Do you know where Dallas is?' I said.

'I can't tell you that right now. You've put a lot of pressure on a lot of people. As a result, there are people who want to talk to you but are afraid. There are too many eyes watching and ears listening.'

'What are you talking about?'

'Your telephone, for one thing. You don't think we know it's tapped? And you yourself. Surely you know you're being followed.'

I didn't think my phone was tapped. The calls came through a switchboard, which made wiretapping more difficult, and any wiretappers would have to obtain a court order. But who could be sure? It really hadn't occurred to me that I might be followed. I knew the reporters had been on my trail, but others: The police, perhaps? Someone connected with Dallas's disappearance? Whether or not I was being tailed, I should have been more alert to the possibility. I had been so singleminded in my search for the missing boy that I hadn't taken precautions that normally were second nature to me.

'If you have information about Dallas,' I said, 'we can arrange to meet in a place that I guarantee is secure. Just you and me.'

'That's my point. I don't think you can guarantee that. I'm not even sure I can trust you. But your reputation is good. You're the best hope we've got, I guess.'

'Well, you have to give me more if you expect me to leave town.'

'I hope you don't feel you're talking to a fool. I'm at a telephone booth, in case you're trying to trace this call. TV shows say you can trace a call in just a minute or so. I know this isn't true.'

'I don't think you're a fool.' He was right; it usually takes ten or fifteen minutes to trace a call, and this assumes that a highly trained crew is standing by at the phone company. 'But see my point. I've set up operations here. This is a very costly, ongoing investigation. I can't pull up stakes because of an anonymous phone call. If you're as bright as you want me to believe, you have an idea of the number and variety of cranks who've called here.'

'See *my* point. I'm afraid to talk to you while you're here. There's too much pressure. You've touched some very sensitive areas. If you were in Texas on a clear telephone line, I'd be less worried than I am. Also, it's less likely you'd betray me if you were in Texas. Not to mention that you wouldn't be so conspicuous there. Here you stand out. And more on the telephone line: surely you have equipment in Texas to assure that no phone of yours is tapped.'

'I do. But if you're so concerned, there are ways to handle this on public telephones right here in Michigan.'

'No way that will satisfy me. Don't you understand that I don't want you in Michigan when you receive this information? If you'll leave, I can assure you that you'll receive a call that might help lead to Dallas.'

'Might? That doesn't make sense. Might. I might be canonized tomorrow. I might not be.'

'Okay. Will.'

'How can I pull up my entire operation on the thin hope you might, I repeat, *might*, know something? My clients wouldn't understand this. They'd believe that I'd taken leave of my senses, getting out of Michigan, where the boy disappeared, and going back to Texas, all because of an anonymous phone call. You tell me you're no fool, and I accept that. But if you were my clients, would you buy such an explanation?'

'I know it's hard, Mr. Dear, but you've probably done stranger things than this to solve a case.'

'How do I know I'll hear from you again?'

'I want this matter resolved as much as you do. You'll understand when you get the call in Texas. Look, there's nothing more to say to you. I have to go.'

'Answer one question, just one, before you hang up? Is Dallas alive? Or am I going to be led to a dead body?'

'I can't talk to you while you're here.'

'If I do what you say, can I get in touch with you?'

'No. I told you, we'll call you in Texas.'

I heard the phone being hung up. I had sat up on my bed when the conversation began to interest me, and now I got up and began pacing slowly back and forth along the length of the room. The caller had not sounded like a crackpot. Ever since I'd come to Michigan, I'd been having plenty of experience with these; why should I believe this one? Often such people start off sounding reasonable, but if you question them about even the most peculiar point, they become hostile and defensive. This person had remained calm and apparently rational. But I knew I couldn't just up and get out of town. That would be embarrassing enough – but what if I had to come back? Supersleuth as superstooge. What the caller had suggested simply was not sound procedure, not that it mattered. The object was to find Dallas, not to go by the book. I'd never seen 'the book,' anyway. I think it is something created for television police melodramas, like the concept that phone calls can be traced in thirty seconds.

I tried to get a mental picture, a fix, on my caller. It was difficult, because he had altered his voice by whatever he held over the mouthpiece. He could be any age from college age all the way up to forty, but I didn't think he was any student. He had talked about 'we,' which bolstered my own impression that more than one person was aware of Dallas's whereabouts. The caller might be a renegade from some group that was holding Dallas, or hiding him. Most important, he was either a very good actor or genuinely scared – of the police, probably. He didn't want the police involved, and somehow he figured that this was less likely if the person solving the case was far away in Texas. I supposed it made a sort of convoluted sense.

I wished Gillitzer would call. He had promised to be in touch at least once a day, and I thought he might have a clue to my caller's identity. Maybe Gillitzer's activities had sparked the phone call; the man's statement that I had 'touched some very sensitive areas' might mean that Gillitzer had carried out my instructions to increase the pressure and that this had brought results. As it was, I had no temptation to leave Michigan. Not after one conversation with an anonymous caller. I was more interested in the remainder of the tunnel search and a hunting expedition of my own.

I called Riddle, Lambert, and Hock. Today was the opening of the Michigan State University football season, a Big Ten game at home, against Illinois, and I told Lambert and Hock to mingle with the crowd and see what, if anything, was being said about Dallas. On a festive occasion tongues might be a little looser; my men might gather gossip, or even hard information. Riddle and I would spend the whole day sightseeing. I'd decided that I could best spend this Saturday in leisurely driving the streets of East Lansing, hoping to find that red Vega whose woman driver had several times been seen in the vicinity of my room. The woman's persistence interested me. She evidently had something that she considered important to say. Crackpots often will keep coming back, but their behavior is unpredictable and erratic. This woman, on the other hand, might simply not know how to give me her message.

Some 70,000 people were expected to pack the big stadium for the game, so while it was still possible to move, Riddle and I drove around campus in one of the Mercury Monarchs we'd brought from Texas. 'Beat

Illinois' banners were everywhere, and brightly dressed, fresh-eyed students lounged on lawns before hiking to the arena, where we could hear the band warming up.

'What about Lopez and Murphy?' I asked Riddle.

'They're away from campus. At home. I'm trying to reach them.'

'Keep after them. I doubt whether they can give us much, but just about anything will be more than we have.'

The search on campus was already depressing me. The sheer number of cars made me think of needles in haystacks. It was like a nightmare, and my mind spun as I thought of the improbability of finding anything on such a day. The cars resembled a giant disorganized army, and in the chaos I had to find one lone red Vega. I was a tiny ant staring at a thousand-foot cliff I had to scale.

We did our best. We spotted several red Vegas, but I knew immediately that none of them was the one we were looking for. I had a picture of the car in my mind, and I thought I would recognize it if I saw it.

Clearly, Michigan State University was valuable for training technicians for the food industry. There was a food science building, an agricultural engineering building, a packaging building, a pesticide research building. I could understand why there was a Kellogg Center on campus, but I was not certain of the connection with names such as Kresge and Fairchild. We cruised Dormitory Road: Phillips Hall, Snyder Hall, Baker Hall, Berkey Hall. We went to the other side of the campus, skirting the football stadium, to the area of WKAR-TV and the Spartan Nursery and the faculty apartments.

We headed east on West Shaw Lane, by the fire station, and got caught in one of those traffic snarls we'd tried to avoid. The game was about to start, and I felt a stab of nostalgia, remembering college games I'd attended in Florida. I still regularly attend the Dallas Cowboys games at Texas Stadium, but the crowds that watch the pros are different from the youthful, carefree bands. Even the cheering is different. The people who attend the pro games have grown up, alas; they know it is all a business, a big business. There's no spontaneous yet organized cheering at Texas Stadium. College ball at Michigan State is big business too, but only the old and cynical view it that way.

We turned north on Chestnut Road, going by the track field, which was right alongside the stadium. The game started. We listened to it on the car radio. We could hear bursts of applause and long, rolling waves of noise like thunder. I could almost feel the huge arena rocking with sound, the foundations shaking as 70,000 people stomped their feet and roared themselves hoarse.

'It would be something,' said Riddle, 'if Dallas were at the game.'

It would be something, wouldn't it? 'He wasn't interested in football.'

'He might show up anyway. If he's playing a game. He might be real confident by now. He'd have reason to be, with us reduced to finding one car out of maybe one hundred thousand. And that car maybe leading to a screwball.'

'He's not at the game.' But what a stunt, if he were. Showing up right in front of 70,000 people. I tried to put the thought out of my mind. If this disappearance was a hoax, I promised, I'd get into another line of work. I just couldn't be so wrong about the case, about the boy.

'Well, he might be,' Riddle persisted. 'What do we know about geniuses?'

'You just want to see the football game.' Riddle loves football, but I knew that wasn't the reason he was talking the way he was.

'Sure, I wouldn't mind seeing the game,' he said. 'This

is frustrating, and you know it. We're not getting anywhere. The tunnels were our main hope, and after that experience I could use some relaxation. But I say he might be at the game because he just might be. We can't eliminate the possibility of a hoax. But it would have become boring by now. We're not giving Dallas any competition. He might feel he has to create suspenseful situations.'

'This isn't a hoax, Riddle. It might have been at the beginning, but not anymore.'

We wound our way through the campus to Harrison Road and slowly cruised north. I imagined that if there were an alert Citizens Crime Watch in East Lansing, we'd soon be discussing our purposes with a cop. That was all right. We were breaking no laws in getting acquainted with this typical college town.

Riddle drove and I looked. Past endless rows of houses that I barely noticed. My eyes searched the driveways, and the curbs in front, where cars were parked. Up Harrison Road, down Center Street, up Beal. I hadn't prayed in the tunnels. Now I did. We needed help. Our investigation was nearly stymied, and we were fast running out of sensible things to do. Fortunately, I thought, it was unlikely that my mystery visitor was a student. The brief glimpse I'd had of her did not imprint 'student' on my mind. Worker, maybe, or housewife.

Down Lotus, up Delta, down Evergreen. East Lansing seemed to me a station-wagon town. Los Angeles was sports cars; Dallas, pickup trucks and Cadillacs. You could usually tell a Dallas pickup truck by the gun rack in the back.

Division Street. Collingwood Drive. Stoddart Avenue. The football game came to an end: Michigan State 33, Illinois 16. The MSU hero was a kicker named Morten Anderson who booted four field goals and three extra points. The radio announcer said that MSU would be a definite contender for the Big Ten championship. Good. I hoped the school made a lot of money. Maybe some of it could be used to start an outstanding program for gifted youngsters. If Dallas was dead, maybe Michigan State could name the program after him.

Then I saw it. All the way up a long driveway, next to a two-story white frame house with an attic, not far from a big lawn in need of a manicure and a lovely, gracious old oak tree in the lawn's center, was the red Vega. This sturdy, middle-class, Middle American neighborhood wasn't where I'd expected to find the car. I'd expected something more rundown, seedier. A drug haunt perhaps, or an off-campus house rented by students.

'Stop at the end of the block,' I told Riddle.

'You sure that's the car?'

'No. Yes. I don't know. It looks like the car. It wasn't very light when I saw it. I always thought I'd remember it if I saw it again. Something clicked in my mind when I saw that car.'

By parking at the end of the block, we could see if anyone left in the red Vega and keep track of whoever visited the house, yet we would be unnoticed. An old-fashioned stakeout. I hate old-fashioned stakeouts. If you are tired, they are okay as long as you have managed to master the difficult trick of awakening from a doze at the first sign of activity. The problem is that many investigators *think* they can wake up but can't. Also, how can you be sure you always do wake up? If you don't, it is impossible to know it. And stakeouts are about as exciting as reading the list of ingredients on a box of cereal, with one difference: the reading might stimulate you to get angry when you learn that the chief ingredient in the cereal is sugar. What you can anticipate in a spur-of-the-moment stakeout such as this one is a visit from the police.

A resident spots a car with two men sitting in it and telephones the law. A patrol car cruises past. The license number is transmitted to headquarters and from there to the National Crime Information Computer. Our car would be clean, but because it bore Texas plates, the police would come back and chat with us – a sure guarantee that we'd draw unwanted attention.

'You sure that's the right car?' Riddle said again.

I wished he'd stop pestering me. 'As sure as I can be.'

'You didn't get the license number?'

'It was dark.' I was supposed to be the boss. Why was *he* questioning *me*?

'There are a lot of red Vegas.'

'Look, I say that's a car we should be watching.'

But nothing happened. The red Vega wasn't driven away; no one visited the house. Dusk turned to dark. Riddle had sentimental 1950s music on the radio and it was driving me crazy.

'I'll show you,' I said. I got out of the car and strode purposefully toward the white frame house. I knocked on the door with authority, ears cocked for the sounds of suspicious activity inside.

'What can I do for you?' The woman was sixty-five, gray-haired, and wore glasses. She was not my mystery woman. Dressed in a blue housecoat and wearing a white shawl over her shoulders, she reminded me of my mother.

'That your red Vega in the driveway?'

'Why, yes, it is.'

'Anyone else drive the car?'

'Oh, no.'

I find it amazing how most people will answer questions. I wouldn't answer questions from someone who looked and acted like me. I guess most people are just nice.

'You never let anyone drive your car?'

'No one ever asks. What do you want, young man?'

Young man?

'Er, I'm selling vacuum cleaners.' No one buys vacuum cleaners from a door-to-door salesman. 'Our vacuum cleaners are cordless.' I didn't know whether there were such things. 'They're great for cleaning cars.'

'Well, come in and show me your vacuum cleaner, young man.'

'It's really very expensive. You probably wouldn't like it.'

'I like you. Such ambition – Saturday night, and you're out selling. Billy Graham was a door-to-door salesman. Did you know that?'

'No.'

'Well, he was. And I just might buy one of your expensive vacuum cleaners. I'll bet you have a family to support. I'll bet that's why you're out working so hard. I admire that.'

'I just remembered, I sold the last one down the block.'

'And you kept knocking on doors. How admirable. Maybe you could come back tomorrow, sell me a vacuum cleaner then.'

'We're out of stock. The one I sold was the last.'

'Shoot! Well, would you like a cup of coffee, or tea? I'm sure you must be tired after a long day.'

'I really should get back to my family.'

'Of course. How nice. I want to thank you for calling, young man. God bless you.'

'I thought that you'd be bringing someone here in cuffs,' said Riddle when I was back in the car.

'Don't talk to me,' I replied.

'Do you want to cruise some more?'

'It's dark.' I immediately realized that this wasn't a

particularly sage observation. 'Let's head for campus police headquarters. Find out that the last leg of the tunnel search drew a blank.'

'I've never seen you so pessimistic.'

'In the short haul, yes. I'm not pessimistic for the long haul. You know me pretty well, Dick. You know we'll find him.'

Whatever the maintenance engineers were paid for that third trip underground wasn't enough; they emerged from the tunnels exhausted and filthy. What they'd found was not Dallas but more of the same: graffiti, beer cans and other litter, evidence of marijuana use, and additional proof of the shocking vulnerability of the campus buildings. One team found hieroglyphics which they thought might be a diagram of a Dungeons & Dragons game, but we couldn't know whether the drawing had any connection with Dallas.

I stayed around campus police headquarters for a few minutes, talking with the engineers. It was almost as if we were war veterans who had just gone through a battle together. 'Did that rush of steam get you?' 'Talk about dark! That was a place where you really couldn't see the nose on the end of your face.' 'The dark was okay, it was the heat. It could bubble your blood.' 'How about that table! Only ghosts could have gotten that table there.' I know I won't forget the tunnels. I doubt if any of the men who went into them ever will.

Riddle and I drove back to the Red Roof Inn, to a pile of messages I'd never be able to get through and more questions from the press.

'Mr. Dear?' He had been waiting for us in the motel lobby.

'You Cliff Perotti?' I had forgotten when he'd said he was coming. California is a long way from Michigan, and I had decided I would believe that this nineteen-year-old was showing up when I saw him.

'I flew in this afternoon. I would have made it sooner if there'd been connections.'

Cliff Perotti was five feet five inches tall and had curly, light-brown hair and a strong chin. He was thin, neat, well dressed; he appeared to be light on his feet, like a boxer, and he had a ready, friendly smile. He was articulate, intelligent, and energetic, the kind of young man you like right away.

'You've gotten your room?' I said. 'I reserved a room for you, near mine.'

'All checked in.'

'Why don't you go there? I have a few things to take care of. I'll give you a call in a while.'

If he was disappointed, it didn't show. I gathered up my messages and headed for my room. As soon as my jacket was off I called Hock.

'Enjoy the football game?' I asked.

'The big schools in Texas play better ball.'

'I hope you didn't start an argument with remarks like that.'

'I tried not to talk about football. Kept bringing the conversation to Dallas. I think the outside world is more interested in him than the students are. The ones we talked to – and there were plenty – thought the disappearance was interesting, but they weren't losing sleep thinking about it.'

'You didn't learn anything helpful?'

'Not unless you believe in an opinion poll that indicates a landslide. Almost everyone believes that Dallas went off somewhere and OD'd. The students know a lot about drugs.'

'It would be nice to think they're acquiring similar expertise in their schoolwork.'

'Yes, well . . . That's it. None of those we talked to

knew Dallas. They base their opinions on hearsay and what they've read in the papers. And, I guess, on just being around the campus and soaking up its atmosphere.'

'What do you think happened, Hock?'

'I disagree with the students. All the evidence points to the fact that Dallas ran off by himself, but either as a hoax – because he couldn't take the pressure – or to commit suicide. Others got involved with him later.'

'You think he's alive?'

'I think he was until recently. He might still be. But he lived for quite a while after the disappearance. Then maybe the others decided he was too much trouble.'

'Don't you think they might decide to cut their losses instead? Nothing that has happened could be worse than murder.'

'We can hope,' Hock said.

Yes, we could. I took consolation from the knowledge that millions of people in this nation's history have disappeared and the vast majority have turned up alive. Some have prospered afterward, and some have been famous, such as U.S. Senator Mike Mansfield, poet Rod McKuen, U.S. Ambassador Clare Boothe Luce, singers Bob Dylan and Neil Diamond, actors Cary Grant and W. C. Fields, comedians Flip Wilson and Danny Kaye, and former President Lyndon B. Johnson.

I leafed through the day's messages, expecting to find nothing of value. Calls from the media, mostly. I suspected that the reporters would not be surprised, after the tunnel search, if I announced that there was little more that could be done. Nonetheless, despite my pessimism, I had two messages that might prove helpful.

The first had been taken down by the switchboard operator: 'Thought we made it clear you had to leave. Disappearance cannot be concluded satisfactorily while you're in Michigan.' My caller from the morning. Of course he hadn't left a number – just the message. Somebody might want me far from Michigan, where criminal indictments most likely would be issued, before revealing Dallas's location, and whoever was involved might also dread a face-to-face meeting with me. Regardless, I wasn't getting out of East Lansing just because of an anonymous voice on the telephone.

The other important message was from Don Gillitzer, who had left a phone number where he could be reached. It was the first time I'd had a number for him since before that initial meeting in the bar.

'What do you have for me?' I asked when I had him on the line.

'Nothing and everything. You don't want to hear about the nothing. The everything is a feeling that we're going to get a break in this case. Maybe you don't want to hear about feelings. Maybe –'

'I never sneer at feelings. Sometimes they're truer than a pile of so-called objective evidence.' Gillitzer sounded excited, hopeful – exactly the way you would expect a man who was on to something to sound.

'I've taken the gloves off,' he said. 'It's not my way of operating, but in this instance I think I can pull it off effectively. There's no excuse for anyone with information not to come forward. I don't care if they do have to incriminate themselves. Anyway, as you suggested, I –'

'I never told you to take chances. I said to leave that to me.'

'I know that. I don't think I'm in danger. But I started leaving hints that you were getting pretty close. I painted you as an ogre, I'm afraid.'

'Good. I can be an ogre.'

'Well, these various people I talked to, three or four of them – I told them that if you had to crack this case yourself, there'd be the devil to pay. I said that maybe a deal still could be made, but time was running out.'

'Who were you talking with?'

'I can't tell you. I don't believe that you tell me your contacts. We have to build up a certain trust – you know about this. I have a lot of faith in your discretion, but I just don't think you can walk in on these people cold and not risk making a mistake that will frighten them into going in the opposite direction from what we want. I'm not trying to withhold any information from you, or making a grab for glory. I just think it would hurt if you jumped in here.'

'I understand.' I did, too. Informants can require very delicate handling. You have to gain their trust and be most careful not to lose that trust with actions that alarm or frighten them. Such as bringing me onto the scene. 'Go ahead,' I said. 'Tell me what you learned.'

'These people are terrified. I mean, it goes way beyond any concern that the gay community will suffer from negative publicity. The fright I'm seeing is personal, or close enough to personal that whatever they know can reach out and involve them. Several days ago I was meeting a wall of hostility. Silence. No one wanted to talk with me. Now they listen and become nervous. No, nervous doesn't describe it. I see pale faces. One man's hands trembled. But it's what I hear that's interesting. They ask about you, want to know if you're reasonable, if you can be trusted. They wonder how much you're motivated by revenge, or whether you simply want to solve the case.'

'I wonder myself. Right now I don't know what happened. How can I know how I'll feel when I don't know what's involved?'

'Those are my feelings. I don't voice them. We have to take one step at a time, and right now we need to get Dallas back.'

'Then you think he's alive?'

'I do. I think I've talked to people who either know where he is or know how to find out.'

'What are the possibilities that I'll be contacted?'

'Well, I hope they're excellent. I may just be seeing what I want to see, but that's not like me. I try not to hope for too much.'

Threats and pressure, without action, lose effectiveness as time passes. I told Gillitzer to make himself visible, in case anyone needed to talk with him, but to avoid saying that I was minutes away from solving the entire mess and turning the case into a vendetta. Besides, the threats and pressure might already have produced results; my anonymous phone caller, whom I didn't mention to Gillitzer, might have been someone he had been talking with.

I called Cliff Perotti and asked him to come to my room. When he entered, the word *dapper* occurred to me, though generally it is applied to much older men. This boy was only nineteen, but he was clean-cut and mature. I explained as much about the status of the investigation as I felt he needed to know, gaining other impressions while I talked. As he had admitted, Perotti was determined, a self-starter. I would have to be careful of him in this last regard, though I felt that his obvious intelligence would serve him in good stead. Another thing was that like most intelligent people, he had immense curiosity.

'How do you see this case in relation to Dungeons & Dragons?' I asked.

'I have a whole possible scenario. Would you like to hear it?'

'Yes.'

'You must remember that the dungeon master, although supposedly an impartial arbiter, can abuse his position and take on the status of God. He can do whatever he wants. If the dungeon master believes that a particular character is weak, he can send that character off on his own. Not just in the game, not just in his head. He can send him on a *real* mission. "You have to prove you're worthy to play with us," the DM might say. "You have to show your mettle. I have a mission that you must complete." Usually the mission is something like spending a night in a haunted house, but it's not hard to imagine that it could be much more demanding. Dallas could have been sent on such a mission. He could still be on it. Or some person or factor could have intervened, as you suspect. But I believe Dallas would have taken the challenge.'

Perotti was very sure of his theory. His voice grew more forceful as he continued. 'A dungeon master can be quite an authority figure, especially to someone Dallas's age. And I understand he's much younger in many respects, a brilliant boy with virtually no social experience. He might very well do almost anything to become accepted by D & D players whom he considers superior. It's very possible that some DM didn't want Dallas in his group, considered him too immature, too much trouble. He might have sent him on a mission that was virtually impossible, never thinking it would go as far as it has. But *we* know that Dallas would go to almost any lengths to gain acceptance. You've told me about his trestling; that seems to me merely a way to show that he has the courage of an adult. Of course it simply demonstrates immaturity, but Dallas might not see that. The same with going into the steam tunnels. Dallas takes life-threatening chances in the hope of gaining friends. The DM I'm talking about, assuming he's not just a sadistic ghoul, might have given Dallas an incredibly difficult assignment, never thinking he would go ahead with it.'

What Perotti said was plausible. But why, then, the concerned reaction to Gillitzer's efforts in the gay community? The people Gillitzer had been dealing with did not seem like the type to play Dungeons & Dragons. They might make up that intervening factor which Perotti had mentioned, though, and have good reason to want to remain silent. Of course, if a DM was initially involved, he would not be eager to step forward, but surely the gravity of the investigation at this late date should have brought forth information from other players.

'What do you think about the corkboard?' I asked.

'I'd think the gun shape represents the old power plant, but I don't believe that the individual tacks are entrances to the tunnels. I'd guess, and it's only guessing, that they're places in the tunnels where obstacles have to be surmounted.'

'Why would Dallas set up the corkboard diagram? If he set it up.'

'I'd say it's his work – a guide, more for himself than for someone else.'

'What about the cremation note?'

'I'd call it a suicide note. I know, you say Dallas probably didn't write it, but I'll bet it turns out he did. I say it's a suicide note, but a *contingency* suicide note. He would kill himself only if he failed. Joining the group could have meant that much to him.'

'A person can get that involved?'

'For sure. You talked about that table your men found in the tunnels– you can imagine the effort needed to get it there.'

'You think Dallas is alive, I take it.'

'I've never thought he was dead. Right from the beginning, just reading about the case, I've believed he was alive. I don't imagine I would have come all this way just to find a body.'

I tried another tack. 'How involved with his character can a person playing Dungeons & Dragons be?'

'I would say completely. You've read of players dressing the part, donning medieval costume and carrying swords and clubs. Sometimes this is for show, to get attention, to do something silly. But sometimes it isn't. People who take the game too far not only dress the part but assume it. I mean, they become the character. They lose their own identity. A thief becomes a thief.'

'How about Dallas? Could that have happened to him?'

'I'd think he would be a likely candidate. He wasn't too happy with his real-life persona and might very well welcome another. You said he believed in reincarnation, and you have to die to be reincarnated. It's a lot easier to become someone else this way.'

'If he assumed another identity, it seems to me, he'd be spotted right away. He'd stick out like a big sore thumb.'

'That depends on the character he's playing. As a magic-user, he'd have to rely on his wits. Become very adaptable.'

'But you don't think that happened?'

'No. I think he'd have been found by now, but not necessarily because he behaved strangely. The publicity has been incredible – this is front-page news in California. No, I told you what I think happened.'

'What I'd like you to do,' I said, 'is get in close with the main Dungeons & Dragons groups here. The scenario you've advanced makes as much sense as anything else I've heard. With your knowledge of the game and your credentials in related areas, you ought to be a welcome addition to any dungeon. See what you can learn. If people seem to be holding back, speculate. Say, "Gee, it seems to me that it might be best to come forward now. Later might be too late. I've heard that this guy Dear isn't someone to screw around with, and the police wouldn't mind looking good with a few arrests." Don't put yourself at any risk. If you have the slightest doubt – the *slightest*

– do nothing. Get in touch with me. Now, tomorrow's Sunday. That's a good day to get started.'

'It probably is. The football game is over, so it's a likely time for Dungeons & Dragons, before people get back to the week-long grind. You said that Dallas played on Sunday too.'

'That's it, then,' I said, standing up.

'Right.' Perotti bounded to his feet. Again he reminded me of a good lightweight fighter. A sharp young man, I thought.

It was late, and I didn't want to make the one remaining call. But I'd promised the Egberts that I would call them every day. I really didn't know what to tell them, but I began to dial anyway.

Chapter 17

The pieces were all in place. Hock and Lambert were keeping an eye on places where drug deals were known to have gone down. Riddle was with me, in the Red Roof Inn, in case we got a call that required a speedy response. Gillitzer was circulating in the gay community, making himself seen but adopting a softer line. Young Perotti was scouring the campus. He'd been up and out early this Sunday, September 9, and when I had asked whether D & D players really started around dawn, he had said he was going to church. That seemed okay – nice, almost – until after he was gone and I had time to wonder. He hadn't said anything about church the night before. I had the unsettled feeling that despite my admonitions, my California friend had struck out on his own mission. This was confirmed not more than a minute after the thought occurred.

'Mr. Dear. Cliff Perotti here.'

I was glad I'd remembered to tell the switchboard to put Perotti's calls through. Sitting in the room with Riddle, doing nothing, was frustrating; I needed someone to yell at, and I was fairly certain I was about to be given just cause.

'Mr. Perotti. How were Sunday services?'

'I didn't go for that purpose. Remember that letter to the newspaper signed J.D.E.? Well, phrases in the letter reminded me of inscriptions I've seen in churches. Regular churches *and* satanic churches. I decided to scout around and check.'

'Did it occur to you to tell me first?'

‘I thought it would be okay. There’s no danger in looking at churches.’

‘No more running off in whimsical directions, Mr. Perotti. I don’t have the impression that you really understand.’

‘I do. I apologize. I wanted to show you what I could accomplish.’

‘You’re not to accomplish anything without checking with me first. Now, what did you find out?’

‘I came across a church with an inscription above the door which read, “In memory of those who made the supreme sacrifice.” Dallas, in that letter to the newspaper, said, “I will make the supreme sacrifice.” There could be a connection.’

‘Dallas didn’t write that letter, Mr. Perotti. We’ve had the handwriting analyzed. It’s not his. Now whoever wrote the letter might indeed have gotten inspiration from that church inscription, but it wasn’t Dallas.’

‘Oh. You didn’t tell me that.’

‘There’s a lot I haven’t told you. Some because I haven’t had time, some because it’s better you don’t know. Will you stay in your area of expertise? People get in trouble when they step outside.’

‘I’m on my way.’

I knew whereof I spoke, and from bitter experience. Occasionally I’ve branched into areas other than investigative work, and while some of these have been successful, I do best when I stick with my profession. Under no circumstances did I want Perotti pretending to be a detective.

I passed time reading an article by Anne Marie Biondo in the Sunday *Detroit News*, which was interesting because it indicated the different approach the campus police were taking from ours. The article read, in part:

> Now police say they have received calls from three people who thought they saw Egbert at a 'Dungeons and Dragons' convention held Aug. 16 through 18 at the University of Wisconsin-Parkside in Kenosha.
>
> 'We've received tips that he could have been there,' said Capt. Ferman Badgley of the MSU police. 'We will be in contact with the [Kenosha] sheriff's department and the people who put on the convention.'
>
> Anna Egbert, the youth's mother, said he attended three science fiction and game conventions in the past year, but had never mentioned the Wisconsin convention.

If Captain Badgley was indeed going to follow up the Wisconsin lead, I wished him well, but I didn't think he would get anywhere. As I sat looking at the article, my mind on fast-forward, I blurted out, 'He just wasn't there!'

'Who wasn't where?' asked the unflappable Riddle.

'Dallas. He didn't attend that convention in Wisconsin.'

'Oh. From the shout you'd let loose, I thought you'd had a revelation. Of course he wasn't at that convention.'

'Badgley says he's checking it out.'

'That's good,' Riddle said noncommittally. He went back to reading the sports section.

It was 1 P.M. when the phone call came. Riddle had gone out for sandwiches and was back unwrapping them, and as soon as I heard 'You're not taking us seriously,' I raised my eyebrows and waved to him to be silent. He put down the food, placed his elbows on the table, and stared intently at my face.

'I told you,' I said to the caller, 'I can't leave town just because I receive advice from an anonymous source.'

'And I told you, the information you need won't be

forthcoming as long as you're in Michigan.'

It was the same voice I'd heard the day before, filtered through some object, possibly a bath towel or a handkerchief. This is a doubly effective method for disguising a voice. Not only is the sound distorted, but the listener is so intent on hearing the message that he or she has little opportunity to concentrate on telltale speech intonations. However, if the conversation is recorded (and I had the rubber suction cup over the mouthpiece of the phone), a voice graph can determine who is doing the speaking – *if* the investigator has a tape of the subject uttering a similar, preferably identical, phrase or sentence in normal conversation as well.

'I'm very busy,' I countered. 'A lot of things are breaking right now. I can't afford to waste time with you, so if you have valuable information, give it to me. Give me something that will justify my leaving Michigan.'

'Like what?'

'Something. Something you haven't read in the press. Then I'll know just how serious you are.'

'I don't know whether I can trust you.'

'That's your problem. I'm in no mood to play games with you. Tell me what your motive is.'

'I think this has gone far enough. I want to help Dallas.'

'I don't believe you. You can help Dallas without my leaving town. You're concerned about yourself.'

'You should be concerned about finding him. I'm offering assistance.'

'Nonsense. You're not giving anything. How about Dallas? Is he alive?'

'I'll tell you when you move.'

'The next time I talk to you, you'll be saying a lot more than just whether he's alive. The police will be with me, and you'll be going on like a broken record, hoping you can make a deal. But deals will be pretty hard to make then.'

There was a hesitation on the other end. I thought I could hear breath being sucked through that cotton, or whatever it was. I looked at Riddle and crossed my fingers for him to see.

'All right. I'll give you this: Dallas went into the tunnels the day he disappeared.'

'Come on. That's not giving me anything. Even a very slow thinker could figure that out from the news clips.'

'You searched the tunnels thoroughly, right?'

'You've got it.'

'Will you believe me when I swear I've never been down there?'

'Look, friend, I wouldn't believe you if you were knee-deep in Bibles. Tell me something only I could know is true.'

'Did you find a milk carton?'

My heart beat a little faster. I shot Riddle a tight smile and a quick nod, a tentative thumbs-up.

'We found a number of milk cartons,' I lied. 'I thought we were in an extension of the city dump.'

'A milk carton with cracker wrappings nearby.'

'What kind of crackers?'

'Cheese. I mean, cheese-and-crackers. You know, crackers with cheese inside.'

'Where should we have found these?'

'I didn't call you to give information. I've already told you more than I should. If you've done your job, you know that what I say is true.'

'You haven't given me enough. You're asking a lot of me, and I'd be a fool not to make sure you have something to offer in return. Now open up with me, or let me get back to business. Where were we supposed to have found these items?'

'Not in the tunnels. In a room off the tunnels. A place hard to get to.'

'And what else?'

'I don't understand.'

'What else were we supposed to have found in this room?'

'I don't . . . oh, he said he might have left a blanket. Did you find a blanket?'

'You're asking me? I admire your chutzpah, but I'm not buying.'

'Well, you must know that what I tell you is fact. Do you do what I ask, or do we take another route?'

'I don't think you have another route, and if you do, you're not being very bright in talking about it. That sounds exactly like a threat. No matter how much trouble you're already in, threats will only dig your hole deeper. You must know how absolutely serious this is. Your calling proves that you do understand. You believe you should bail out, if you can, and you're right.'

'I've told you all I'm going to. I shouldn't have gone this far. I need to know if you're going to leave East Lansing.'

'If I do leave, what assurances do you have that I won't come back? You see, I don't understand you. I don't like dealing with people I don't understand. It's clear enough that you're scared. But I don't believe that you're stupid.'

'You won't have any reason to come back.'

'Well, I'm not going to make a decision right now. But assume I do what you suggest: how long before I hear from you again?'

'I want all your men pulled out. You have four of them. It's not enough that you go.'

'How do you count four?' I wished this hadn't spilled out of my mouth. I pride myself on my skills in dealing with informants. I've even lectured on the subject. Of course this caller would think there were four: Riddle, Hock, Lambert, and . . . Gillitzer.

'I'm being straight with you. You have my word that I'll deliver. But you've got to be on the up-and-up with me. I want you and all four of your men out. No leaving anyone behind to botch this deal.'

'I thought I explained to you that your word doesn't mean a lot to me.' Often a good offense can cover up a mistake. 'But yes, if I decide to go along with you, all of us will leave.'

'It has to be that way. Otherwise I can guarantee that you're acting very irresponsibly.'

'I told you, pal, I don't cater to threats.'

'I want you to know that I don't have a lot of choices.'

'If I leave, when will I hear from you?'

'Arrangements would have to be made. It would take a while.'

'How long?'

'Three or four days at most.'

'Can't you make it sooner?'

'That's it. And I suggest you move as quickly as you can.'

I heard the click on the other end, and then a dial tone. Riddle had heard my end of the conversation, and now I played the whole dialogue back to him. My memory is excellent, but it was valuable to hear the exchange on tape.

'What do you think?' I asked.

'About time we got a break.'

'You believe that's what it is?'

'It's either someone who has direct knowledge of what's going on or a person with a friend in the police department or maintenance department. Or – this is less likely – a policeman or maintenance engineer.'

'What do you think about pulling back?'

'I'm not for all of us leaving. We could make a show of it but have someone double back, check into a different motel under a different name. We'd have to figure out a plausible way, one that guarantees that our man wouldn't be detected, but I think it could be done.'

'I'm not so sure. The caller knew about Gillitzer. And none of our faces is unfamiliar. We've made ourselves very visible on purpose.'

'Well, you know the Riddle Rule: When you play the game of who-can-you-trust, the answer is invariably no one.'

'The caller knew about the milk carton, cheese-and-cracker wrappers, and blanket.'

'And might be a friend of a maintenance engineer or a cop. No rule says these people can't have weird friends. Besides, you know, the temptation is strong to talk about your exploits. Especially something as unusual as the tunnel search. Get a few beers in you, surround yourself with cronies, and you want to blow about the interesting things you're doing.'

'It's possible, I suppose. Dick, why don't you let me be alone for a while. Go watch the pro game if you want. I'd like to sit here and see if I can figure out what we've got.'

What I really wanted to do was to listen to the tape of the conversation, stopping it each time the caller said something that was possibly critical. I needed to make a decision that could be crucial to the case, and it had to rest solely on the telephone call.

The tape was barely under way when I stopped it. '*The information you need won't be forthcoming as long as you're in Michigan.*' Clearly the caller wanted me to leave, probably because somehow I was a threat to him in Michigan. This meant that he himself was probably in Michigan. But he might be afraid of telephone tapping also. He had mentioned taps in his first call, and had known a lot about them. If indeed my motel room telephone had been tapped, he was taking a big risk in calling me. Probably he figured that it was not tapped, but would be when the really important information was exchanged.

It takes anywhere from a few seconds to forty-five minutes to trace a local call, depending on the equipment available at the exchange where the call is received. But everything changes with long-distance calls. They are virtually impossible to trace. The telephone company can verify that the call came through the long-distance exchange, but it cannot tell you what city the call came from, much less which telephone the call originated from.

I turned the tape back on and listened again to our maneuvering for position: he, wanting me to act on blind trust; me, attempting to extract every particle of information possible. Next came the admission that *he knew about the milk carton and cheese-and-crackers wrappings*. Although right from the start I'd suspected that Dallas had gone into that room, I hadn't confided this hunch to any of the other searchers. Riddle's suggestion that the caller might be an acquaintance of a policeman or maintenance engineer seemed to me unlikely, and even more so because of what the caller had chosen. Why not mention that fantastic table? Or the eerie witch's hieroglyphics? Why did my caller choose the milk carton and cheese-and-crackers?

'*Oh, he said he might have left a blanket.*' Unless my caller was a consummate actor, he had let slip something he didn't intend for me to know: that he had talked with Dallas. 'He said' indicated a face-to-face meeting. And the statement seemed spontaneous, off-the-cuff – in many cases, the most truthful sort of statement. Yet the caller might be just a good actor.

'*Or do we take another route?*' There were two things to chew on here. First, the 'we.' That indicated more than one person, which was what I'd suspected all along. I didn't believe that a single third person was stage-managing this entire operation; the evidence simply didn't point in that direction. Gillitzer had found several people who behaved suspiciously, the student population was suspicious because many people who had played Dungeons & Dragons with Dallas had not come forward, and even if the disappearance was related to drugs, a coterie would probably be involved. No, the lone chicken hawk Gillitzer had mentioned could not have pulled it off for this long, nor could a lone anybody. And the strange people who want to talk to me don't say 'we'; it's 'I.' Only 'I' possess the knowledge that you, William C. Dear, need to solve this extremely puzzling matter. My caller had given himself some unexpected authenticity with that 'we.'

The mention of 'another route' was no more than I'd expected. If Dallas was alive (and I felt more confident than ever that he was) his captors probably rightly perceived that they couldn't hold him much longer. I was the best outlet for his release – perhaps the *only* outlet. If I refused, they would take 'another route.' That had several connotations, each of them sinister. The most obvious was that he would be killed. I thought about that for a few minutes. Killed. It did not fit with a game of hide-and-seek, a super Dungeons & Dragons spectacular intended to outwit Dallas's elders. It did make sense if Dallas had been sexually abused, or if the drug crowd was involved.

'*You won't have any reason to come back.*' That seemed clear enough. To find Dallas – and what else could be the purpose? – I would not have to return to East Lansing. Clearly the boy, or his body, was to be released to me, but not in Michigan. Another possibility occurred to me: the people involved might have an urgent need not so much to get *me* out as to get *Dallas* out of Michigan. He might still be in the East Lansing area; to move him safely might require absence of the most determined and dangerous hunters.

'*Three or four days at most*.' This had been the answer when I had asked how long it would be before I heard from the caller after I left the state, and it indicated that the people would need time to arrange the transfer of Dallas to us. What if they just want time to take the boy to a safer spot? I thought. It would be almost criminal if I were close to breaking this case and pulled out, only to give whoever was involved a second life. But that was just the point: if I was about to find Dallas, I wasn't aware of it. This phone call promising help seemed the best hope I had.

The decision would have to be made. The arguments against leaving were that the caller might be a crank (not likely) or might have a sound reason for wanting us out of the state – but no intention of assisting us. If he did now want to move Dallas to another area, how could we prevent that anyway? No one would put Dallas on public transportation, because people at stations and airports had been alerted to look for him, and media coverage had made his a well-known face. If they moved him by private vehicle, we'd be helpless to stop it. Roadblocks had never been a reasonable alternative in this case. Dallas had been missing for twenty-six days. A twenty-six-day roadblock?

The big reason in favor of our leaving was quite simply that this might be the break that resolved the disappearance. The call was a textbook example of how such cases usually are concluded. And if I did leave, I could always come back, although that would be expensive and inconvenient. The caller probably wanted a well-publicized withdrawal, and I was eager to give it to him. In addition, there did not seem that much more for us to do in East Lansing. We had searched the woods, the tunnels, and every conceivable public place where Dallas (or his body) might be. Short of an illegal house-to-house hunt, there was nowhere else to look.

Yes, I decided, we would return to Texas. In reality I couldn't force Gillitzer to do anything, but I imagined that he'd be amenable to my request that he go back to New York. And what Riddle had suggested – a less-than-complete pullout – was still possible. What I hoped to leave behind in East Lansing might turn out to be a weak reed to lean on, but it was something: Perotti. Mr. Perotti would have to receive a quick and effective course on how to follow orders, with heavy emphasis on the need and value of restraining his usually admirable yen to self-start, but he could be valuable as my eyes and ears in Michigan. If anything that required my presence occurred, I could be on my plane and on the way in minutes.

It was just after three o'clock, too early to use the radio to call everyone in, so I thought again about that informant – if such he was. He had not even mentioned the reward. Five thousand dollars is a powerful lure to most people, and I have resolved numerous cases with rewards of much less. Not asking about the reward indicated guilty knowledge; the caller must know that there was no chance of getting any money, that the best he could hope for was to avoid criminal charges.

Further speculation seemed fruitless. There was no telling who held Dallas, or for what motives. I felt that I could eliminate students perpetrating a hoax, who might have been involved at the beginning of Dallas's odyssey but had surely not been part of it since then. They might provide insights into the first day or two of his disappearance, but why fill in step by step from the beginning when we might be able to jump right to the end? This was not a good novel we were reading, but a real-life whodunit in which the ending was everything. I hoped very much that Dallas himself would fill me in on the middle.

Well, arrangements had to be made, and I thought there wouldn't be a better time to start. I was worrying about Gillitzer when right on cue, an example of wish-fulfillment, the phone rang and the gay detective was on the other end of the line.

'What have you got?' I asked.

'No more than yesterday. I didn't expect anything. I've been doing what you said, which is making myself visible but not saying much.'

'Don, something has come up. I may have gotten a break on this case. Can I impose on you to go back to New York no later than tomorrow morning? It's very important for all of us to be gone by then.'

'Of course I'll do what you say. Can you give me some of the whys?'

'I really can't. Believe me when I tell you it's vital.'

'I guess, then, that this is good-bye.'

'Call it "so long." I've really appreciated your valuable help. Maybe the time will come when we can do it again.'

'I'd like that.'

'Don, I'll let you know how this turns out. We'll have lunch in New York together. And when I have Dallas back and tell him all you've done, I'm sure he'll want to meet you as much as you want to meet him.'

'That's all I've wanted from this case.'

'I know that. So long, Don.'

'So long.'

I rang the front desk. 'I've got good news for you,' I said.

'You've found Dallas.' The woman on this shift had performed stalwart duty, as had all of her coworkers.

'Not yet. I can promise you, though, that that's going to happen.'

'You've gotten the gifts you promised from Neiman-Marcus.'

'Alas. But they'll be coming, I assure you.'

'What, then?'

'I and my whole crew will be checking out tomorrow morning. Life can return to normal for you.'

'That's not good news. It's been exciting here, being involved in a big mystery and all. Listen, can you tell me about Dallas? Is he going to be all right? Are you going to find him?'

'Just between us, yes, I am going to find him.'

Next I called Captain Ferman Badgley. I told him that we were pulling out, a piece of information he must not have found particularly depressing. I also called Wardwell and Lyons. They were good young detectives, and I wanted to tell them that their cooperation was appreciated.

By 7:30 P.M., when my three men and Perotti were gathered in my room, I had notified everyone (save the Egberts) who needed to know that I was leaving. I explained to the four men that I thought we had done about all we could in Michigan and that going back to Texas and letting the matter simmer for a while might produce more results. We had certainly made our presence conspicuous. But any more pressure, I said, might produce negative results. Of course Riddle knew about the phone call I'd received, but I settled on telling the others only that I expected results soon from the good work we'd done.

I had to be very careful, firm, and precise with Perotti. I knew he'd be very disappointed by the sudden pullout, since he had come all the way from California only the day before. When he said he'd like to stay on a little longer, I agreed.

'Mr. Perotti,' I said, 'you actually can play an important role here. But you're going to have to let me be the director. I was disappointed by your actions this morning.'

'I understand.'

'Quite simply, I want you to serve as my eyes and my ears, but not my mouth. You don't even breathe my name. I don't want anyone to know there's a connection between us. I have good reason to believe there's a break in this case, and you can play a big part in whether we succeed or fail. You can continue to nose around campus if you like, pursuing Dungeons & Dragons leads, but I think you'll be more effective staying near the motel. Watch for people who come around looking for me. Try to find out who they are without letting them know who you are. A clever person can do this, Mr. Perotti, and I know you're very resourceful. You can say, "You looking for that investigator? He left," or some such approach. Whatever, *you are not connected with me*. Don't antagonize the police. Call me collect the minute you have something, and call me every day anyway. I'll expect to hear from you tomorrow evening, at the latest. Now, do you have all that?'

'I understand,' Perotti said again. 'You'd prefer that I stay close to the motel.'

'Yes. But if you feel you can learn something useful by pursuing role-playing games on campus, go ahead. You have a big responsibility. You're the only contact I'll have here.'

Arranging for transportation back to Texas should have been easy, but it wasn't. Riddle and Hock readily agreed to drive the two company cars, and of course Lambert and

I intended to fly the plane back. I asked Lambert what kind of weather was expected, and he called the airport.

'It's good here for tomorrow,' he reported a few minutes later. 'We'll hit thunderstorms about halfway to Texas, but that doesn't bother me.'

'I'm sure it doesn't. But it bothers me. I'm not flying through thunderstorms in that plane. I'll take a commercial flight. You stay around until the weather clears.'

'Bill, you know I'm a good pilot.'

'You're a *great* pilot, Lambert. But I'm taking a big, solid jet. They're harder to knock out of the air.' Actually, I'm a bit afraid of flying, despite all the statistics that say it's the safest way to travel. Those statistics seem to be based on mileage, not time spent traveling. Somehow I figure I'll live longer in a car than in a plane.

'Imagine trying to crash-land a 747 in a field or on a highway.'

'I'll take my chances. I'm not flying with you through that godawful thunderstorm. And stop talking about crash landings.'

'Mr. Macho. Wait till I tell that cute reporter I've met that you're afraid of a little rain. I can see the headline now: "Cowardly Detective Exposed." I can mail it out to all your clients in Texas.'

'You're going with a reporter? What happened to the coed?'

'Don't change the subject.'

Hock, Riddle, and Lambert left for their rooms to pack, and Perotti was dismissed with another lecture on following instructions to the letter. I called the airport and made reservations, with a change of planes in Detroit. I'd be safe and sound in my home by six o'clock. Next I called several reporters and asked them to spread the word that I was leaving in the morning. I wanted maximum coverage of the event. It would be a disaster if I left and that anonymous caller believed that I was still in East Lansing. Then I dialed the Egberts' number in Dayton.

'Anna,' I said when she picked up the phone, 'I have what I believe may turn out to be good news. A tip that I feel could be the real thing. It's going to require us to return to Texas, but be assured that this is a necessary move in the investigation. We're not in any way giving up. The truth is, we feel we may be close to finding Dallas.'

'You're not just giving me an easy brushoff, are you, Bill?' she asked, her voice tight with feeling. 'It would be terrible if you've become discouraged and feel there's no more you can do, but it would be easier to know now than to be let down lightly.'

'Unless I'd been lied to by a client, I would never quit a case voluntarily. Anna, I mean it. This could be good news. I don't want you to get too high, but subdued hopefulness is called for here.'

'Can you tell me what you have that's causing you to leave?'

'I would if I could. Believe me, it's very promising. Try to keep an even keel. You've shown a lot of strength so far. I can only imagine how I'd feel if my boy were missing.'

'You are confident?'

'I've never been more.'

'Stay in touch, Bill.'

I figured that took care of everything. As I pulled the bedcovers over my shoulders, I was sure that this case would be solved. And that wherever Dallas was, the case would be solved in Texas.

Chapter 18

The trip from Michigan to Texas was uneventful. At the stopover in Detroit I heard my name paged and briefly hoped that Mr. Anonymous would be telling me that I was far enough from East Lansing and that the demand for me to go all the way to Texas was merely a test of my good faith, but the pagers turned out to be a troupe of reporters who wanted to know the latest about Dallas's disappearance. I told them the same thing I had told their brethren in East Lansing.

Frank Lambert, flying my private plane, arrived in Dallas four hours before I did. The thunderstorm had indeed turned out to be a few raindrops, and he had accomplished his trip without any of the hassle of standing in line and waiting for baggage. A private plane really is the answer in most situations. I told Lambert, who was waiting at my home, to keep himself available in case we had to make a very quick return trip. Hock and Riddle, who left East Lansing in the company cars, also arrived back in Texas on Monday evening and I told them to keep themselves available too.

Not too long after my arrival I heard from Cliff Perotti, whose IQ, I suspected, was not a great deal lower than Dallas's. Perotti had nothing to report and was thinking of returning to California the next day. I preferred for him to tough it out a little longer in East Lansing, but I couldn't bring myself to ask him to stay. But shortly after midnight on Tuesday, September 11, I received a second telephone call from him. His voice was excited; I could tell he was trying to contain himself.

'You know that mystery woman you told me about.'

'What about her?' I gripped the phone tighter.

'Her name is Cindy Hulliberger.'

'How do you know that?'

'I have her here. I think we have the breakthrough we need.'

'You have her *there*? Right next to you? She can hear what you're saying?'

'Not right here like right here. But she's at the motel. I've talked to her. She's waiting for me, wants me to go with her.'

'Start at the beginning. Tell me what happened.'

'I was out talking to people about Dallas. Then I came back to the motel and the desk clerk told me there was a woman looking for you. How she could not know you'd left I don't know. The desk clerk pointed to a car in the parking lot.'

'A red Vega?'

'The very one. I told you, the woman is here. She said – she, that's Cindy Hulliberger – that she didn't know you'd left. Her motivation, she says, is a desire to help Dallas. She says she knows where he is. She claims she's seen him. Dallas ran away because of pressure from his parents. But he became ill. She talked about maybe its being a mental breakdown.'

'This woman a doctor?'

'Of course not. But she wants me to go with her. She says she can take me to places he's been since the disappearance.'

'Places he's been? Why not where he *is*?'

'I asked. She says he's been moved several times. At a given moment he might not be at a specific location. But she says we can find him by asking around. She wants me with her.'

'Why you?' I had a fairly good idea.

'I told her I was associated with you. That I was in continual touch with you.'

I'd told Perotti not to mention our relationship, but I supposed I would not have acted very differently in his shoes. He knew, at least to a degree, how much I'd wanted to talk with the person I'd dubbed the 'mystery woman.' Probably Perotti felt he had to establish credibility in her eyes.

'What do you think?' I said. 'Is she a screwball?'

'I believe she's telling the truth. Just from talking to her. She appears genuinely concerned about Dallas. I've known a lot of people, plenty of them weird. You can imagine, given the business I'm in. Cindy Hulliberger strikes me as sane and sincere.'

'Why all the sneaking around? Why didn't she just contact me?'

'She also strikes me as very frightened. She says the people involved in Dallas's disappearance might hurt her if they knew she'd come forward. Under no circumstances, she says, would she talk to the police. And she says she'll only take me around while it's dark.'

I thought back and realized that her visits to my motel room had always been at night. And her behavior certainly had been consistent with someone who was afraid. I still was concerned about her claim that this time she had come to see me. My departure had been well publicized. Could she possess all the knowledge she claimed and not know that I had returned to Texas? It did not seem farfetched to assume that Cindy Hulliberger might be connected with the person whose call had prompted my departure from Michigan. She could be checking to see whether I had left. If that were the case, I wasn't sure what effect Perotti's admission that he had been left behind as my associate would have.

'What does Cindy Hulliberger look like?' I asked.

Physical appearances, I think, mean a lot. I'm an avid people-watcher, and I try to guess people's occupations and personalities merely from looking at them. I confess, I've occasionally even followed people whose appearances have fascinated me, just to see if my speculations are correct.

'She's maybe five feet seven. I'd say twenty-four years old. Heavyset. A pleasant enough face. Looks like she could take care of herself.'

'Did you get her license plate?'

'RZB-385.'

'You did good, Mr. Perotti.'

'Should I go with her? She wants me to go with her.'

'Where does she live?'

'She lives in Lansing. She's a clerk in a department store.'

'That's not enough, Mr. Perotti. Get the *address* at both home and work.'

'I will. But she's waiting for me now. Can I go with her?'

'Yes, you can ride with her. Learn anything you can. But if she stops somewhere, wants you to go inside somewhere, you simply flat-out refuse. You call me before you do anything other than take a ride.'

'You've got my promise.' Perotti sounded eager.

'Just hold those horses you're on. Listen to me. This Cindy Hulliberger says she's afraid. She may have good reason to be. You could get yourself hurt very badly, or killed. You take no chances at all. Well, that's not true – you're taking a chance just going with her. But do nothing else. Call me immediately as soon as something looks promising. I know you're cocky, but believe me, you're not able to handle anything rough. This case could get very rough.'

'I'll call you the minute I have anything.'

'I'll be right here.'

And I was. I stayed at the telephone all through the long early-morning hours of September 11. There was really nothing to do but wait, and hope and pray that Perotti wasn't in over his head. Several times I was close to picking up the phone and dispatching one of my men back to East Lansing, but each time I stopped short. It could be that Cindy Hulliberger was perpetrating a hoax.

The call from Perotti came at 6 A.M. He sounded even more excited than when he'd called before, and for a moment I thought maybe he even had Dallas in tow. When I learned that this wasn't the case, I asked him to slow down. Then: 'What have you been doing for five hours?'

'Riding around. Learning the most fantastic things. Cindy Hulliberger is a goldmine of information.'

'Give me a sample.'

'She told me she knows who killed Laurie Murningham.'

Perotti obviously expected a reaction. 'Who's Laurie Murningham?' was the best I could offer.

'Laurie Murningham was the daughter of Max Murningham, mayor of Lansing from 1965 to 1969. She was abducted during a holdup at a gift shop where she worked on July 9, 1970. She was found July 20, 1970, in a swampy area near Mason, twenty miles from where she had been kidnapped. She'd been strangled to death. The case was almost as sensational as Dallas's disappearance.'

'That was more than nine years ago, Mr. Perotti.'

'It would be incredible to solve it after this long.'

'What about Dallas? We're looking for Dallas.'

'Just give me another minute on Laurie Murningham. Cindy said she was killed because she knew her kidnappers. This was an important case, Mr. Dear. There was $16,500 in rewards posted for Laurie Murningham's return. After she was found dead, $2,000 was offered for her killer.'

'Has Cindy Hulliberger mentioned the reward in this case?' I was afraid she had. Rewards tend to bring forward a galaxy of informers, each with an improbable theory that might by chance pan out and thus give him or her a claim, however shaky, to the money.

'She never mentioned a reward.'

'Well, that's something. What did you learn about Dallas?'

'One more thing about Laurie Murningham. The woman who owned the Lansing gift shop says that a black man abducted Laurie, but Cindy claims that there were two murderers. Surely she knows enough details about the case not to add another murderer if he didn't exist.'

Actually, just the opposite would probably be true. A clever imposter would want to add important, previously unknown 'facts.' The intended effect might be exactly what Perotti was experiencing: Why would she say something so fantastic if it weren't true?

'I don't want to hear any more about Laurie Murningham right now,' I said. 'What did you find out about Dallas?'

'We've been driving around all this time, driving and talking. Lansing and East Lansing, all through the MSU campus, out into farmland. She took me by a gray, two-story frame house just a block from the campus. She said Dallas had been held there, that she'd seen him there, but he'd been moved. She said he'd been held in a room. He was wiped out on drugs and didn't know where he was. She repeated that she thought Dallas suffered a mental breakdown.'

'What else did she say?'

'She wouldn't elaborate. She's very afraid. She did say that several people were involved. I think she was being honest. There was no hesitation about saying that she didn't completely trust me. She insisted that she wished you were here to talk with.'

'I was there. If she was afraid of being seen with me, she could have called.'

'She said she was afraid the conversation would be taped. She came around at night hoping she wouldn't be noticed.'

'I imagine you'd like to check out that house she showed you.'

'You bet.'

'Don't. I don't want you to do anything. We could be treading in very dangerous waters. You say Cindy Hulliberger is frightened, and that you believe she's on the up-and-up with you. Believe, then, that she has a reason to be afraid. *You do nothing*. Do you understand?'

'That's going to be difficult. Cindy has set up a meeting for me for tonight with a person who she says can put us in touch with those holding Dallas.'

'Who is this person?'

'She didn't say.'

'Did you ask?'

'Yes. She wouldn't tell me.'

'Damn, Mr. Perotti. Did you find out where she works?'

'Myers Department Store.'

'And where she lives?'

'I have her address.' Perotti gave it to me. 'It's on the west side of Lansing.'

'All right. That's good, Mr. Perotti. Now tell me about this meeting you're supposed to have.'

'It's for nine o'clock tonight. Cindy will have her friend

come to the Red Roof Inn parking lot at that time. He's supposed to be able to put us in touch with the people holding Dallas.'

'He?'

'Yes. A male.'

'I guess you can go ahead on this. But let Hulliberger and her friend do all the work. If they can negotiate Dallas's release, that's fine, but I don't want you involved. We really could be dealing with rough types. You're my eyes and ears in East Lansing, nothing more. At the slightest whiff of danger, get away from it and call me. Regardless, I'll be expecting to hear from you as soon after nine o'clock tonight as possible.'

'Would you like me to see if I can learn anything more about the Laurie Murningham murder?'

'Forget Laurie Murningham. Do nothing except keep that nine o'clock appointment. If I were there, I'd lock you in your room until then. Can I count on you just to stay put?'

'Yes. I'm very tired now. I think I'll grab some sleep.'

'Sleep all morning and all afternoon.'

I had been up all night also, so I lay down with three phones within a couple of feet of me, and woke up at noon, angry because I'd slept so long. Clearly nothing had happened. It probably wouldn't have happened even if I'd been awake, agitating, stirring matters up, but I was nonetheless upset because I'd been out of it for more than five hours. I was convinced I hadn't missed any phone calls. The ring of a telephone instantly awakens me from the soundest sleep, a fact the doubting Frank Lambert refuses to concede. 'You're like the clown who says he doesn't snore,' Lambert once sneered. 'How does he know he doesn't snore? He's asleep. How would *you* know if the phone rang and it didn't wake you up?'

More out of boredom, impatience to be doing something, than anything else, I gave an interview to Ruth Eyre of the *Dallas Morning News*. It appeared the next day and read, in part:

> DESOTO – Back behind the electronically controlled iron gate at his flashy estate here, private eye William C. Dear is still full of scenarios, theories and leads he is confident will solve the case of a 16-year-old genius who disappeared at Michigan State University.
>
> 'Something may break in the next 72 hours,' he says from his desk on his rolling acreage with its heliport, tennis court and swimming pools and his staff of secretaries and assisting detectives.
>
> The teenager, James Dallas Egbert III, disappeared Aug. 15, and police have searched without success eight miles of steam tunnels underneath the campus where Egbert was believed to have played a medieval fantasy game called 'Dungeons and Dragons.'
>
> At East Lansing, Mich., MSU police were much less optimistic than Dear. Capt. Ferman Badgley called an end to the daily news briefings that have been part of the spectacular investigation and said there was simply no solid evidence of where the missing youngster might be.
>
> 'I personally think if he's alive, he's playing . . . we're pawns in this game and we're being utilized to satisfy his own needs,' Badgley said.

I was interested to learn that Badgley thought that Dallas might still be playing a game. I disagreed, though I believed that the boy was still alive. In fact, the idea that Dallas might be dead rarely entered my thoughts as the day wore on. Everything about the case indicated to me that he was alive, although probably not in too good condition. The most promising hope, it seemed to me, was still that anonymous caller. His specific knowledge of what we had found in the tunnels was much more substantial, at least so far, than Cindy Hulliberger's broader but unproved claims.

Again I let the idea roll around in my mind that Cindy Hulliberger was connected with the caller. No one could have known that I had left Perotti behind; Hulliberger would have discovered his presence when she came to check whether I had indeed left Michigan. That first long car ride in the early-morning hours might have been a rapid, necessary adjustment to reality, prompted by Perotti's admission that he was associated with me, and Hulliberger could have used the time spent driving around to size up the young games expert. I suspected that there were people who wanted this case to end almost as much as I wanted to find Dallas, and the presence of Perotti would not deter them.

I phoned Riddle, Hock, and Lambert and asked them to come to my home. I caught them up on the news about Perotti and told Hock I wanted him ready to leave for East Lansing at a moment's notice. I told Lambert and Riddle to be ready too, because I expected to have to hurry off soon to pick up Dallas. I had a strong conviction that we were not dealing with genteel types so I wanted a strong presence available at the critical moment.

I was alone once again at 9 P.M., when the phone call from Perotti didn't come. I'd been watching the hands of the clock, which assured that they would move more slowly than usual, but as the magic moment came and went my impatience and frustration became almost unbearable. Once again it was clear to me how ill-suited I was for waiting. It was my own fault, mine alone. I had dubbed 9 P.M. the magic moment, even though I knew that the call might come much later. Perotti's *meeting* was at 9 P.M.; there was no telling how long it would take for him to report back.

I calmed myself as best I could with the thought that if Perotti called immediately, it meant that the meeting had been postponed or cancelled. But nothing was going to help very much. This was the twenty-eighth day Dallas had been missing. The time elapsing was intolerable.

The call came at 9:15, just as I was growing reconciled to a long wait. When I receive an important phone call, one in which the news will be either good or bad, I try to get a jump on what I'm going to hear by listening to the tone of the voice. Perotti sounded excited and optimistic. How could this be? What could he have accomplished in fifteen minutes?

'How did the meeting go?'

'It didn't. Cindy's contact was just driving into the parking lot when a state police car appeared. It must have spooked him. He never stopped, just spotted the police car and drove off.'

'Terrific. So you don't have anything?'

'Cindy will set up the meeting for tomorrow night. We'll arrange it so nothing can go wrong. I really think we're on the right track here.'

'How are you going to do that? Set up another meeting, that is.'

'I don't know. We'll work on it. Don't worry. I'll be very careful. I'll check with you as soon as we have the plan.'

'I take it you don't think this woman is playing games with you.'

'I really don't. What worries me is the police. That was quite a coincidence, that police car showing up when it did. Do you think I could be under surveillance?'

'I don't know.' If he hadn't maintained an extremely low profile, the chances were excellent. The police had to know of my optimistic proclamations, which contrasted so starkly with their own admitted impotence. It has happened before: the police, unable to develop their own leads, start tracking the private investigator. It's called investigating the investigator, and it provides a warm feeling of knowing that you are doing something right.

'Where is Cindy Hulliberger now?' I asked.

'She's with me. At the motel.'

'Would she talk to me?'

'I don't see why not. Let me ask.'

Just a moment elapsed before I heard the woman's voice. 'Hello? Mr. Dear? This is Cindy Hulliberger.' Her tone was tense, raspy. It was the sort of voice I would associate with the description Perotti gave me.

'I appreciate your trying to help us, Cindy,' I said. I wasn't sure at all that this was the case, but it seemed as good an opening as any.

'The people involved with Dallas.' Her voice had an urgency that would be hard to fake. 'There have to be assurances that they won't be prosecuted.'

'What have they done that would warrant prosecution?'

'I don't want to talk about that. I need to know that they won't be in a lot of trouble. Cliff said it could be taken care of.'

Cliff, I thought to myself. He had no more authority than any other man on the street to promise there would be no prosecution. Mr. Perotti and I would have to have another talk.

'I can tell you this,' I said. 'My interest, and the interest of the Egberts, is in getting the boy back. Right now no one is thinking of revenge. We want Dallas safe and sound.'

'Well, that's why I've come forward. It's reached the

point, Mr. Dear, where Dallas will have to be killed or released.'

There it was. That was what I had imagined was happening. The pressure we had exerted in East Lansing was going to bring results. Too often people – even the police – see only their own side of a case, imagining that a robber who has pulled a bank job is laughing at his victims and living it up in Las Vegas or the Riviera on his ill-gotten gains. The truth is that he is probably very frightened and lonely, hearing footsteps and jumping at shadows. No, I had never believed that any people who might be involved in Dallas's disappearance were having a high time at our expense.

Cindy Hulliberger's credibility had greatly increased, in my opinion. 'Let me assure you,' I said, 'that I don't want Dallas harmed. He's a minor child. In many respects he's not much more than a baby. I'll go anywhere to get him, go see and talk to anyone who can help me find him. I can also guarantee that if he is killed, I will move heaven and earth to bring those responsible to justice.'

'I don't want him hurt either. That's why I'm talking with you.'

'Why don't you just tell me where Dallas is?'

'I don't know where he is. I know where he's been. I can put you in touch with those who can deliver him to you.'

'Who was the person Perotti was supposed to meet tonight?'

'I can't tell you. We'll meet him tomorrow.'

'Cindy, I'm being truthful with you. I expect the same in return.'

'Can't you understand, Mr. Dear? I'm afraid for *my* life, too.'

'Did you have anything to do with taking Dallas?'

'No. I swear I didn't.'

'How did you acquire your information?'

'Through the circle of people I know. I won't tell you any more than that.'

'You say Dallas's life is in danger, yet you want to wait until tomorrow night. Don't you think we should move faster?'

'I can't do any better than I am. If the police hadn't made an appearance, the matter might be decided by now.'

'What's your role in all of this? Are you a go-between?'

'I know about these people. I know they want the pressure taken off. I think it's best for everyone if Dallas comes out of this safely.'

'That's not answering the question. What is your role?'

'I'm not telling you any more. Just assume I'm concerned about Dallas. And I'm concerned about myself also.'

'Can you tell me this: Is Dallas in the East Lansing area?'

'I'm not saying any more than I already have. Helping you get Dallas back should be enough.'

'But Cindy, we have only your word that you can do that. You haven't given us anything yet.'

'I showed Cliff a house where Dallas was held.'

'Only your word, Cindy.'

'Well, it will have to be enough.'

'Cindy, it would be very unfunny if it turns out that you're just leading us on.'

'I'm not laughing, Mr. Dear. I wish you could see me. I'm flat-out scared.'

'I hope for your sake that you are leveling with us, Cindy. Put Perotti back on the line, will you?'

I told Perotti to stick close to the motel and not even to leave his room unless he absolutely had to.

'One reason to stay in your room,' I emphasized, 'is that I may want to call you. I expect there might be something important, and I'd need to get in touch right away.' I couldn't imagine what this would be, but I thought it would help keep him in his room. I also told Perotti to go ahead and make plans with Cindy Hulliberger for tomorrow night but to be extremely cautious, and to call when he had the scenario sketched out.

Next I called Jim Hock at his Dallas apartment. 'I want you in East Lansing tomorrow,' I said. 'Commercial flight. I'll arrange to get you out as early as possible. I think something's coming down real quick there. I don't want to be frozen out. I need you to size the situation up very discreetly. Don't let the police know you're in town. Under no circumstances should you talk to the press. The police in particular could be a problem, because they know you, but I think you were the least visible of any of us.'

I didn't want Hock to be discovered by my mysterious caller and thus endanger anything on that front. Still, talking to Cindy Hulliberger, hearing the tension in her voice, I felt that I couldn't afford *not* to have an experienced man on the scene.

'Do I contact Perotti?' Hock asked.

'I don't know. Call me as soon as you reach East Lansing. I'll have a clearer idea by then.'

It was not yet 10:30 P.M. when I set down the phone, rose from behind my desk, and extended into a mighty stretch. I knew I'd be up late again, waiting for Perotti's next phone call, but in any case I'd be unable to sleep for many hours. I would rest when exhaustion set in. I suspected that this would be the last rest I would have before the case was solved – however it might turn out.

Chapter 19

I stayed at Dallas–Fort Worth Airport on Wednesday, September 12, watching Hock's flight until it was off the ground and in the air – until it was a dot in the big, wide, clear Texas sky, and then nothing. Hock might very well be flying off to solve the case, I thought, and my heart was up there with him. I suppose I envied him. He might be in on the moment of truth. Walking through the mammoth airport terminal, though, I didn't think he would be. I brushed against several people as I went, immersed in thought, again trying to sort this most illogical case into logical pieces.

The broad outlines were clear to me. The person whom Cindy Hulliberger wanted Perotti to meet was one and the same as the caller who wanted us out of Michigan. Cindy had been sent to see if we had left, had been discovered by Perotti, and had decided to cooperate with him. What else could she have decided? Perotti had her license number. She couldn't refuse to assist him; my agency and the police would be on her like a swarm of bees, and hers would be the worst of all possible worlds. Not only might Dallas be killed, but those involved in or with knowledge of his fate, including herself, could expect no mercy. Perotti's presence had forced her hand, and the hand of her male friend. Surely he knew now that we would find him.

With head down, I shuffled through the cavernous air terminal. Even when I realized that I was lost, I kept going a little longer. I came out of my reverie long enough to ask a passing flight attendant where my parking area was, and from her soft laugh and shaking head I could tell I was about as far away as possible.

I found a taxi driver and told him where I wanted to go. He was hostile. It had taken him an hour to get to the front of the line and he wasn't moving for anything less than a fare to downtown Dallas.

'A trip to another part of the airport?' he said. 'Buzz off.'

'I'll give you ten dollars.'

'Walk it, buddy.'

'It's a long way. I'm in a hurry. Twenty dollars.'

'You know what you can do with your twenty dollars?'

I thought of explaining things to him in a language he could understand. But he had to make a living too. 'Thirty,' I said. 'And don't give me any back talk. Buddy.'

'Get in.'

Increasingly, I couldn't think of any reasonable motive for the caller to want me out of Michigan except a return of Dallas. I mulled this over as I drove on the busy freeway through Irving, home of Texas Stadium and the Dallas Cowboys, on the way to my DeSoto home. I was becoming more and more convinced that Hock was going to find our missing genius. This was the twenty-ninth day of the disappearance; even the most determined searchers could be expected to lose some of their vigilance. Life goes on; there were other matters to concern the police. Assuming the call had not been an outright hoax, it must have had something to do with the *way* Dallas was to be released.

It was just after 1 P.M. when I reached home, where my secretary reported that Perotti had just hung up. I went straight to my private office and called the Red Roof Inn.

'You've got the agenda for tonight?' I asked, as soon as Perotti was on the line.

'Yes. And Cindy's here with me if you need to talk to her.'

'It's daylight.'

'I can tell you she's plenty nervous about that.'

'What have you decided?'

'She's coming to the motel tonight at ten thirty. She'll drive me to a meeting with the guy we just missed last night.'

'Where is the meeting?'

'She won't say. I get the impression that all of this is very delicate. She doesn't want to give me access to anything she doesn't have control over. Maybe she fears I'd act on my own.'

'A smart lady.'

'What's that?'

'Never mind. So she's taking you somewhere tonight. That's all you know. Wouldn't you say that this is pretty risky?' I could tell from Perotti's voice that this was precisely the way he was thinking. Some of the glow of his initial enthusiasm had worn off, as it increasingly struck home that this wasn't a game.

'I'm nervous, I'll admit it. You couldn't spend time with Cindy and not catch the tension. She's afraid, and she's beginning to persuade me that she has good reason.'

'Do you want to back out?' I didn't want to spend much time on this topic. I knew, and Perotti didn't, that the experienced Hock would be on the scene well before the scheduled meeting, and Hock wouldn't allow the young Californian to get hurt.

'Of course I don't want to back out. I'm just saying that I'm not afraid to admit I'm feeling a little queasy.'

'Let me talk to Cindy.' I had a plan, and I hoped I could make it work.

'Mr. Dear?' The same raspy voice.

'Cindy, I hope nothing goes wrong tonight.'

'I don't think it will. This time we're going to pick up my contact. We'll make double sure we're not followed.'

'It sounds like you're taking quite a chance.'

'I am. I'm afraid of what can happen.'

'I wish I could be there. I have experience with tight situations.'

'That would be good. I'd feel better if you were here.'

'I'm happy to hear that, Cindy,' I said in a reassuring voice, 'because I will have a man there before ten thirty. His name is Jim Hock. You can have the same confidence in him that you would have in me. He's got the best possible training, and will be invaluable if there's an emergency. He's not there to get anyone in trouble. He will be around to protect you and Cliff if it's necessary.'

'He's not coming to turn people over to the police?'

'His concern is the same as mine: to find Dallas.'

'I'm just wishing he could be invisible. It could ruin everything if he called attention to himself.'

'Mr. Hock has been told that. He's a professional, as I said, and knows what to do. He's coming to protect you and Cliff. And in case he's needed for Dallas. Now I want you to help me. I need to know the name of the person you're meeting with tonight.'

'I can't tell you. Can't you understand that people don't want to get involved? That was my condition before I agreed to help.'

'Look, I'm doing all I can to protect you. But you're going to have to show me something in return. So far we have nothing from you. Even the meeting last night turned to zero. I need the name of that person so I know that you're being as straight with us as we are with you.'

'You won't rush over to see him?'

'We won't do anything until you take us to him tonight.'

'Well . . . his name is Mike Barnes. He lives in Lansing.'

'How old is Mr. Barnes?'

'Nineteen.'

'Is he one of those holding Dallas?'

'No. I don't want you thinking that, even for a moment. I think he can put us in touch with those who are holding him.'

'Tell me who they are.'

'No.'

'Cindy, we have to trust each other. How can I help you if you hold back information?'

'I'll never tell you that.' Her voice had risen several octaves, and was tinged with panic. 'I was clear on this right from the beginning. My purpose is to help you find Dallas. Nothing else.'

'How quickly can we have him? I could find him without you.'

'Maybe tonight. Yes, maybe this can be settled tonight.' I could tell she didn't like the idea that we might find Dallas without her help. She wanted some control over the situation, and I could think of several reasons why. 'I think people want this over with,' she said.

'You gave me the alternative.'

'Yes.'

'Cindy, I hope for your sake that we can trust you. Put Cliff back on the phone, will you?'

I told Perotti, who had already guessed, that Hock would be in East Lansing before the 10:30 P.M. meeting. I said that he should stay in his room until Hock arrived. Anyone who wanted to reach him could contact him there, and if anything new arose, he should call me immediately. Perotti was becoming edgier by the minute. I thought he might be right to be afraid, and wished that that plane Hock was on could go faster.

After I hung up I again had a very strong feeling that I would have Dallas before my head once again touched a pillow. My desire to be in East Lansing for the climax was enormous. I knew I could still make it: a call to Lambert, and we could be off in my plane within the hour.

I had no proof whatever that Mike Barnes was the man who had called to demand that I leave Michigan, but I believed that he was. The man on the phone had certainly feared police involvement, and according to Cindy, it was the sight of the state police car that had prompted Mike Barnes to flee the night before.

Barnes was nineteen, Cindy in her mid-twenties. Gillitzer's idea about the chicken hawk had not been prominent for several days now. Attention had shifted to a younger crowd. Cindy, who said that she had actually seen Dallas, had mentioned that those involved were connected with her own circle of acquaintances, whom I (perhaps wrongly) assumed were young. Once again I had to consider the possibility of a drug angle. Friends of Cindy's and Mike's might be too young to fit the chicken-hawk category, but not to belong to the group most widely associated with drugs. Dallas had used large amounts of drugs; in fact, he had made them, and his skills in this area might be considered valuable enough to have something to do with his disappearance.

This Wednesday was torture for me. I stayed in my private office all day. I tried to read a book but couldn't concentrate. I played solitaire and lost. Newspeople around the country, and a few from overseas, called frequently, but my secretary had instructions not to put them through.

Just after 7 P.M. I heard from Hock. 'I'm here in East Lansing,' he said, 'at the airport. I've just rented a car.'

'Get over to the motel. There's a meeting with Cindy Hulliberger at ten thirty. She's supposed to take you and Perotti to see a nineteen-year-old named Mike Barnes. According to Hulliberger, Barnes can put us in touch with those who are holding Dallas.'

'Hulliberger and Perotti know I'm coming?'

'Perotti's happy about it. He's got an understandable case of the jitters. Hulliberger also professes delight. You can judge that for yourself. I can't tell you whether Barnes knows. You'll find out soon enough, I guess.'

'Right. What do you think?'

'I think we'll have Dallas soon. Be careful tonight. Call me just as often as you can. Call before you leave the motel to let me know what the plan is.' This was important. I was serving the same purpose for Hock that a police command post serves for an officer who is about to enter a building or talk with a suspect. The person at the command post needs to know where the officer is and what he intends to do. Nothing could be worse than for trouble to occur when the people in charge have no idea what the man in the street is doing.

Again the hands of the clock crept ever so slowly around, not helped by my constant checks of the time. Night had fallen, and inside my office it was very dark and quiet. A lone desk lamp was the sole illumination. The silence was almost as complete as it had been during my first day in the tunnels – an eerie, apprehensive silence that raised goose bumps on the arms.

Hock called just before 10 P.M.

'Okay,' he said, 'this is how it's going to come down. Perotti and I are going to follow Cindy to Mike Barnes's residence on Devonshire. She'll pick him up, and in separate cars we'll proceed to Edgewood Boulevard in Lansing. An apartment complex. Hulliberger and Barnes will enter to see an Archibald Horn. Evidently they believe he's the key to leading us to Dallas.'

'Have you talked with Barnes? Does he know about this trailing business?'

'No, I haven't talked with him. I'm taking Cindy's word for the fact that he knows.'

'What's your opinion of our friend Cindy?'

'I'm not sure. She appears to be telling the truth. She's certainly scared enough.'

'Why the separate cars?'

'According to Cindy, it's for the benefit of Horn. She doesn't want him to know of our existence until she and Barnes have talked to him. She's a stickler for precautions. Says she doesn't want to risk his seeing us when we pull up to the apartment.'

'Well, good luck.'

'As they say, if I'm good, I won't have to be lucky.'

'Don't believe that.'

It was fingernail-chewing time again. This maddening wait was the worst yet. From my desk I could see out through jalousie doors to the swimming pool, where the moon, shining through pear, pecan, and pine trees, sketched strange shapes on the water. I constructed a little game, a fantasy, around the figures dancing in the pool. It was beautiful out there, and as still as a church sanctuary.

I couldn't keep it up for long. My mind was a thousand miles away, in Michigan. I like to be in on the deciding moments of a case, and usually am. More important, since many of my cases involve potential danger, I do not like others to take risks that rightly should be mine. But I told myself that this was simply a situation where it was impossible to be along. I had to be in Texas in case that phone call came. This rationale accomplished no good, and the hands of the clock seemed to slow in direct proportion to my growing impatience. I even began to think dark thoughts about Hock. By 11:30 I was wondering how I could ever have hired someone so irresponsible. Surely he knew how much I wanted to hear from him, learn what was going on, find out about every single happening. In my mind I knew that Hock was doing just fine, but my heart operated on a different level.

The hands of the clock moved past midnight. Day

thirty. Thursday, September 13. I am not a superstitious person, but I wondered whether the number thirteen would be unlucky for us.

The phone rang just after 12:30 A.M. I was saying hello before the first ring had stopped.

'Good news or bad?' I asked before Hock could identify himself.

'Can't tell,' he said.

Good Lord, I thought. I'd almost rather have bad news than 'can't tell.' This case has been filled with 'can't tells.'

'Give me the rundown from the beginning.' I imagined Hock could hear the disappointment in my voice.

'Perotti and I followed Cindy Hulliberger. We were in the rental car, she in the red Vega. She wouldn't have been aware that we were behind her if she hadn't been part of the planning. She picked up Mike Barnes on Devonshire. He was waiting for her in the driveway.'

'Did you talk to him?'

'No. He got in the car, she drove off, we followed. As planned, we went to the apartment complex on Edgewood Boulevard, and Hulliberger and Barnes went inside.'

'So you still hadn't talked to him?'

'That's correct. At that point it would have been inadvisable. Their purpose was to speak with Archibald Horn, and they didn't want him to know about our presence. In any case, we arrived at the apartment complex at eleven o'clock and they were inside for fifteen minutes – the second-longest wait I can remember.'

'Don't tell me about time moving slowly,' I said. 'It's a lot better when you're waiting for something more than a phone call.'

'It turns out that that's what we were soon doing. After those fifteen minutes Cindy came out of the apartment and told us that they were waiting for a telephone call from a person or persons holding Dallas. She said we would have to wait outside a little longer.'

'Those were her words? Waiting for a phone call from those holding Dallas?'

'It could be one person; it could be more than one. She went back into the apartment, and then came the *first*-longest period I can remember. By my watch it was forty-five minutes. It was right on midnight when Cindy came out of the apartment, and Mike Barnes was with her. He invited us up to the apartment.'

'Barnes did?'

'Yes.'

'Describe him to me.'

'Five feet seven. Slim build, fair complexion, blond hair, blue eyes. Nineteen years old and lives with his parents.'

'So you went with them?'

'Yes. The four of us – Barnes, Cindy, Perotti, and me – went to the door, and Barnes knocked. Archibald Horn answered and asked us to come in.'

'What were you able to find out about Horn?'

'I was able to establish that he's gay, and spends a good deal of time on Michigan Avenue, in the gay section of Lansing. He admits that he's had male teenagers in his apartment, but says he has no idea where Dallas is. He denies knowing Dallas or anything about him.'

'Do you believe him?'

'No. But what good is that?'

'Well, what came next?'

'He had a boy in his apartment, maybe eleven years old. This sent Perotti into a spin. He said that if Horn didn't tell us the truth, he'd be in a lot of trouble.'

'It was probably a mistake to let Perotti go along.'

'He can get overly enthusiastic.'

'What did Horn do?'

'He asked for my identification. I showed it to him and then he demanded that we leave. Said he'd call the police if we didn't. That was an unnecessary touch.'

'You left right away?'

'Of course. He was saying he knew people in high places and could make things rough on us. That didn't impress me at all, but as you know, if a person wants you out of his place, you get out.'

'What about Cindy Hulliberger and Mike Barnes?'

'They left with us. Cindy said that Horn knew how to deliver Dallas to us if he wanted. I asked Barnes what he thought. He wouldn't say anything. Was like a clam. But he didn't contradict Cindy.'

'How about the phone call they were expecting? From those supposedly holding Dallas.'

'Evidently it didn't come.'

'So you sent Barnes and Hulliberger off on their own?' I knew he had. I knew what a good investigator would do next.

'Yes. Cindy will contact us tomorrow – later today, actually. I set up a surveillance outside the apartment.'

This was the perfect time to keep watch. If Horn had been shaken by the visit, he would probably act in haste. He might very well go see someone. People move quickly after a traumatic experience; call on a robbery suspect, and he will probably act swiftly to contact any confederates he might have, to alert them to danger or to develop stories that will mesh under intensive questioning. The good detective realizes this and lies in wait, hoping to garner important leads.

'Any luck?' I asked.

'An unmarked sheriff's car pulled up. I suspected that it was a police vehicle and ran a license check just before calling you. A white male got out and went directly to Horn's apartment. I assume the man is a sheriff's deputy, but I can't prove it. Anyway, Horn seemed to be waiting for him. He stayed in the apartment maybe thirty minutes, then came out and drove off.'

'And that's when you left?'

'Yes.'

The visitor almost certainly was a sheriff's deputy, which meant that at least one policeman, and probably many, now knew we were back in town. Horn would have told the officer about Hock; that probably was the primary purpose of the meeting.

'I want you to find out all you can about Archibald Horn.'

'As soon as the world is up and about.'

'And that sheriff's deputy, if that's what he is.'

'Right.'

'Keep in close touch, Jim.'

I laid the phone down and leaned back in my chair. It was 12:45 A.M., and fortunately, I wasn't the least bit tired. I had a great deal to think about and digest.

Even more fortunately, it was a long time before I was able to do this. In just forty-five minutes, at 1:30 A.M., the phone rang again. I picked it up on the second ring, having first to untangle myself from my lying-back posture. On the other end of the wire was the voice I'd waited so long to hear.

Chapter 20

'Mr. Dear?'

'Yes.'

'This is Dallas.'

It was indeed! Never did I doubt it was him, and I wanted to shout to the world that he was on the phone with me. Two emotions at once seemed to flood my entire body: enormous, unmitigated, body-relaxing relief that he was alive, and pure, get-up-and-celebrate jubilation because the great quest was probably near its end.

'Dallas, are you all right?' It was important to keep my voice benign. I felt ecstatic, but calm concern was the best emotion to portray.

There was the briefest of hesitations, then: 'Yes. I'm all right.'

His voice sounded simply pathetic, like that of a frightened, injured animal filled with terror and doubt and pleading to be cuddled and squeezed and made safe. My heart wanted to speed across those telephone lines to be with him.

'Dallas, where are you?' I asked.

This time the hesitation was longer. The phone's receiver was already slippery in my hand; in fact, my entire body was so wet with sweat that I might have been back down in the steam tunnels. It was as still as a tomb in my office. I could hear the boy breathing on the other end of the line, but this was the only sound to disturb the silence.

'Keep it cool, man. Keep it cool.' This new voice came, I guessed, from someone standing behind Dallas. It belonged to a male adult and was low and urgent, as if it came from a coach whose nervous charge might forget his instructions and panic into error.

'Dallas, *can* you tell me where you are?' I thought that if he was being held, he might be able to provide only yes-and-no answers.

There was no answer. Just the breathing.

'Is someone holding you?'

I heard a sob. Then he started to cry. He was weeping.

'I want you to hang in there, son. You don't know me yet, but I care a great deal about you. I want us to get together, because I just know we can be friends. You can't imagine how many people all over the world care about you and are rooting for you. When we meet, I know you'll be able to tell how special you are to me.'

The crying was no longer coming from deep in his stomach in wrenching, involuntary bursts. It had turned to sobs, each spaced a little further from the preceding one. Very little affects me more than the crying of a child who is in genuine pain, and it required no particular sensitivity to figure out that this boy had known experiences bordering on the unspeakable.

'Take your time, son,' I said. 'I give you my most solemn promise that I am only concerned about your safety. I can't think of anything I want more than your safety and happiness.'

Now there was only the breathing on the other end, more measured but still reminiscent of a tiny, terrified animal who might at any moment bolt and run. I could imagine Dallas's heart pounding in his chest.

'Can you tell me where you are?' I repeated.

This time I guessed that the wait was caused by a hurried conference between protégé and coach. I heard a brief whispered exchange but was unable to make out the words. The voices were Dallas's and the 'keep it cool' adult's.

'Dallas,' I said, 'I only want to bring you back from wherever you are. Son, that's the only concern I have. Nothing else matters to me but your safe return.'

Still not a word. Just the breathing of a creature; a rabbit perhaps, or a deer. That was good enough for me. I thought it would be bang-my-head-against-the-wall time if he hung up.

'You can trust me, son. I wouldn't let anything in the world hurt you. I wish you knew all the things I've done to find you. It's because I care. And right now there's nothing more I could ever care about than finding you and bringing you back to safety. I'll go anywhere to get you, son. I'll leave right away. You tell me where to be and I'll be there.'

'You really do care about me?' It was more a plea than a question.

'I wish I had the words to tell you how much.' He was talking and I didn't want him to stop. My hand gripped the phone hard, as if that would hold him. 'Tell me where you are and I'll be there as swift as the wind.'

'All you want is to bring me back?'

'That's all, son. To make sure you're safe, and always will be. If you want, though, I'd like for us to be friends. I could use a friend, and I think you'd be a very good one.'

'Mr. Dear, I can't tell you where I am right now. It's just not possible. I'll have to call you back.'

What could I do? I felt I might have won at least a small measure of his trust; pushing the issue could shatter the fragile structure of our very slight relationship. But I didn't want to let him get away from me, either. As in most of my cases – except much more so in this one, because of its compelling nature – a great deal of planning had been done to get to a critical crossroads, and I would be crushed if I let the solution slip away now.

'When will you call back?' I said.

The hesitation. The coaching. 'In an hour,' said the frightened boy. 'Two hours at the most.'

'Would you do me a favor, son? Would you call your parents? Let them know you're alive. This is very important, to them and to me. I could call them, but I know how much it would mean to them to hear your voice.'

This time the silence lasted perhaps ten seconds – a long time on the telephone. 'Can you call them?' I asked. 'Are you able to?'

'I'll call them.'

'Is there anything else I need to know? Are you sure you'll be okay?'

'Just wait for me to call back, Mr. Dear.'

'You bet I will. I'll sit right here where I am. Son, will you tell me where you are when you call? Will you tell me where I can come and get you?'

One last hesitation. 'I think so,' he said. 'I hope so.'

Then he was gone, and immediately I was assailed by self-recrimination. *Why did you let him go?* I asked myself bitterly. There's no guarantee you'll get him back. He's just a boy, and you didn't get anything from him. Not a single clue to his whereabouts. What kind of detective are you? Not a *single clue*. If he doesn't call back, you're not a whole lot further along than you were the day you took this case.

That wasn't true, and when I stopped criticizing myself, I thought that maybe it had gone all right after all. The more I analyzed, the more I felt that I probably couldn't have accomplished more in the conversation with Dallas, and with a different tack I might have fouled it up irretrievably. If that voice in the background came from a captor, he might have wanted to test my reaction. My assurances that all I wanted was Dallas's safety must have had a welcome ring to his ears. If I had pressed for more information, I might have been cut off entirely. Or, if Dallas was acting on his own, say with a friend or acquaintance in the background to lend moral support, he might himself have wanted to make a judgment. Could I be trusted? Was I worried mainly about him, or about capturing the others who were involved?

I did not doubt that Dallas was terrified. From the overall flow of the conversation I guessed that he was not in fear of his life from others. But then there were the last words he said, 'I hope so,' in response to my asking where he was, and I wondered whether he really had any control over what was happening on his end. In fact, if he *was* operating on his own, why call me? He'd never even met me. He could easily have learned my name by following news stories about his disappearance, but why choose me to contact? His parents, or even the police, would be a likelier choice.

Why had I received the call at this time? I could not believe that it was just by chance. Cindy Hulliberger had told Hock and Perotti that she, Barnes, and Horn were waiting in Horn's apartment for a telephone call 'from those holding Dallas.' It evidently had not come (who could be sure?). But might not it have arrived later? After Horn had not-so-politely demanded that Hock and Perotti leave the premises, might he have done something that led to Dallas's calling me? Or did he take that action after the visit from the person in the unmarked sheriff's car? This last seemed to me the most likely.

I decided I would know the answers to all my questions soon enough. I called Riddle, then Lambert, and told them to come to my house as fast as the speed limit would allow. It was necessary to be ready. I didn't want valuable time to elapse between Dallas's disclosure of his location and our arrival there to pick him up. We could make preparations for the trip now.

I turned on a few more lights in my office and started a pot of coffee brewing, even though I hate coffee. Maybe my hospitality would partially stifle any grumbles about 2 A.M. phone calls and low pay. I thought of breaking a long-standing rule and setting out an ash tray for Riddle, but that was going too far.

The call came at three o'clock, before Lambert and Riddle had arrived.

'Mr. Dear, this is Dallas.' I could tell he had been crying just a moment before but had managed to gain some sort of control.

'Are you okay?'

'Yes, I'm okay.'

'Will you tell me where you are?'

Again I heard that voice in the background.

'I'm going to have to call you back,' he said in a slow murmur. 'I'll give you the time and location then.'

'Why can't you tell me now, son?'

'It's just not possible. You don't understand.'

'Try to make me understand.'

'I can't do any more right now.' Dallas's voice was charged with emotion. He wasn't hysterical, but he was walking on an edge. It occurred to me what it had to be.

'You can't imagine how much people care about you,' I said. 'You have a lot of dear friends you don't even know about. One fellow I want you to meet came all the way from New York to East Lansing to try to find you. Another, not very much older than you, flew in from California. These people paid their own expenses. Their only concern is you. And there are so many others – I've had thousands of messages from people who are hoping and praying that you're all right. I mean it when I say that you have many friends, and I believe I'm one of your best friends. I'd like to have you visit me at my house, maybe stay a while as my guest.'

'What is your house like?'

'It's big. And it's isolated. Really isolated from everything. Swimming pool and tennis courts. Lots of gadgets – James Bond sort of things. You might enjoy looking them over.'

'There really aren't many people around?' Dallas's voice indicated that this was a highlight.

'Privacy, I can guarantee you, I've got.'

'That must be nice. A place all alone where you can think.'

'I'd love to have you stay here.'

'Maybe . . .'

'It's your choice, son. I just know we'd have a good time.'

'I can't promise you now.' His tone was wistful, sad. I wanted to keep him on the phone a long time, until I was sure he was all right.

'You could teach me a lot,' I said. 'I'd love to tell you about my business, see if you have any ideas. I get a lot of cases that are really challenging.'

'You use a computer?'

'I have. But I don't have my own computer. Maybe that would be a good thing to buy.'

'I'd like to talk to you before you do.'

'That would be good. A computer might be just what I need.'

'It's important to get the right one. That's the trick. Get the wrong computer, and it's really worse than useless.'

'Well, we can talk about that. I definitely want you to stay with me for a while. We'd have a good time.'

'It might be possible.'

'I wish I could come and get you now. I'm really eager

to meet you. I feel that you're a good friend already, but it will be a lot better when we're together.'

'I can't tell you where I am now. Things have to be worked out.'

'Can you tell me when you'll call? You must know how concerned I am. I won't believe you're safe until I see you.'

'I'll call you before ten this morning.'

'Can you tell me any more than that, son? I'm very worried about you. You must know that anything encouraging that you can tell me will be a help.'

'I just can't say any more right now. I'll call you before ten o'clock with a time and place.'

'I'll be waiting right here at the phone. What I told you still stands. I'll come anywhere to get you, and I'll leave right away. There's nothing I have to do but make sure you're safe.'

'I will call you. Don't doubt that.'

'I haven't, even for a moment. And I'll bet you called your parents like you said you would.'

'I did. They told me to call you. They didn't know I already had. They wanted to know where I am. I wouldn't tell them. The only person who'll know is you.'

'They told you how much they missed you?'

'Yes. They said they loved and missed me very much. Both of them were crying, and I was too. It was strange.'

'They do love you, son. Very, very much. I can tell you that from firsthand knowledge.'

'A lot of things have to be worked out.'

'They will be. Give it time. Let me help you. We'll be the best of friends.'

'Maybe it can happen,' Dallas said, his voice faraway. 'Maybe not.'

'It can,' I said. But I was talking to an empty line.

I needed to make a fast decision whether to take a

gamble. If you don't hang up the telephone right after the other person does, sometimes the line doesn't disconnect, and if the person who has called you picks up the receiver to telephone someone else, you can come on the line, pretending to be the operator. Disguising your voice, you can ask for the person's phone number on the pretext that there is trouble on the line. In this case, though, there was unacceptable danger in trying the stunt. It seemed to me that I had won a measure of Dallas's confidence, but I could irretrievably lose it if he caught me attempting to trick him. And it was likely that I would be caught. I'm good at changing my voice, but probably not good enough for someone as brilliant as this boy, who almost certainly knew more about telephone stunts than I did. It would be irresponsible to gamble.

It would be doubly irresponsible because I understood perfectly the primary reason for Dallas's delaying tactics: considerations of suicide filled his head. I'd done my best to dissuade him, but from sad past experiences I knew there was no guarantee of success. Dallas might indeed also want time to orchestrate a scenario for his rescue that would protect others who might be involved, but primarily he was thinking of killing himself. This meant that he had, or would have, some freedom of movement, which indicated in turn that the voice I'd heard in the background did not belong to a captor, or if it did, the captor would soon be out of the picture.

Many suicides make last-minute phone calls and/or leave a note behind, either to say goodbye to someone or to determine whether there is a reason to live. This is why we have suicide emergency centers. These calls really are life-and-death matters, and usually the potential suicide needs to be convinced that someone cares. The person doing the persuading is often someone at a suicide emergency center who has never met the suicidal person, and because these people are often successful at preventing a tragedy, I thought my conversation with Dallas might make the crucial difference.

I called the telephone company, and by sheer persistence, even though it was 4 A.M., I managed to get a supervisor on the line who seemed to know what she was talking about. I knew it was fruitless to ask where the two calls from Dallas had come from; it was something the phone company didn't know. I harangued and pleaded, however, for the company to place the equipment needed to trace a call on my line. A boy's life was at stake, I said. I pointed out that here was a chance for this much-maligned corporation to earn some good will, and I promised personally to report its good deed to the press. But a trace just wasn't possible, because of the time factor. Dallas's call was due before 10 A.M., and it would take more than six hours to get the necessary people and equipment in place.

Riddle and Lambert arrived while I was butting heads with the phone company, and I caught them up on what was happening as soon as I was free. I said that we had to be ready to go on an instant's notice and that I thought that Dallas's taking his own life was now the biggest danger.

'So it's going to be a cliff-hanger to the end,' Lambert said.

'Nothing's easy when it can be difficult,' I agreed.

Riddle put it best: 'This boy is worth whatever.'

I checked in with the Egberts. They were filled with hope, and I tried to bring them down to a more even keel without introducing negative thoughts. It wasn't just that I felt that Dallas might snatch himself from us at the last moment. I had attempted to lift their spirits during the darkest times of the investigation, following the adage that things aren't as bad as they seem, which is usually true. But things generally are not as bright as they seem, either. I kept the possibility of suicide to myself and assured the Egberts that as soon as we had a location, we would not lose a moment in going after their son, and yes, of course I would keep them updated, and yes, I was feeling the tension and anticipation too.

The tension really was terrific. It helped to have Riddle and Lambert with me, but even so I lapsed into long silences several times and paced the floor like a caged animal. I could tell they were deeply concerned too.

None of us would even venture an opinion as to where Dallas might be. Newspaper speculation had focused on Michigan, where he went to school; Ohio, where he lived; and, oddly, Texas, because he had relatives here and had wanted to attend his cousin's bar mitzvah. I didn't know, and it was useless to speculate. But it wasn't useless to begin making preparations.

I called Avia Jet, a private airplane company that I had used in the past, and explained a bit about the case I was working on. The person I talked with said that he'd been following it closely. I said that I needed to have a Lear jet standing by and that I would probably be leaving before noon, but I couldn't be sure. I said that under no circumstances was our destination to be made public; I did not know what to expect, but I wanted to be prepared for a rescue operation that could be both delicate and dangerous, and I was sure I didn't want the police or the press arriving before we did and fouling up the works. The Avia Jet representative assured me that he would not tell anyone about our destination, 'which right now I don't know.'

'I don't either,' I said, and left it at that.

I'd decided to charter a Lear jet rather than take one of my own planes because of the time involved. The Lear is much faster. Also, if we were to encounter bad weather, the Lear would probably have little difficulty in flying above it. But the most important consideration was speed. An operation such as this is almost always best handled swiftly. People who have witnessed police at work often are surprised by their decisiveness, the whiz-bang manner in which they take a suspect into custody. Of course Dallas was not a suspect, but there was no telling whether others would be with him, and it would be best to have him in my custody before possible haggling arose. In short, the thing to do was to get him first, as rapidly as possible within the bounds of safety and reason, before he or others had a chance to react, and *then* talk about the matter.

Everyone at some time or another has experienced a maddening wait, at the end of which will be reward or disappointment. These times can seem interminable. The wait that morning for Dallas's call ranks among the two or three worst I've known. He finally called, just a few minutes before ten.

'I'm so eager to see you,' I said, 'that I've been pacing holes in the carpet.'

'I guess you want to know where I am.' His voice was quiet, with a certain unhappy resignation. The tenseness was still there, along with nervousness and fright. He was not jumping up and down at the prospect of our meeting.

'I do want to know where you are. That's the only way I can help you.'

'I need a few promises from you first.' His voice was soft and sad, and I had to strain to hear.

'What are they?'

'I want you to come promptly at five o'clock tonight. I want you to stand exactly where I tell you.'

These requests again raised the possibility that others were involved, that the meeting was being set up for their protection. Well, I didn't have a choice. Dallas was about to tell me where he was – information that, as this is being written, has never been revealed to anyone, not even Mr. and Mrs. Egbert. Only Riddle, Lambert, and myself have known, and we had good reason for keeping it a secret. I have been offered thousands of dollars just for the name of the town where Dallas was, but until now the time was not right to release that information. I must confess that I have enjoyed the numerous wild guesses, some of them offered as fact, that have appeared in newspapers and on television. None of them have been correct.

'Of course I'll agree to your conditions,' I said.

'I'm in Morgan City, Louisiana.'

I'd never heard of the place (and later, when I saw it, I wished I still hadn't). I wrote the name on a sheet of paper and slid it over to Riddle, who had a map in his lap. I could have spent a lifetime guessing Dallas's whereabouts, and I would not have hit on the answer.

'Morgan City,' I said, as though this were the most logical location in the world. 'I can be there by five o'clock.' I thought I really could be. If it was so remote that no airfields were nearby, we could go in one of my planes and Lambert could land in a field. But this wasn't going to be necessary. Riddle was handing me his map, with Morgan City circled. The town was a hundred miles from New Orleans, in the southeastern part of Louisiana, close to the Gulf of Mexico. How Dallas Egbert had gotten there from Michigan State University was beyond my comprehension.

'Come to the corner of Front Street and Everette,' Dallas said, his voice still low and nervous. 'Stand on the west side, at the corner. I want you to wait ten minutes.'

'That's easy enough.'

'After ten minutes, walk across the street and go south on Front. About halfway down the block, on Front Street, between Everette and Freret, you'll come to a glass door with metal bars. You'll have to get inside. Go down the hallway to the first opening on the right. Head in that direction to the first door on the right. Knock on that door.'

'Are you going to be there, son?'

'I'll be there.'

'Dallas, I'd appreciate it if you don't go anywhere. If you stay right where you are. I'll be there when you say and you'll be okay.'

The boy agreed, and the line went dead.

I told Riddle and Lambert where we were headed. Riddle, not an emotional man, shook his head.

'It might as well be there as anyplace else,' I said.

'It's not that. Hurricane Frederic is going through Louisiana. We may not be able even to get into the state.'

How could this be possible? I wanted to scream. We knew where Dallas was and we might not be able to get there? I was sure he wouldn't wait past five o'clock, and I didn't want even to think of what the boy would do if we didn't show up. If he was going to get off to a decent start back in conventional society, he needed to know that he could count on people's promises. I didn't want to break the very first one I made to him, that I'd go anywhere to get him, even if I had an excuse as good as a hurricane.

I also didn't want to call the local police. This was a matter that might require the delicacy of a surgeon, and I doubted whether Morgan City's finest – no matter how much I explained this fact to them – would understand enough to apply a light touch in handling the rescue. Dallas wanted me to stand on a street corner for ten minutes. I guessed that this was so he or others could check me out before I went to his actual location. In all likelihood the people involved knew what I looked like. Someone else standing there might cancel the entire rescue, and if the police just headed for the building where Dallas said he would be, they might very well find nothing.

We decided to go to the airport to learn the news. I don't know about Riddle and Lambert, but I needed to get out and do something. Prudence told us we must be prepared. The sinister possibilities of this case had not been eliminated – drugs, kidnapping, murder – and we needed to be ready for the unexpected. I decided to carry a Walther PPK .380. Riddle and Lambert were with .38-caliber police specials.

At Love Field the news was good, at least for us. Although nearly half a million people across a three-hundred-mile swath of Florida, Alabama, Mississippi, and Louisiana were being moved to safer ground, and Frederic was every bit as powerful as Camille had been in 1969, smashing everything in its path, the hurricane was not threatening Morgan City or anything else between that town and Love Field in Dallas.

I thought we should get in and out of Morgan City fast. I didn't want to be suspected of sneaking around prior to 5 P.M. Our movements might be monitored as soon as we landed in Louisiana, and if so, all the observers were going to see was an operation strictly within the parameters Dallas had set down. I would get to that street corner at 5:00, pick him up at 5:10, and leave town.

We arranged for Hertz rental cars to be ready when we landed at Patterson Airfield, ten miles from Morgan City, then we departed from the Cooper Aeromotive terminal at Love Field at 3:25 P.M. Avia Jet's Lear crew consisted of pilot John Rowland and copilot Charles Roork. We told them enough about our mission to impress them with its seriousness, and made certain that when we arrived at Patterson Airfield they would remain there, ready for an immediate departure. The route was 420 statute miles, carrying us over Beaumont, Texas, and Lake Charles,

Louisiana, and took less than an hour to fly. We arrived at 4:20.

Lambert and I transferred to a 1978 Ford LTD, and Riddle followed us in an identical car as we drove Highway 90 to Morgan City. I was amazed that Dallas could have ended up in such an area. The landscape was gray and depressing, dotted with dilapidated shacks and rusted, abandoned machinery. It seemed to me that when the Great Depression hit this unfortunate countryside, it forgot to leave. The airport in Patterson surely existed only to serve oilmen, whose business was undoubtedly the sole reason anyone lived here at all. Billboards advertised the area's chief tourist attraction: Swamp Gardens.

The country, however, was paradise compared to Morgan City itself. Although some 16,000 people lived there, everywhere I looked the houses were old and there were shanties in a terrible state of disrepair. Morgan City was abysmal, seedy, rundown, disreputable; it was an oil town filled with transients. I imagined that the police had long ago stopped trying to control the ubiquitous, casual violence that I seemed to sense everywhere.

We drove past the city hall and courthouse in downtown Morgan City, and a *half a block away* was Railroad Avenue and a sight to rival the planet's seediest red-light districts: prostitutes strolled the block, peddling their wares to roustabouts and roughnecks (and probably politicians and businessmen too), surrounded by a solid phalanx of dimly lit bars with names like Star Bar, Tony's Bar, Happy Time Club (which had a sign in the window reading, 'Don't open door to wide'), La Petite Lounge, and Blowout Lounge. A few winos crouched in doorways with paper sacks. Burly bouncers looked this way and that through windows. The area seemed to have enough pawnshops to serve a city of a million or more. One hundred yards from these monuments was where Dallas had told me to find him.

I was standing on the southwest corner of Front and Everette promptly at five o'clock. Front Street seemed to be Morgan City's main downtown drag, and it wasn't much. The buildings were old, undignified, and depressing. If we were looking for trouble, this was the place to come. The pickup trucks, as numerous as in small-town Texas, sported bumper stickers that said 'I Got Drunk at Homer's,' 'Stay Out Of My Way,' and 'Redneck Heaven.' Confederate flags outnumbered American ones. I had to be a sight. I was wearing a three-piece, blue-striped Pierre Cardin suit, eelskin boots, and several big gold rings. I was as foreign to this Louisiana backwater as it was to me. Even a lady of the sidewalk, venturing a few yards from her usual patrol, could bring herself only to look at me, not to make an approach. A couple of roughnecks carrying cans of beer eyed me with distaste, but when I returned their glances, they let the matter pass.

Lambert was window-shopping across the street. The reliable Riddle, parked in his rental car some fifty yards up Front Street, was our backup.

I could see across the street and south to the doorway Dallas had directed me to enter. It was set between a series of stores and could lead into anything. The top half of the door was mainly a glass pane guarded by iron bars. I saw several men, but no one entered. It seemed certain that I was being watched, but from where I couldn't tell. I glanced at my watch every minute or so for the benefit of those eyes. In case they didn't know me, I wanted it clear that I had arrived, and on time.

I would have attracted myself if I'd been a police officer in Morgan City, but there was no sign of the law in this town. There was also no sign here of Frederic; it was a bright, clear, sunshine-filled late afternoon.

At 5:10 I crossed to the east side of Front Street and

headed south – a short trip, maybe forty yards. I passed Lambert without giving any sign of recognition, and sensed that he was casually moving his window-shopping in the same direction. Behind me, I knew, Riddle was tracking my progress through powerful binoculars.

The door was locked and barred. Failing to open it by turning the knob, I knocked, firmly at first but then loudly. There was no activity at all behind the door. I didn't want to break it down, so I headed back north on Front Street, east on Everette, and south to the rear of the building. Maybe I could get in from there; I knew Lambert would stay in front to monitor any activity in that area. But the back yard was guarded by an eight-foot chain-link fence topped with barbed wire. Someone trying to scale the fence from either direction would be ripped to pieces. It's a prison, I thought; it looks just like a prison.

I returned to Front Street and the door with the iron bars. I was angry and frustrated by this last barrier to what I prayed would be the successful conclusion to a very long case. Lambert had moved his shopping still closer to the door, and could hear as I pounded in vain for attention. Passersby on the sidewalk seemed to find this behavior not at all unusual.

I stepped back to stare up at the building, to see if there was any way to get in from above, and at that moment I heard a door buzzer, like those in apartments that release the front-door lock. The door swung open, and a man who too much resembled a derelict not to be one emerged onto the sidewalk. I grabbed the door with my left hand and slid inside, and as quickly and silently as a shadow, Lambert was right next to me. I had had no idea he had gotten that close; either I was slipping or he had perfected his skill to state-of-the-art.

We let the door close behind us, and I undid the button

on my suit jacket and the snap on my holster. Stretching ahead of us was a dimly lit corridor perhaps five feet wide, illuminated by a single bare light bulb dangling overhead some fifteen feet away. Where the corridor led I had no idea. The building itself, with its creaking wood floor and peeling paint, might have housed small offices in some long forgotten time.

It was ten feet to the corridor where Dallas had told me to turn right, a corridor as twilit and depressing as the first, and I knew that Lambert, at my rear shoulder, was watching behind us to be sure we wouldn't be surprised. I didn't think we'd been led into a trap, but it wasn't impossible. We proceeded slowly and quietly, though no one could step on those floorboards without causing creaks, and we kept our ears cocked for any other sounds. There were none.

Six feet after we turned right we found the door: old, but with sturdy wood. I listened, my ear an inch from the door. Not a sound. Not a rustle. My heart beat faster. I knew this was the moment. Would I find Dallas alive behind that door? Would he be dead? Never before or since have I felt such sharp, piercing anticipation – trepidation –as when I lifted my fist to knock.

No answer.

I listened, but the building was as still as those Michigan State University steam tunnels.

I knocked again.

Nothing.

Dallas was gone, or he was dead inside that room.

I reached for the doorknob. If it didn't turn, I was going to knock the door down.

The door swung open inward and I stepped inside, Lambert so close that he was brushing my back.

I saw Dallas immediately, and had to blink back my shock at his appearance. *He was so small*. He didn't look sixteen years old. My first impression was of a child of perhaps seven. A *waif*. Dallas sat on the edge of a low army cot, feet barely touching the floor, hands clasped between his legs, head so bowed that his chin was on his chest. He might have been a little boy pounded by blows and torture and now defeated, with no defiance or fight left in him at all, only a pitiful, accepting despair. Whatever he had experienced had crushed him. Hunched over, Dallas might have been mistaken for a gnarled little old man, all huddled up into a small package and trembling from a cold that didn't exist.

Dallas's head didn't move as I entered the room, but his eyes briefly and without real recognition flickered up to mine. There were scratches on his face. Tears were tracking down his cheeks, and his crying was the worst kind: noiseless, coming from deep within but stifled before it became sound, perhaps because no sound could truly portray his misery. He emitted such an air of tragic helplessness and loneliness; it was absolutely genuine, entirely devoid of guile or play-acting. I can't recall ever being so affected by the sight of another human being.

The room was maybe twelve feet by ten feet, with worn, tattered army cots on each side. It took only two steps to reach Dallas's side, but I had to duck to keep from hitting my head on a rod stretched across the length of the room, six feet off the floor. I assumed that it was for hanging clothes, but there were no clothes in this room, or anything else except those two army cots. No sink, no chest of drawers, no chairs, no lamps, not even a window. The room would not have met the standards of a prison cell.

'It's going to be all right, son,' I said to Dallas, putting my left hand on his right shoulder. I've read a lot about the mothering instinct; I think that what I was experiencing was the fathering instinct. I wanted to pick this wretched boy up in my arms and hug him and make him safe.

Dallas had nothing to take with him. I slid my left arm all the way around his shoulders and helped him to his feet. He stood tentatively, wavering, leaning against me, his head touching my side below my chest. He was five feet three, but crouched and shaking like a tottering old man, he seemed much shorter.

Lambert had his instructions. If we encountered any trouble from other people, he was to take Dallas and hurry him straight to our rental car, parked fifty feet away on Front Street. From there they were to go directly to the airport and back to Texas. I would be able to find my way home on my own. I wasn't playing hero, and Lambert knew it. My only responsibility now was Dallas's safety.

My arm around his shoulder, I guided the boy out the door of the miserable room, into the narrow, dark hallway, to the intersecting corridor, and down to the door that I'd had so much difficulty getting through. Next to me Dallas was nearly limp, listing on rubbery legs and leaning disjointedly against my side. When we reached the door, I slipped to his other side, put my right arm around his shoulders, and turned the knob with my left hand. With Lambert right behind us, we stepped outside.

There were four of them, big, husky, ready for a fight. 'What's movin' here?' said one of them, stepping forward.

'Come any closer,' I replied, 'and I'll take your head off.'

These unfortunates *liked* to fight. In Texas they're called shit-kickers, and pain doesn't affect them. Not yours. Not theirs.

'You movin' that boy?' This from the one who had come front and center. He had yellow-black teeth and stupid little round button eyes. 'You ain't movin' that boy nowhere.'

Lambert had Dallas by the shoulders and was about to

start him toward the car. Lambert can be a terror, and I wondered whether the thugs had any idea whatever how lucky they were that he was removing himself from the scene. But I wanted to get out too – right away. Maybe there was one thing these ugly lumps would understand.

I reached inside my suit jacket, removed my Walther PPK .380 (I have an easy-draw holster), and held it pointed sideways against my chest. The weapon looks fearsome, and is. If anything were going to bring a glint of intelligence and reason to the dull eyes of these menaces, it would be this gun. And the look in the eyes of the person who held it.

Time froze. Later I deduced that the delayed reaction was caused by the inordinate length of time it took the brains of these Neanderthals to sort out and judge the message their visual sense had just transmitted.

Drawing a gun, even the rawest rookie cop can attest, is inviting trouble of the worst kind. A good policeman only does so as a last resort, and I mean last. But there was no other way with the foursome we faced. Violence was first nature to them, and they could strike, even as they smiled, which at this moment they weren't doing. I guessed that they were transients working an oil field, in town like cowboys of the Old West after a cattle drive, looking for trouble. They were Morgan City's version of the muggers of New York, the sadistic bikers in California, and the drug gangs of Florida. I couldn't believe that they had any connection with the slightly built, highly intellectual Dallas, who came from a genteel midwestern family. But what did I know? What did I know about the missing thirty days in the boy's life?

The leader took maybe a quarter-step back. I don't think that in what passed for his mind he had decided what to do, but the fact that he was looking at the gun and retreating, however slightly, decided *me* to attempt to leave with Dallas and Lambert. Tucking the gun back in the shoulder holster (I had purposely been careful that no one on the street other than the four would see it), I accompanied the boy and Lambert past them on the sidewalk and toward the car. They stared us all the way into the vehicle.

Dick Riddle, seeing the potentially dangerous confrontation develop, had moved his car nearer the scene. If I had been overwhelmed, I'm sure he would have come to my assistance, but his instructions were to follow Lambert and Dallas to the airport. The boy was what counted.

Once we were in the car, we made as quick a getaway as we could. I drove the speed limit, with Dallas sitting between me and Lambert and Riddle following behind. I snatched glances at the boy when I could. He sat in the car just as he had in that desolate room: hands clasped between his legs, chin down on his chest. He was trembling, but there were no more tears. If not for the trembling, Dallas could almost have passed for catatonic. It did occur to me as we pulled up to Patterson Airport that he hadn't uttered a single word.

We escorted Dallas onto the waiting Lear jet and made him as comfortable as possible, then Riddle and Lambert stood guard outside the plane while I checked the rental cars in (each had been driven twenty-two miles). I had two phone calls to make before we could depart.

'Dr. Gross? This is Bill Dear.' Dr. Melvin Gross was Anna Egbert's brother-in-law, Dallas's favorite uncle, and the man who had recommended me to the Egberts.

'Bill! Who could ever have imagined the direction of this case! It's good to hear from you. How is your hunt going?'

'I've got Dallas. He's with me now.'

'Why . . . why, that's just marvelous. How is he? Where are you? This is just the best possible news.'

'I don't know how Dallas is. That's why I'm calling you. I'm no doctor, but I don't think he has a serious physical injury. I have worries about how he is mentally. I imagine he's gone through an awful ordeal and is in some sort of shock. I'm bringing him to Texas, and I think you ought to look at him.'

'Of course. Immediately. I'll arrange for him to be checked into Irving Community Hospital. What time will you arrive?'

'I can't be sure. Maybe eight thirty. Could you be ready before then?'

'You bet, Bill. I don't know how you did it, but you sure have the gratitude of a lot of people.'

I called the Egberts.

'I have wonderful news for you,' I said when they both were on the phone. 'I have Dallas. He's safe.'

There was a squeal of joy from Anna Egbert's throat, an elemental eruption of the purest relief and elation.

'Bill,' she said, 'you've given us the finest present anyone could ever receive. This is the answer to all of our prayers. Bless you, Bill.'

'I've been in touch with Dr. Gross,' I said. 'We're going to check Dallas into a hospital, just to be sure he's okay mentally and physically. I'll get in touch with you later to give you more details, but for now, be assured that we'll take good care of him.'

The jet left Patterson Airfield at 6:10 P.M. Lambert sat up front near the crew, and Riddle was across the aisle from me. Dallas had the window seat directly on my right. I'd told Lambert and Riddle not to talk with the boy unless he spoke first, and for twenty minutes or so I debated whether I should say anything. No conversation could be better than the wrong one, and I wasn't sure what to say.

At least Dallas's chin was off his chest. He was looking uninterestedly out the window.

'I'm not going to ask you any questions now,' I said, both to break the ice and to reassure him. 'I do want you to feel absolutely sure that you're safe.'

Dallas didn't reply, but he had heard me. You can tell whether a person has heard or is far away and can't be reached.

'I meant what I told you on the telephone. I'd like very much to be your friend. We could have good times together.'

His eyes no longer were directed straight out the window. His head had dropped a bit and he was looking down, as if in thought.

'I'd like you to come and visit me. As often as you like. Yes, I'd just love for you to see my place.'

'I'd like that,' Dallas said. These were the first words I'd heard from him, other than over the phone. He lifted his head and again looked out into the darkening sky.

'You'll be seeing your uncle, Dr. Gross,' I said to Dallas when we were ten minutes away from landing. 'I guess you know how happy he'll be to find out you're safe.'

We arrived at the Cooper Aeromotive terminal at 7:05, fifty-five minutes after we'd left Patterson Airfield. I'd had a radio message sent ahead asking Bill Courson to meet us. Courson, a friend and former deputy sheriff, worked for me on and off, and I wanted his presence as an extra precaution. I didn't particularly fear any intervention from whoever might be involved in Dallas's disappearance, but it was my responsibility to guard against all eventualities. I suspected that sometime before we delivered Dallas to his uncle, we might have an encounter with the press, and from experience I knew that reporters could be difficult to shake.

As soon as we arrived I headed for a telephone to call my office. It was as I had feared. My secretary told me that there were more than two hundred people milling around on the grounds of my property. Word had leaked that Dallas had been found, and every television station and newspaper in the area had representatives waiting for the arrival of the celebrated, long-missing boy. Only a very small number of people knew that Dallas had been located, and I was fairly certain which one had given out the information. I was positive when my secretary informed me that the same mob scene was occurring at Irving Community Hospital.

I called Dr. Gross at the hospital. 'We can't have all these reporters jostling Dallas,' I said. 'It's unthinkable to put the boy through a media circus. I imagine that his nerves are nearly shattered already, and this isn't going to help at all.'

'What do you think we should do?'

'I'm going to take I-35 north to Belt Line Road. I'll park just west of I-35 on Belt Line. Meet me there and I'll turn Dallas over to you.'

It was a miniprocession: Dallas, Lambert, and I in the lead car; Riddle behind us; Courson trailing Riddle. We parked on the shoulder of Belt Line, in the town of Carrollton. It was 8:30 P.M. Dr. Gross was already there, and I opened the passenger door and let Dallas out.

It was like a scene out of a motion picture: two people eyeing each other at a distance and then running to embrace. Mainly I watched Dallas. He raced along the shoulder of the road and flew into his uncle's arms. Bear-hugging each other beneath a bright, clear Texas sky, they did a full-circle pirouette. Dallas was crying, but this time I could tell they were tears of joy.

'Don't worry,' I heard Dr. Gross say to Dallas. 'You don't have to go home until you want to.'

Then he called to me as he let Dallas into his car. 'Bill, you did a great job. We really appreciate it and won't forget.'

Chapter 21

I returned home to eerily lit chaos. A large band of nomads seemed to have congregated under searchlights on my front lawn, which resembled the site of a gigantic accident, replete with hordes of reporters, police, and curious onlookers. I have never seen the press turn out in such numbers. A neighbor said he counted to three hundred before giving up the effort. Two helicopters had landed, one on my helipad but the other on my yard!

Even though I couldn't recall the last time I'd slept, exhaustion had not yet crept in. I still was riding the high of having found Dallas, so I gave in and held a press conference. I stood behind so many microphones that a U.S. President announcing an important treaty might have been envious. Parts of the conference were televised live, as stations broke into their regular programming, and excerpts were shown coast-to-coast and throughout much of the world the next day.

The only matter I felt the reporters had a right to be disappointed about was my refusal to divulge where we had found Dallas. Until I could learn why and how he had gotten to Morgan City, I didn't want reporters digging up and printing information that would needlessly embarrass the Egberts and, more important, that might be harmful to Dallas. I wasn't going to tell even if they asked a million times, which for a while it seemed they would.

The press couldn't decide whether to be elated or let down by my description of the events leading to Dallas's discovery. The juicy part was the sudden, out-of-the-blue phone call from the young genius, which the reporters really shouldn't have been so surprised about, since I'd been predicting his imminent recovery. I talked about the caller who had demanded that I leave East Lansing, about Hock's activities just hours before I heard from Dallas, about the intense pressure we exerted on and around the MSU campus which must have loosened tongues and inspired those with knowledge of the case to apply the brakes before a calamity could occur.

I told the reporters what they asked to hear – that is, how Dallas was dressed when I found him (incredibly, he was wearing the same clothes he'd had on when he left Karen Coleman in the Case Hall cafeteria: blue jeans, brown T-shirt, tennis shoes); whether the boy was all right (physically, yes, I thought so; emotionally, I was without qualifications to judge); whether Dungeons & Dragons had played a role in the disappearance (Dallas had been through a jolting experience and I hadn't wanted to question him on details); whether Dallas had gone into the steam tunnels (I had evidence that he had, but had not asked him directly); where he had been for thirty days (same answer: the time and place had not been right to question Dallas); what was the significance of the corkboard and suicide note (I had ideas, but it was better not to speculate at this time); when they could see him (I didn't know; Dallas had been put in the care of a doctor); what was the reaction of the Egberts (great happiness, obviously); whether the Egberts would be coming to Texas (yes, they would be arriving on an early-morning flight); and whether Dallas would be returning to Michigan State University (I almost choked when I heard this question, and I amazed myself with my restraint by saying only that I didn't know).

Always the questioning came back to where I'd found the boy. A few of the reporters tried to trick me into answering, slipping the query among questions about an unrelated area of the investigation, but there was no way that the information was going to come from my lips. My firmness in this regard did not discourage them.

'Was it in Texas?'

'No, it was not in Texas.'

'Ohio. Did you find him in Ohio?'

'Not in Ohio. Listen –'

'How about Michigan?'

'No, Michigan is wrong.'

'We have evidence that one of your planes was flown to Michigan today.'

'Your evidence is wrong, unless the plane was stolen.'

The news conference lasted more than an hour, but even when I said, 'No more questions' and walked away as a gesture of dismissal, determined stragglers attempted to learn the little something extra. It was 11:30 P.M. before I was alone and could shower and put on fresh clothes. It was after midnight, in the early hours of September 14, before I was on my way to Dallas–Fort Worth Airport to meet the Egberts.

They arrived on an American Airlines flight just after one o'clock, the radiance of relief and joy shining through their fatigue and through the lines on their gray faces, etched deeply and probably permanently by their son's disappearance. I was now very exhausted too, having deflated from the tremendous pressure (mostly self-inflicted) like a rubber inner tube that is suddenly punctured and becomes flat and flaccid.

Anna Egbert was crying, and Jim Egbert, normally reserved, couldn't stop talking. Mostly he went on about what an excellent job my agency had done; he thanked me so often that it became embarrassing. He was just glad his son was back safe and sound, and talking was a way to fill up the time until he saw him.

We drove to Dr. Gross's home in Irving. He and his

wife were waiting for us on the front lawn and took us inside. Dallas was in a bedroom, resting, and I went to get him. He was lying down with his eyes open, and he seemed much more relaxed – not, I hoped, only because of the sedative Dr. Gross had given him. He smiled weakly when he saw me.

'I told you everything would be all right, didn't I?' I said.

'Yes, sir.' This was something. He was talking.

'Your mom and dad are outside. Would you like to see them?'

'Not right now. Maybe in a few minutes.' He sat up. He was still weak but remarkably improved over the first time I'd seen him.

'Is something wrong?'

'I'm afraid of something.' And I could tell he was. His hands shook, and his voice was low and hesitant.

'You can tell me what it is,' I said. I meant what I was going to say. 'I want to be your friend, Dallas. I believe a real friend is one you can trust. You need to know you can trust me with anything. If you're afraid of something, you can tell me.'

'You wouldn't say what it is?'

'Not if you don't want me to.'

'It's Mom. She'll want to know everything about what's happened since I disappeared. Do I have to tell her?'

'No, you don't. If that's what you prefer, you don't have to tell her. I know you've had trouble with your mother. I hope now everything will be better.'

'It won't be better, Mr. Dear. She'll be okay for a few days, but then it will start again. Always pushing me. Always complaining about what I do. It won't be better.'

'She's had a lot of time to think, son. I really believe things might improve. It's going to take some effort on your part too.'

'Well, I hope things can change. I just can't see it happening.'

'You've both been through a lot. Just this incident is more than some people experience in a lifetime.'

'I wish Dad would stand up to her.'

'Dallas, so much might be changed. All anyone can ask is that you meet your parents halfway. I want you to try.'

'I will.' He was off the bed and on his feet, another improvement. I doubt whether he could have walked without support when I first saw him.

'Good. And I'd like you to visit me today after we all get some sleep, if your uncle thinks you're up to it.'

'That would be fun. Tell me about your detective agency and we'll decide if you can use computers.'

'You've got a deal.'

We went out into the living room and the next scene happened very fast. Mrs. Egbert and Dallas had their arms around each other, and Dr. Egbert's arms were around both of them. All three squealed with delight, laughing and crying together. There was plenty of 'I love you' and 'I missed you' and 'I'm sorry.' It was a wonderful, beautiful family reunion, and all differences were suppressed or forgotten – forever, I hoped. It was time for optimism and thankfulness and new beginnings.

I stayed maybe twenty more minutes. I'd asked the Egberts earlier not to grill Dallas about what had happened, which was probably an unnecessary precaution, and had advised them chiefly to show him a great deal of love and affection, advice which, I could see, they surely did not need. Comfortable family matters were being discussed, and after we all decided that it would be best for Dallas to visit my home the next afternoon at one o'clock, I said good-bye and headed for home. I had a serious struggle not to fall asleep at the wheel.

I knew I'd be asleep the moment my head touched the

pillow, but in the rush of events I'd forgotten an important item that needed my attention. I called Hock in East Lansing to give him the good news.

'Congratulations,' he said as soon as he answered the phone. 'It's great that you got him.'

'You know?'

'It's the big story on the news here.'

'I guess all I can tell you then is to come home.'

'Was it what Perotti and I did here that led to the break?'

'I don't know yet. It doesn't matter. We did it, Hock, that's what counts, and you deserve a lot of credit. Tell Perotti, will you? Thank him for me.'

Bedtime. Seven o'clock in the morning. I turned the sheets down. I slipped beneath them. I had lowered my head to within an inch of my pillow, which meant that I was an inch away from being asleep, when I heard a rapping on the sliding glass door that leads from the lawn into my bedroom. What in hell? I thought. What now?

I had my Walther PPK .380 out from beneath my mattress and was gliding toward the glass door when I heard the noise again. It just wasn't possible, I thought; no one could get right outside my bedroom without my knowledge. Then I remembered: I must have been more tired than I thought, because I'd forgotten to turn on the alarms attached to the fences surrounding my home, an oversight that had *never* occurred before. But what about the dogs? Houdini couldn't get by my dogs . . . Right, if they were roaming the grounds, but I'd locked them up because of the news conference.

Wearing undershorts, I decided that the direct approach was best. Down in a crouch, lightning fast, I slid the glass door open and pointed my gun directly toward the stomach of Bob France, reporter for the *Dayton Journal Herald*. France had been among the very best of the reporters covering Dallas's disappearance.

'I'm here,' he said, ignoring the gun. 'Came as soon as I heard. Couldn't make it in time for the news conference, but this might work out even better.'

'I'm glad you're here because that means you can leave. Get lost, France. I need sleep.'

'Is this any way to greet a friend? Look, about where you found Dallas, why not –'

'How did you become my friend? I'm getting some sleep. You're getting off my property.'

'After I came all the way from Dayton? Climbed those fences and trudged a quarter-mile uphill to get here? Almost was shot?'

'Who almost shot you?'

'Some guy in undershorts.'

I let him in and we talked for an hour. Not just because it was one-on-one but because he's a good reporter, Bob France acquired information about Dallas's disappearance that enabled him to write stories on the case that were superior to almost all I later read. I didn't tell him where I had found Dallas, but there were plenty of details the press conference hadn't brought out. I liked Bob France, and later we did indeed become friends.

We finished talking at about eight-fifteen. France left, after making an appointment to see me again, but this time I didn't even make it under the covers before I was interrupted. It was a telegram for Dallas, care of me, from Don Gillitzer in New York – a poem, with just a short message at the end.

> I know how it feels
> When you can't figure the game
> But still somehow think you should win.
> I know how it feels
> On the outside looking in.

> I know how it feels
> When you don't know where to look
> But still somehow long for a home.
> I know how it feels
> To be young and alone.
>
> You've been much on my mind. I'm glad you're alive.

I later showed the telegram to Dallas, and it appeared to have considerable meaning to him. I also told him about Gillitzer and how he had come all the way to Michigan on his own money and put himself in dangerous situations, because he had cared enough to help. Gillitzer had said that all he wanted from his efforts was to meet Dallas; I knew the boy would enjoy a meeting too, but I told him there was plenty of time.

I slept until one o'clock on this Friday and woke up if not refreshed, at least excited. We had done it! We had found the boy! I realized that it really hadn't dawned on me until now. Why, it had been only yesterday! Twenty-four hours earlier we hadn't even left Love Field for Morgan City. I stretched out on the bed between the crisp sheets and savored the triumph.

Now I had time to take care of something I'd promised to do. I drove to the original Neiman-Marcus in downtown Dallas and picked up gifts for the staff at the Red Roof Inn. I knew I would be going back to East Lansing in a week or so and could deliver them then. As I was reaching for my credit card, I noticed the three slips of paper I'd stuffed inside my wallet back on August 22, our first day on the case, when Lambert, Riddle, Hock, and I had guessed how it all would turn out. I had guessed a suicide. When I got back to my car, I read what the other three had thought.

'Murder' was written on Dick Riddle's slip of paper.

'Runaway,' Hock had scrawled.

'Kidnap' was Lambert's speculation.

I had said that the person closest to the truth could have bragging rights about being the best detective. Riddle and I had been wrong, but had Lambert and Hock been correct? It was painfully apparent that although we had brought Dallas back, we had little idea of where he had been, or why. I hoped Dallas would provide the answers, but probably it would be a long time, if ever, before anyone other than a psychiatrist should probe deeply enough to learn what had happened.

That evening Dr. Egbert held a news conference at my home. It drew a large media turnout, and Dr. Egbert handled himself exceptionally well in front of extremely discontented reporters. The press had been told that Dallas would not be available for questioning – it would have been madness to subject the boy to this – but evidently they didn't take us seriously. Reporters were openly hostile because they couldn't meet the boy and disbelieving when Dr. Egbert said he couldn't provide many of the answers they wanted. The truth is, he simply didn't know. Nor did I, not nearly as much as I wished, and precisely this thought was on my mind as I settled in after the news conference for what would be my first real sleep since August 21, the day before I received Dr. Egbert's call about Dallas's disappearance.

The next day, Saturday, September 15, I felt fresh and alert. Looking forward to an enjoyable day with my new friend, I picked Dallas up at noon at Dr. Gross's home, as planned, and headed back for my house. I intended to fix sandwiches for the two of us, then let the afternoon proceed as it would.

Dallas still wore jeans and a T-shirt – blessedly, not the same ones I'd found him in – and he seemed rested and relaxed. But in comparison to what? What was rested and relaxed for him? He certainly wasn't chattering away; in fact, he barely said anything, but his demeanor was bright and he showed interest in his surroundings. He had asked me to bring news clippings relating to his disappearance, and these I now handed to him in two bulging manila envelopes. Dallas thumbed through them, stopping occasionally when something caught his interest. I got the impression that he was amazed by the attention the case had drawn.

'I called Karen Coleman,' he suddenly said, looking up from the pile of stories on his lap. 'Was that okay?'

'Sure,' I replied. I wondered why he felt he had to ask.

'I just wanted her to know I was all right.'

It wasn't until I reached DeSoto that I decided it might be pleasant to eat in a restaurant. Sue's Place is a little country restaurant with good hot lunches.

'You'll love the special for the day,' I said. It was chicken-fried steak, mashed potatoes, and gravy.

'Could I have a hamburger?'

'If you want.'

We sat across from each other at the small table, and Sue herself waited on us. She didn't recognize Dallas, though his picture was in the papers. Dallas had brought the clips inside with him and became increasingly absorbed by his own story. He shook his head a lot, which I took as a criticism of the journalists' accuracy. Through one hamburger and then a second he silently read the story that both of us had been living.

'I guess it's not so bad,' he said at last, 'given what they had to work with.' He put the clippings aside. 'I suppose you'd like to know what really happened.'

'Sure I would.' I looked at him closely. I didn't want him to think he had to tell me anything. Youngsters are sometimes very good at knowing whether a person is being sincere with them. If Dallas could see inside me, he would recognize that I had nothing but hope that his life could be straightened out. 'But you should tell me only if you want to.'

'I'd like to tell you.'

'You let me know what you think you should. Just be sure it's the truth. A friend doesn't lie to another friend.'

'It's pretty bad.'

'No, it isn't, Dallas. You *think* it's pretty bad. I can't persuade you otherwise. But I'll tell you, and I know you have a good imagination – I've read your poetry – you couldn't make up a story that would shock me. Try as you might, you couldn't do it. What happened was caused by many things we're just not intelligent enough to control or understand.'

'It's my fault.'

'No. It's not anybody's fault. Besides, fault doesn't matter. It's what we do now. I've made many mistakes, too, done things I'm ashamed of.'

'I don't want anyone else to know. It has to be a secret between us. It's bad, and I couldn't face others if they knew.'

'I won't tell.'

'You must not go after anybody. You have to promise me that. I don't want to get anyone into trouble.'

'I promise.'

Dallas stopped for a moment, then asked if he could have a Coke. It was 1:45 and we were alone in the restaurant. The boy's face had grown exceedingly grim, graying almost before my eyes, and I knew tears weren't far away. I went to get him the soft drink and asked Sue in a whisper if she could keep herself busy in the kitchen while we talked.

'I guess it's never going to be easy,' Dallas said when I got back to the table. His hand shook so violently I could hear ice cubes clink in the glass. Then he began.

'I'd been planning to disappear for a long time, Mr. Dear. I thought about it for maybe nine months, or more. At different times I had different reasons. I planned just to go somewhere and kill myself. A place where no one would find me. I didn't think anyone cared, and I didn't want anyone to have to bother with burying me. No one was nice to me while I was alive, so why should I let them be nice when I'm dead? I even studied drug dosages so I'd know what would be fatal. Getting the drugs was no problem. I didn't think dying would be too bad, the way I had it planned – like just feeling all warm and going to sleep. I even planned what I'd dream about before I drifted away.

'But other times I thought it would be better to disappear and not kill myself, disappear and never be seen again. I was being cruel at times like this, and I didn't like the thoughts I was having. It was just revenge against my mom and dad. Especially Mom. I had the feeling she'd never let up on me. It would have been bearable if I thought she wanted me to improve, to do well, because it would help me, but it was to make *her* look good. Well, if I disappeared, I felt that would really be a punishment for them. They'd never be able to rest, worrying about me. Maybe once every five years or so I'd see they got a note or something to indicate that I was still alive. You see, if I was dead they could blot me out, but if I was alive they couldn't. It would be sweet revenge for the way they messed up my life. Every five years a little reminder that I was out there somewhere.

'Other times I didn't want suicide or revenge, but I thought I'd just go away for a while and think. There was always pressure – school, parents, sometimes a job – and never time to do what I wanted to do. What I really wanted was just to lie in bed and read good science-fiction books and not have anything at all to worry about. It wasn't possible and I knew it. But I thought that if I could just get away alone, without interruptions, all by myself, I'd be able to reason things through and come up with a way of living that would be not just bearable but pleasant. These times were fun, when I imagined thinking everything out, getting it all in a neat little plan, and then laying it on the line to my parents. "This is the way it's going to be, or else." The trouble was, I couldn't be sure of the "or else." Maybe I could live with my uncle in Texas, that would have been good, but I was afraid to ask, and what if my folks just said no? I had to get away and think. Get my plan together – something so reasonable to everyone that there couldn't be any doubt that it would be accepted. It would be best for me, for my parents, for everybody. The key was getting away by myself to work all this out. I needed time. There was never enough time, the way I was living. Interruptions. Pressure. My parents hounding me. I wanted my life to get simpler and it just got more complicated.

'Well, that's it. At different times I had three different reasons for wanting to disappear. Disappearing itself was on my mind all the time, for maybe nine months, as I said. But all I did was think about it. No action. All show and no go. I started to talk to myself – not out loud, you understand, but in my mind – and I kept telling myself that I had to act. I was just a think factory. Finally I couldn't take the inaction anymore. *Just do it*. That was August fourteenth. *Just do it*. Act, and then see what happens.'

'Karen Coleman was the last person you talked with?' I was skating on razor-thin ice. I didn't want recollections of the disappearance to overwhelm the boy, but an investigator knows that the moment of revelation has to be seized or it may be lost forever.

'Yes. I had lunch with her. I knew what I was going to

do. I didn't have much money – just a few dollars – and I wanted food in my stomach before I left.'

'You went to the steam tunnels, didn't you?'

Dallas seemed surprised. 'How did you know that? I didn't read it in any of the stories you gave me.'

'I just know. I've done nothing but think about you for a long time, and I've learned a lot about you. Tell me, where did you enter the tunnels? Through the basement of Case Hall?'

'Tell me how you guessed that.'

'Once I knew you'd gone into the tunnels, I figured you'd done it right away, and in the surest way so you wouldn't be seen. That would be to slip right down into the basement and from there to the tunnels.'

'Right. I'd practised before. It was easy.'

'Before we go any further, Dallas, tell me about the note. A lot of us thought it was a suicide note. For a while I believed it was.'

'It was, sort of. I had three things on my mind, remember? If suicide was what turned up, I'd said my good-bye. And I'd said what I wanted: to be cremated. No remains to be buried, that hypocrites could stand over and pretend to be grieving. I also said "should" in that note. "Should my body be found." I didn't think it would be, that anyone would find the place I went to in those tunnels.'

'I found it.'

'Really?'

'You took milk and a blanket and cheese-and-crackers down with you.'

'I didn't know how long I'd be there. Once I'd gotten to the little room, I wanted to be able to spend time there. To think. No one would disturb me there. I didn't want to have to start foraging for food just a few hours after I settled in.'

'Foraging?'

'I could get to almost anywhere on campus through those tunnels, Mr. Dear. Getting food would be no problem at all.'

'I know you played Dungeons & Dragons in the tunnels. How many times did you go down there?'

'Maybe two hundred. Sometimes I'd go four or five times a day. It became a hobby with me, learning all about those tunnels. It helped when we played D & D, but it was more than that. I could go down there and no one would bother me. Once some kids didn't want me in their game anymore. I went anyway. They walked right past me and never knew I was there.'

'But the note,' I said. 'We were talking about the note. You wrote it?'

'I did.'

'How?'

He knew why I asked. 'You got a ballpoint?'

I slid the pen over, and on a napkin Dallas wrote the following, with his *left* hand:

TO WHOM IT MAY CONCERN:
SHOULD MY BODY BE FOUND,
I WISH IT TO BE CREMATED

The handwriting was a virtual duplicate of that on the note found in Dallas's room. The wording *was* a duplicate. I made a promise to myself to have a talk with my handwriting-analysis people. The Michigan State Police analysts had believed that someone other than the missing boy had written the original note, and this opinion had not helped our investigation. In fact, we had wasted valuable time in wondering which third party could have printed the message.

I looked at Dallas, back to the note on the napkin, and

once more into his eyes. He smiled, then shrugged. There was no sense of triumph in the gesture.

'I thought the handwriting might throw someone off,' he said.

'One more thing, if I may,' I continued. 'That corkboard was obviously left for someone to see.'

'Right. I meant it as a combination map and suicide note. The map would show where I was, if you could find me. The note, the message I intended to convey, was that I was dead. Of course, if that's how it turned out. I really didn't know what would happen. The gun shape on the map represented both a gun and a power plant on campus. The meaning of the gun, I thought was obvious, as in shooting yourself. Suicide.'

'You took a gun with you?'

'No, a gun is the most obvious way to indicate suicide. I made it pretty easily with those pushpins. The other pushpins and thumbtacks represented alcoves I knew about in the tunnels. Like the one where I went. I tried to space them to a personal scale. I think I know all the alcoves in that section of the tunnels, and the only one I left out was the one I was in. Once you realized that each tack was an alcove, you could look for the only one that was missing. It wouldn't be easy. To know what the tacks represented, you'd have to find the alcoves below ground and then compare them with a map of the campus. If you'd done that, you'd quickly have seen that the alcoves were in the same position relative to the power plant as the tacks were to the gun shape.'

'Why use the power plant?'

'It's where we often started D & D games. I thought the searchers – you and your men, as it turned out – would discover that fact fast enough. Also, if you look at the power plant on a map, it's shaped like the gun I drew.'

'You really enjoyed Dungeons & Dragons, didn't you?'

'Playing the game – for real, I mean – was total escape. I mean, I could get into it. Scramble through those tunnels like a monkey. And you can use all your brains. There's nothing to constrain you except the limit of your imagination. When I played a character, I *was* that character. Didn't bring all my personal problems along with me. It's a terrific way to escape.'

'You used the corkboard to leave messages.'

'Yes, and anyone could figure out that that last configuration was a message. I also used the corkboard to map out D & D games. I could come up with some wild ones. I thought I'd make a good dungeon master, but older players figured I was too young and far-out.'

It occurred to me that Dallas *had* been, in a way, a dungeon master. By disappearing, leaving clues, and setting up alternative outcomes for his adventure, he had created a game in which the other adventurers – me and my men, his parents, anyone who was involved – never knew what to expect. In Dallas's ultimate game of Dungeons & Dragons, his only real opponent had been death.

I forced a laugh. 'How about the trestling?'

'That was because I didn't give a damn. I'd be down because of a teacher or my parents, really depressed about everything – not low enough to kill myself, but I just didn't care. Maybe the train would do the job for me. If something wanted me dead, this was its chance.'

'Didn't you also do it for attention?'

'I suppose.'

'Weren't you afraid out there on those railroad tracks?' I shuddered when I thought of my own experience.

'No, I wasn't. I told you, I didn't care. And after a time or two, I knew that if I lived through it, I'd feel a lot better. I was never depressed when it was over.'

It was hard to believe that this boy had ever not been

depressed. He seemed to be shrinking before my eyes; telling me what had happened was terribly hard for him. But it was also terribly important, to both of us, that I know.

'Did you ever play Dungeons & Dragons on the tracks?'

'No. I thought of it. The train as the dragon.'

'What do you enjoy, Dallas, besides Dungeons & Dragons?'

'Computers. I'm really happy when I can work with computers. I think what I'd like most in this world is to open a computer store.'

Dallas's eyes brightened as he said this, and I wondered whether someone of his ability could be happy selling computers. But now was not the time to pursue it. Though I knew my next question would be painful, I had to ask it. I smiled in what I hoped was a kind way and asked, 'What happened when you went into the tunnels that day?'

Dallas's hands trembled, but he answered softly and quickly. 'I went straight to my alcove. I'd never shown this one to anybody else. I wanted to be alone so I could make some decisions. I knew what the three choices were. I sat down against the wall, so I could lean against it. It was chilly and I was wrapped in my blanket. I had food within reaching distance. It was heaven, Mr. Dear. I'd done it – I'd taken the first and most important step. Things would be better, whatever it was that came of this. For ten minutes or so I didn't think of anything. Enjoyed the silence, the being alone. I lit up a joint. It had been a long time since I'd felt so mellow. Then I started to think – hazy, pleasant thoughts at first. Mostly about my life and what I wanted it to be. Going to school was fine, and I needed that, but the pressure had to be taken off. If I didn't get an A, I didn't want somebody screaming at me, my mother or a teacher. I didn't want always to have to perform and be the hotshot. I'd learn what I wanted to, not what someone else thought I should. I'm really good with computers, Mr. Dear. You'd be amazed at the things I can make them do. But little things, too, I had to work out. I didn't want people complaining about my sloppiness, how my notes weren't in order, my room was always a mess. I'd try to do better, but people were going to have to give me some room.

'The same way with the drugs. I'd gone too far, I'll admit, but I didn't need to be hassled about going cold turkey. There is nothing wrong about relaxing with a joint. It seemed as if everything about my life had to be a secret. And the gay thing. I'm gay, and that's the way it is. But do you think I could have an honest talk with my parents about that? Well, all of these issues were going to have to be hashed out. I started imagining a conversation with Mom, where we just worked everything out, and that's when the nightmare began. Going over this talk with her. "Mom, I'm gay, and we're going to have to discuss that fact and learn to live with it. First, I think –" "Dal, you don't know what you are right now. If we discover that you really are gay, we can discuss it then, but I think you ought to examine everything very closely. We can get help for you, people who can decide whether this is really true." "It is true, Mom." "You *think* it's true. We should find out. Maybe you're not gay at all." You see, Mr. Dear, a talk wouldn't be possible.'

Dallas paused and took a deep, trembling breath. 'Take the question of grades. "Mom, I've decided that being near the top of my class isn't the most important thing." "Fine, Dal. We just want you to live up to your potential." "I don't know what my potential is. I don't want always to feel that I have to do great. I want to lay back, let the learning come. It's not laziness. There are things in school I *want* to do. I'd rather do them than the things other kids do for their leisure. But other aspects of school are boring. I don't want to have to perform drudgery just to get grades." "All of us have to do things we don't like. Your parents, for example. We do things we don't want to do. It's part of growing up, Dal. But maybe I have been too hard on you about grades. I can make an adjustment. It's just that it's easy for you, and it makes us proud – and I'd think it would make you proud too – when you do well." I could go on with this, Mr. Dear. But every conversation I imagined ended up unsatisfactory. I thought she wasn't going to accept anything I felt I needed to do. Like maybe working in a computer store for a while, instead of going to school. And it wasn't just Mom. Nobody was going to understand me or take me seriously. And they couldn't help even if they did. What could a teacher do? Talk to my mom? He wouldn't have any more luck than I would, and most likely he would be won over to her side. "Keeping your room clear, Dal, really is a very small price to pay. It's not as though some of the things we're asking take a lot of time."

'Then there was the matter of friends. I didn't have any. I tried too hard. I knew that, but what was the alternative? If I kept my distance, nothing developed. A few times I did find people willing to be friends. I'd tried hard and succeeded. But then I'd find out I didn't want them as friends. I'd made such an effort to win them over that I'd never stopped to ask whether we had anything in common. It seemed that I'd never have anyone close to me. I can hear Mom saying, "You're only sixteen, Dal, it can take a long time," and that's true, like you said, but it doesn't help. Anyway, I was the sorriest, loneliest person I could imagine. It might be okay if I could get out on my own, but I didn't see how I could, without help from others, and if that was forthcoming at all, it would be with plenty of strings – "We just want you to try a few things our way" – which meant the pressure and the disapproval would never stop. So a talk, a let's-straighten-it-all-out-and-start-over-again talk, wasn't going to help. I realized that as clear as could be.

'I was amazed I hadn't seen it before, all those months I'd been thinking about having talks like that. I thought it was good that I'd come down to my room, I should have done it sooner, because I could think there and see how things really were. Analyzing how the conversations would go eliminated my second option too, the one where I would disappear and get revenge on my parents for forcing it on me. Contact them every five years just to make sure their pain didn't go away. If disappearing was so easy, why had I ever thought of the conversations in the first place? It was obvious to me that I needed other people, but that I couldn't have them under any circumstances that would be tolerable. I couldn't make it on my own right now. Oh, I'd made myself believe that I could, but it wouldn't work out, I saw that now, and it would just end up with someone like you finding me and bringing me back to my parents. It would be the worst kind of humiliation, and for what purpose? No, it was clear to me what had to be done. I was depressed and miserable and not even sorry. I should have done it before. Life was no good for me, and this was the best and only solution. I'd brought Quaaludes down with me, more than the book promised would do the job. I took them all. Swallowed them with the milk. I didn't want to wait one second longer, didn't want my brain working so it could tell me I was wrong.'

His face was contorted with pain. The memory was bad enough, but now he felt guilty too, or so I imagined.

'When did you wake up?' I asked as gently as I could.

'I didn't know at the time. It was the next night.'

'The sixteenth.'

'Yes.'

'Do you want to go on, Dallas? I know the remembering is hard for you.'

'I'd like to tell you. I've started, and I might not want to another time. But now I'm going to have to count on you. I don't want names released. I don't want people in trouble.'

'If someone hurt you, Dallas, it will be very hard for me to keep a promise.'

'No one hurt me.'

'Are you sure?'

'Not in any way that mattered.'

'What do you mean?'

'I want to talk to you, but I won't unless I have your promise that others won't be dragged into this.'

'If you tell me you weren't hurt, I'll promise.'

'I wasn't.'

'I'll keep what you tell me between us.'

'You'll have to promise me again.'

'I promise again.'

I meant what I said, and apparently Dallas believed me, because he went on. 'It was terrible when I woke up. I'll spare you the description of how I felt. It was the worst. I wished I was dead. But I had a feeling that I wasn't going to die, and I had to do something about the pain. I crawled out of the tunnels and virtually all the way to a friend's house, more than a mile away. Oh, I tried to walk, but I couldn't keep on my feet and kept falling down. I don't know which was harder, crawling that far or the terrible pain. I expected that someone would see me, but it was night and no one did. A bunch of times I just lay down and went to sleep, but the cold ground would wake me up. I must have started about nine o'clock at night. It was nearly dawn when I got where I was going.'

'What did you intend?'

'I didn't know. I wanted the pain to stop. All I could think was that I didn't want anyone to find out what I had done.'

'This friend – who is he?'

'An older guy. I met him a number of times in a bar we went to. I'd been to his house before.'

'What do you mean by "older"?'

'Early twenties, maybe. He was from the East Coast.'

'Why did you think he'd help you?'

'We'd always gotten along. I'd talked to him some.'

'Is he gay?'

'Yes. Mr. Dear, I don't want any trouble for anybody.'

'I gave you my promise. Go ahead and tell me what happened.' It was obvious that Dallas didn't want to talk about this part.

'My friend took me in and said he'd call for help. I begged him not to. I told him I'd kill myself for sure if I had to go back to what I'd left.'

'So he agreed to help.'

'Yes. He carried me up and put me to bed. He took care of me. He made me glad I wasn't dead.'

'Was sex involved?'

'I don't want to talk about that, Mr. Dear.' He looked up at me, his eyes pleading.

'Dallas, you can't shock me. And I've promised that I won't involve others. I think you know my word is good.'

'There was no sex at first. Later there was, but nothing against my will.'

'Later? How long did you stay in this house?'

'The first one? A week, maybe.'

'There were others?'

'Two others.'

'Why did you move?'

'My friend became very nervous. He'd talked to

someone, maybe one of your men, and I think it scared him. He said I'd have to go someplace else, but it would be okay.'

'What did you do while you were there?'

'I took a lot of drugs, Mr. Dear, I was stoned almost all the time.' His voice was dull, joyless.

'Only your friend knew where you were?'

'Others came. We did drugs together.'

'Do you know Cindy Hulliberger, Dallas?'

'The name rings a bell somewhere. Is she important? I can't be sure, but I think I met her.'

'What about the second place? It was also a house?'

'Yes.'

'In East Lansing?'

'All three were houses, and all in East Lansing.'

'What happened at the second house? That was August twenty-fourth or twenty-fifth, I guess.' Hock, Lambert, and Riddle had the investigation well under way by then.

'More drugs. I never went out. You can understand that. But I want you to know that I had no idea of the fuss that was being made. I didn't really know about that until you came to get me.' Tears welled up in his eyes.

'You didn't read newspapers? Watch TV?'

'All I did was stay high. I guess nobody wanted me to read newspapers or watch TV.'

'The second house – was the occupant another friend of yours?'

'I knew him, but not well.'

'People coming and going again?'

'Not a constant stream. But there were people, yes.'

'How were you treated?'

'At first, good. Not so good later. I was told that I had caused a lot of trouble. A few people screamed at me, and I didn't understand why. One man got so mad he threatened to hit me.'

'Were you ever struck?'

'No.'

'What happened to cause you to leave the second house?'

'The man just woke me up in the middle of the night, said I would have to go right away. I didn't even know the person at the third house.'

'When did you get there?'

'I'm not sure. Maybe the first or second of September.'

'And did things change?' I suspected that they had.

'It was completely different. I began to get afraid.' There was no doubting this statement. The memory of the house made Dallas's face tighten, and he seemed to shrink even more.

'Did the drugs stop?'

'Yes. And I felt miserable. It was like the worst hangover ever.'

'Were people still coming and going?'

'No one. Just me and the man in the house. He kept telling me that he was going to have to do something with me.'

'This frightened you?'

'I told you it did.'

'Were you afraid for your life?'

'I was toward the end.'

'You couldn't leave?'

'I was told not to.'

'At the other houses, were you told not to leave?'

'It didn't come up. I guess everybody just assumed I wouldn't.'

'But you were held at the third house?'

'I don't think I could have left.'

'The man in the third house – what else did he say to you?'

'Mostly he made it very clear that I wasn't wanted. That

he would have to do something with me. Once in a while he'd curse me, call me a "stupid damn kid," and worse things. He cursed other people too. The ones who'd had me before.'

'How long were you at the third house?'

'Two days. The man at the house and another man drove me to the bus station at night. They bought me a ticket to Chicago, and gave me money besides. They said that I should take a train to New Orleans, that I had enough money for that and a little extra. They gave me a phone number to call. Made me promise I'd do it. They said I'd be in bad trouble if I didn't call, or if I did anything besides what I was told.'

'What kind of trouble?'

'I think they meant they'd hurt me.'

'That would have been about September fourth, when you were taken to the bus station?' Dallas and I both had been in East Lansing for perhaps a week. He had already left town by the time we searched the tunnels.

'I don't know. I suppose.'

He knew. The 'I suppose' was a request that I not make him be too specific. He was still hurting deeply from the rejection by his 'friends,' and I had no intention of making his ordeal any worse by forcing him to give me details he would rather keep to himself.

'Did you do what you were told?'

'Yes. The bus to Chicago, a train to New Orleans. I didn't have any trouble finding Grand Central Station in Chicago. I've spent some nights on the streets in East Lansing. I can get by better than you might think.' Even as he said this I could see the doubt in his eyes.

'You knew why you were being sent to New Orleans, didn't you?'

'No. Except that people didn't want me around,

because I was missing and they were afraid they'd get in trouble for keeping me.'

I could think of another reason. If something was going to be done to Dallas, it was better for it to happen far away in New Orleans. This was only guesswork. But there could be very substantial reasons why those with whom Dallas had stayed did not want their involvement known to the police.

'So you made it to New Orleans.'

'It was a terrible trip. Coming off the drugs and all. I was really down. Started telling myself I couldn't do anything right, not even kill myself. And that nobody wanted me, and why should they? It would always be that way, I told myself. I'd thought for a while that I'd been welcome in those first two houses, but even those people didn't want me. I just decided that there wasn't any hope, and that this time I'd do it right.'

'Kill yourself?'

'Yes. I had maybe fifty dollars left of what had been given to me, so I went to a drugstore and another store and got the ingredients I needed to make cyanide.'

'You know how to make cyanide?'

'I can make almost anything, Mr. Dear. Sure I can make cyanide. I bought the ingredients and then rented a hotel room.'

'You didn't call the number you'd been given?'

'Not then.'

'What happened next?'

'I went up to the room, mixed the cyanide in some root beer, and drank it.'

'I'm glad you're not very good at this sort of thing, Dallas.'

He smiled without a trace of mirth at my poor attempt at humor. 'Well, I sure wasn't that time. I woke up the next day, weak and sick as a dog. I mean stomach-upside-down sick. I never want to be that sick ever again. I had dry heaves for two days.'

'You stayed in the room for that long?'

'There was no money for that. I called that phone number I'd been given. It had been disconnected, so I telephoned East Lansing, the house where I'd first stayed. I could tell that my friend wasn't happy to hear from me. He said I'd been sent out of East Lansing because people could be in trouble for keeping me, and that things were getting very hot. He told me that if I was found, I mustn't ever tell who I stayed with. I was perfectly willing to promise this. I didn't want anyone in trouble because of me. My friend said he couldn't help me right now but to stay in touch, he'd be able to do something for me soon. He told me not to talk to anyone, not to breathe a word of who I was.'

'How was he going to help?' I was certain I knew what he had had in mind. He wanted to be able to reach Dallas. He wanted to be able to arrange the circumstances for the boy's reappearance. He wanted to have some cards to play when the time came, as it had to, for Dallas to surface. Getting Dallas away from Michigan had helped. Now it was a matter of extracting promises that not too many inquiries would be made about where the youngster had been.

'I guess,' Dallas said, 'it had something to do with a place to stay.'

Wrong, I thought. 'Where did you stay?'

'I told you, I can take care of myself. I stayed in an empty building. There are lots of those in most every city. I walked around during the day, stayed in a building at night. I felt miserable. I'd suspected that I wasn't wanted, but being told just to stay away, not ever to come back, really hurt my ego, and at a time when I didn't need it. Here I was in New Orleans, which isn't the best city I've ever seen. At least the parts where I was. I didn't have any money. Didn't know a soul. Already I could feel the depression coming back.'

Now was a good time for a question I'd wanted to ask since I'd found him. 'I know clothes aren't important to you,' I said, 'but just out of curiosity, why were you wearing the same clothes when I found you that you'd been wearing when you left Karen Coleman?'

'I didn't wear them the whole time.' He gave me a weak smile. It was better than nothing. If he was going to survive, he had to remember how to smile.

'Well?'

'I took them off at my friend's house, after I came out of the tunnels. I was told to put them on before I left the third house to get on the bus for Chicago.'

'You didn't see them in between?'

'No. My friend had clothes I could wear.'

'Well, how did you get to Morgan City? I assume you went from New Orleans to there.'

'I met a fellow from New York. He bought me a few drinks and we became pals. He could see I was out of money, and he said that picking up quick cash was no problem. Roustabouts were always needed; there were temporary labor agencies that even sent vans around to pick people up. The companies provided housing and meals, which they deducted from your pay. It sounded just like what I needed, and I said let's go.'

'The New York guy went with you?'

'Yes. Where you picked me up was where we were living.'

'You actually worked in the oil fields?' I couldn't imagine it. Why would anyone hire such a small boy to do physical work?

'For four days.'

'Pretty rough neighborhood where you lived. And I've seen better rooms than the one where you stayed.'

'Dangerous, too. There were fights every night in the hallways, and prostitutes came in if one of the guys happened to have money.'

'No one knew who you were?'

'Not then.'

'Did you stay in touch with East Lansing?'

'Once a day. I was told that something would break soon. Then just a few hours before I called you, my friend in East Lansing told me that it had gone far enough. He said I could be in a lot of trouble and that others might be too. He said that it had to end. He made me promise again that I wouldn't reveal what had happened or mention any names. I told him that that's what I had intended all along. Then he told me to call you. "Dear's a smart guy" is what he said. "Whatever trouble you're in, he'll be able to help."

'And then you called?'

'No. I talked some more with my pal from New York. He thought I should get in touch with you, too. He was with me when I called you.'

It was almost over. He had one more painful admission to make. I looked him in the eye with what I hoped was a tender friendliness.

'Why all the phone calls? You called me three times.'

'I didn't know whether I wanted to be found. I wanted more time to think. Having you wait on the corner was just to see whether you could be trusted.'

'How did you pass the time while you waited for me?'

'Thinking. Wondering if I was doing the right thing. Getting depressed, imagining what lay ahead.'

'And?'

'And then you found me.'

Epilogue

Mr. and Mrs. Egbert returned to Dayton after about a week, but Dallas stayed behind with Dr. and Mrs. Gross. He felt comfortable at his uncle's home, and after our first talk he wanted very much to stay near me. Besides, he would have felt too much pressure too soon if he had been sent back to his hometown right away; he needed time to mend, to grow stronger.

I flew to East Lansing on September 18 to talk with Cindy Hulliberger, who was now claiming the $5,000 reward. I rode around East Lansing with her in the red Vega. Both the Lansing and the East Lansing police department had me wired for sound, because we were going to talk not only about Dallas but about the Laurie Murningham murder as well. What Cindy had to offer was not helpful in the Murningham matter, but she did point out a house where, she said, Dallas had been held. That part of her story seemed to be true, but in the end I had to reject her claim to the reward, chiefly because of an incident that had occurred with Cliff Perotti. As he was leaving for the airport to return to California, *many hours* after news of Dallas's recovery had been made public, Cindy approached him and said, 'I think I have some more information for you.' How instrumental could she have been in Dallas's safe return if she didn't know I had found him?

The best part of the East Lansing trip was delivering those gifts from Neiman-Marcus to the sterling staff at the Red Roof Inn. The staff deserved all the thanks I could give them, and I was a little embarrassed to find *them* thanking *me*.

Later I received a letter signed by both of the Egberts, and their thanks make me warm each time I reread it. It's one of those small pieces of a person's life that make you feel it hasn't all been in vain:

> Dear Bill,
>
> Anna and I can never repay you and your men for locating and saving the life of our son Dallas. There is no doubt in our minds that if we had not hired you, but simply let the police 'do their job,' we would never have seen Dal again.
>
> We know some of the personal risks you and your associates took in locating him, and I can't imagine anyone doing a more professional job. Your associates Richard Riddle and Jim Hock were also very supportive through the whole ordeal and are certainly a credit to your team.
>
> We spoke to Dal tonight in Texas and he just went 'on and on' about what your friendship means to him, and of course we feel the same. Thanks for a 'JOB' well done.

Dallas and I were in fact laying the basis for a solid friendship. He called me every day, sometimes more than once, and in addition to the day when he gave me his remarkable account of the missing months he spent four long afternoons and evenings at my home.

I didn't push him at all for further specifics about his disappearance, but he added details that he had left out during that session at Sue's Place. For example, he told me that he made many of the drugs he and his 'friends' used at the first two houses where he stayed, and that in New Orleans a policeman had stopped him, asked his name and gotten it, and then merely told him to move on.

What had happened, he said, was 'our secret.' He emphasized specifically that he would never tell his mother – no good could come of it, he said – and this was a conviction from which he never wavered. On December 21, 1979, more than three months after Dallas surfaced, he granted an interview to Bob France of the *Dayton Journal Herald* in which he 'said he was "never going to reveal any details" – even to his parents, James and Anna Egbert.'

I believe that Dallas was simply so embarrassed by the events of his disappearance that talking about them was unbearable. Of course, something much deeper than embarrassment was also at work. Two near-successful suicides had left memories and wounds a lifetime couldn't heal.

Dallas several times told me how much he feared that his younger brother, Doug, would be hurt if the truth became public. He had a deep affection for Doug and expressed the hope and even belief that his brother would grow up under happier conditions than he had. He did not want Doug to endure cruel asides from his classmates and friends about his 'faggot brother, the dope addict,' and he emphasized this as another reason that I should remain silent. I thought he was right to be concerned, and I held off writing this book until Doug was out of high school.

But stories did appear, although they were not based on fact. Dallas gave me a letter Karen Coleman had written him. She realized that she had made a mistake with the press:

> It's hard for me to recall all the hassles I was put through once you were discovered missing. If I had known that you considered me one of your close friends I believe I could have kept a grip on myself a little better. Of all the campus police and Dear and his associates I'd have to say

> Mr. Dear made me the most nervous. The way he questioned most every statement I made bothered me a great deal. For making me silent his questions about whether you were the type of person who would leave clues to make a game out of finding you worked well. The truth is I know hardly a thing of what kind of person you actually are. Don't get me wrong, I like it this way, you're one of the few people who can make me smile just by looking into my eyes.
>
> The problem I've created with the news media I really don't have an explanation for. It was sort of like a way to theorize with myself as far as reasons or situations for your absence while in the presence of some reporters. In person I've talked to two, from the Free Press + Monthly Mag, and on the phone I imagine near a dozen – God knows where from. Please punch me a good one if ever you see me again – I feel I do deserve to be shit on for playing such a gossip.

But each time Dallas came to my house he looked better. He was getting good solid care from Dr. and Mrs. Gross; there was color in his cheeks, and he bounced when he walked. He laughed a lot too, and I thought, You just might come through this time after all. We took long walks and drives together, had quiet talks in my den, tossed a softball back and forth on the front lawn. He talked excitedly about computers, and I didn't have to understand to enjoy listening. I told him about cases I was handling, and if his solutions were not sensible, they were at least imaginative. One night I raced him from my front gate to the front door.

Dallas stayed in Texas with Dr. Gross for perhaps a month, and then returned to his family's spacious split-level brick home, set on a wooded lot in the Dayton suburb of Huber Heights. Returning to Michigan State

University was out of the question. He enrolled at nearby Wright State University, majoring in computer sciences.

At first he called me at least once a week sounding chipper and spry. Our talks were long and friendly. He still saw me in the role of rescuer, confidant, and friend. As he went on enthusiastically about his new life, my hopes increased that his story might turn out to have a happy ending.

The first discordant notes were sounded in early December. Dallas told me that he was having disagreements with his mother. I held my breath and hoped the trouble wasn't beginning again. A few days later came another call and a report that the battle had escalated. Several days after this, Dallas asked if I would visit him at Christmas, and I promised I would.

I took him to dinner in Dayton, and afterward we had one of our good long talks. He told me that things were better at home than before his disappearance, particularly with his father. 'He's really trying hard, Mr. Dear,' Dallas explained. 'We've had better times together than ever before.' Relations were better with his mother too, but Dallas felt that they were beginning to deteriorate. 'She's also been trying hard,' he admitted, 'but she's beginning to insist I do everything the way she wants. I'd hoped we were past that stage. She won't learn that I'm grown up, or nearly so.'

I tried to emphasize the positive, saying that his parents were trying and he should try too. I told him that his mom and dad loved him very much and he had a friend now whom he could count on. I told him that I looked forward to his phone calls and he should get hold of me any time he wanted. Dallas promised me that he would give the situation his very best effort.

It didn't improve. Each week or two I heard a growing litany of complaints over the telephone. He was being pressured about grades, about his dress, about the hours he kept, the friends he had. He said that the depressions he'd known were returning, and in late March 1980 he told me that they were growing worse.

I wondered whether Dallas might be better off in Texas, or whether my having a talk with Dr. and Mrs. Egbert might help. I knew that they had provided Dallas with psychiatric help and would attempt to move heaven and earth if it would help their son. Over and over I wondered what I should do, what I could do.

Dallas quit Wright State University on April 14, 1980. Grades of course were not the problem. He told me that he was wasting his time in school. What he said he wanted was to work in a computer store, 'or any place where I can use computers.' Instead he went to work at one of his father's three optometric shops, grinding lenses part-time.

In late July Dallas moved into a furnished one-bedroom, $155-a-month apartment with an acquaintance of his, Kevin Bach, aged twenty-three. He asked me what I thought of the move, and I told him I thought he should stay at home and think about getting back into college. He told me that that was just impossible; 'I'm telling you, Mr. Dear, it's unbearable at home.' I agreed that if his moving really was a last resort – if there really was no other way – then maybe he should go. I was in Miami when he called me, and Dallas asked whether I would loan him money. It was the first and only time he ever asked me for anything. I told him yes, of course I would loan him money. I said that he should call my secretary in Texas, who would send whatever he needed. But Dallas never made that call.

I talked with him one more time, in early August. He sounded excited about the new apartment, and because I wanted him to be happy so much, I let myself hope that it would all work out. Maybe getting out on his own was just what Dallas needed, I told myself naively.

On the morning of August 11, 1980, seated on a couch alone in the living room of his apartment, Dallas put a .25-caliber automatic pistol to his right temple and squeezed the trigger.

I learned later in the day what had happened. I was on a camping trip in Colorado with my son, Michael, and two other boys, and heard the terrible news from my secretary. I immediately called Dr. Egbert and told him how sorry I was.

Dallas wasn't dead. He lay in critical condition in the intensive-care unit of Grandview Osteopathic Hospital, his lungs and heart functioning only because of life-support machines. *My friend*, I said to myself through the tears, *thank God you were never any good at killing yourself*.

I was wrong, of course. Six days later, on August 16 – a year and a day after he had disappeared – the wonderful brain no longer gave off waves, and the machines were disconnected.

Dallas's kidneys were donated to recipients in Tennessee and New Jersey. Patients in Grandview Hospital were to see through his eyes. His skin tissue was given to the Shrine Burn Institute in Cincinnati. Even his name was to live on: Dr. and Mrs. Egbert established the Dallas Egbert Memorial Fund, which they hoped would be able to help other gifted but troubled youths.

When I returned to my office I found, in a pile of messages, a note that Dallas had called on August 9. I hadn't known about the message, and I wondered whether it would have made a difference if I'd gotten it. I guess I'll always wonder. But I knew I had had a relationship with him that made me good at talking him into and out of things. There was a reason for this:

> He was a boy, a man,
> who was born and died
> before his time.
> Who cared?
> I did.
> I was his friend.

The Journals of RACHEL ROBERTS

NO BELLS ON SUNDAY

EDITED AND WITH A DOCUMENTARY BIOGRAPHY BY
ALEXANDER WALKER

'Everyone has not only a story, but a scream'

The story this book tells is a true and extraordinary one. The form it takes makes it rarer still. For it is written by Rachel Roberts herself, right up to her suicide.

On stage and screen she portrayed characters of strength and power, yet Rachel Roberts' real life was one of addiction, obsession and emotional turbulence. Despite an international reputation as one of Britain's finest actresses she was locked into a chaotic downward spiral of alcoholism that ended in suicide. With painful clarity she recorded her own disintegration in a series of remarkable journals – the professional triumphs and outrageous social behaviour, her ill-fated marriage to Rex Harrison, her longings and agonies of self-hatred – the final entry coming on the eve of her death.

Alexander Walker, film critic of the *Standard*, has taken Rachel's words and skilfully woven them into a documentary biography with contributions from those who knew Rachel professionally and privately – Albert Finney, Jill Bennett, Lindsay Anderson, Karel Reisz, Athol Fugard, Richard Gere and many others. The result is a unique book, the compelling story of a talented, passionate woman, haunted by a terrifying self-destruction.

'She wrote lucidly . . . her last agonised performance.' *Daily Telegraph*

AUTOBIOGRAPHY 0 7221 8866 8 £2.95